ANTI-ZIONI
CONTEMPORARY WORLD

*Also by Robert S. Wistrich*

HITLER'S APOCALYPSE: Jews and the Nazi Legacy
REVOLUTIONARY JEWS FROM MARX TO TROTSKY
SOCIALISM AND THE JEWS: The Dilemmas of Assimilation in Germany and
    Austria-Hungary
THE JEWS OF VIENNA IN THE AGE OF FRANZ JOSEPH
THE LEFT AGAINST ZION: Israel, Communism and the Middle East (*editor*)
TROTSKY: Fate of a Revolutionary
WHO'S WHO IN NAZI GERMANY

# Anti-Zionism and Antisemitism in the Contemporary World

Edited by

**Robert S. Wistrich**
*Professor of Modern European and Jewish History*
*Hebrew University of Jerusalem*

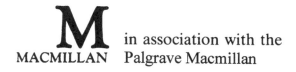 in association with the
Palgrave Macmillan

First published 1990

Published by
THE MACMILLAN PRESS LTD
Houndmills, Basingstoke, Hampshire RG21 2XS
and London
Companies and representatives
throughout the world

British Library Cataloguing in Publication Data
Anti-Zionism and antisemitism in the contemporary
world.
1. Jews. Racial discrimination by society
I. Wistrich, Robert S. (Robert Solomon), 1945– II.
Institute of Jewish Affairs
305.8'924
ISBN 978-1-349-11264-7      ISBN 978-1-349-11262-3 (eBook)
DOI 10.1007/978-1-349-11262-3

# Contents

# Acknowledgements

This book had its origins in a conference sponsored by the Institute of Jewish Affairs (IJA), London, the Centre for the Study of International Antisemitism at the Hebrew University of Jerusalem, and the Programme for the Study of Political Extremism and Antisemitism, Tel Aviv University. The conference took place a number of years ago and was organised by Michael May, then Assistant Director of the IJA and now its Director. Since that time a number of contributions have been added and others amended, revised and updated where possible, to take account of more recent developments. The editor would like to thank the Institute's former Director, Dr Stephen J. Roth, and his dedicated staff for their support in bringing this project to completion. He is especially grateful to Antony Lerman, Director of Research at the Institute, for his invaluable assistance in overcoming the editorial and organisational problems which occurred *en route*, as well as for his constructive involvement in the conception and publication of the book.

*London*                                                      ROBERT S. WISTRICH

# Notes on the Contributors

**Shlomo Avineri** is Herbert Samuel Professor of Political Science at the Hebrew University of Jerusalem. A former Director General of the Israeli Ministry of Foreign Affairs, his books include *Israel and the Palestinians* (1976) and *The Making of Modern Zionism: The Intellectual Origins of the Jewish State* (1981).

**Yehuda Bauer** is Professor of Holocaust Studies and Chairman of the Vidal Sassoon International Centre for the Study of Antisemitism at the Hebrew University of Jerusalem. Among his books are *From Diplomacy to Resistance: A History of Jewish Palestine 1939–1945* (1973), *American Jewry and the Holocaust: The American Jewish Joint Distribution Committee 1939–1945* (1981) and *A History of the Holocaust* (1982).

**David Cesarani** is Lecturer in Politics at Queen Mary College, University of London. He is a specialist in the history of Zionism in Britain.

**Theodore H. Friedgut** is Associate Professor of Russian and Slavic Studies at the Hebrew University of Jerusalem and a member of the International Advisory Board of *Soviet Jewish Affairs*. He is the author of *Political Participation in the USSR* (1979).

**Zvi Gitelman** is Professor in the Department of Political Science at the University of Michigan and has been Director of its Centre for Russian and East European Studies. He is the author of *Jewish Nationality and Soviet Politics* (1972), *Becoming Israelis: Political Resocialization of Soviet and American Immigrants* (1982) and *A Century of Ambivalence: Jews in Russia and the Soviet Union* (1988).

**Julius Gould** held the Chair of Sociology in the University of Nottingham from 1964 to 1987. A member of the Editorial Board of *Patterns of Prejudice*, he has written widely on aspects of Jewish society, including *Jewish Commitment: A Study in London* (1984), and co-edited, with Shaul Esh, *Jewish Life in Modern Britain* (1964).

**Raphael Israeli** is a Senior Lecturer at the Institute of Asian and African Studies, a Fellow of the Truman Research Institute and Director of the Centre for Pre-Academic Studies, all at the Hebrew University of Jerusalem. Among other works he is the author of *'I, Egypt': Aspects of President Anwar Al-Sadat's Political Thought* (1981) and *Peace is in the Eye of the Beholder* (1985).

**Antony Lerman** is Director of Research, Institute of Jewish Affairs, London and Editor of *Patterns of Prejudice*. He is the Editor of *The Jewish Communities of the World: A Contemporary Guide* (1989) and Assistant Editor of the annual *Survey of Jewish Affairs*.

**Natan Lerner** is Visiting Associate Professor in International Law at Tel Aviv University and Director of the International Centre for University Teaching of Jewish Civilisation, Jerusalem. He has written many articles on the Jewish position in Latin America and is the author of a commentary, *The UN Convention of the Elimination of All Forms of Racial Discrimination* (1980).

**Ronald L. Nettler** is a Fellow in Muslim–Jewish Relations in the modern period at the Oxford Centre for Postgraduate Hebrew Studies. His publications include studies and articles on contemporary Islamic religious doctrine on the Jews and Israel, and he is the author of *Past Trials and Present Tribulations: A Muslim Fundamentalist View of the Jews* (1987).

**Earl Raab** is the Executive Director of the Jewish Community Relations Council of the San Francisco area and has taught at the University of California, Berkeley and at San Francisco State College. He co-authored *The Politics of Unreason: Right-Wing Extremism in America 1970–1977* (1978) with Seymour Martin Lipset and is the author of *Major Social Problems* (1964).

**Barry Rubin** is a Fellow at the Foreign Policy Institute of Johns Hopkins School of Advanced International Studies in Washington DC, and a specialist on Third World dictatorships. He is the author of *The Great Powers in the Middle East 1941–1947. The Road to the Cold War* (1980), *Paved With Good Intentions: The American Experience in Iran* (1980) and co-editor, with Walter Laqueur, of *The Israel–Arab Reader: A Documentary History of the Arab–Israeli Conflict* (1985).

**Emmanuel Sivan** is Professor of History at the Hebrew University of Jerusalem and Editor of the *Jerusalem Quarterly*. He has published numerous articles on Islamic fundamentalism and is the author of *Radical Islam: Medieval Theology and Modern Politics* (1985).

**Norman Solomon** is Director of the Centre for the Study of Judaism and Jewish–Christian Relations at Selly Oak Colleges, Birmingham, England and Editor of *Christian Jewish Relations*.

**Robert S. Wistrich** is Professor of European History and holds the Erich Neuberger Chair in Modern Jewish History at the Hebrew University of

Jerusalem. He was editor of the *Wiener Library Bulletin* from 1974 to 1981. His books include *Revolutionary Jews from Marx to Trotsky* (1976), *Socialism and the Jews: The Dilemmas of Assimilation in Germany and Austria-Hungary* (1982), *Who's Who in Nazi Germany* (1982) and *Hitler's Apocalypse: Jews and the Nazi Legacy* (1985).

# Introduction

Forty years after its creation the state of Israel is still not formally recognised by the majority of its Arab neighbours. At the simplest level of analysis this denial of Israel's right to a sovereign, independent form of political existence in what was formerly the British mandate territory of Palestine, might appear to lie at the root of anti-Zionist ideology. The enemies of Zionism, whether they be Palestinian nationalists, Islamic fundamentalists, Pan-Arab radicals, Soviet, East European or Chinese Communists, Trotskyists, Third World ideologues, neo-Marxists or Western liberals, all contest its legitimacy as a movement of national liberation and in varying degrees challenge the right of the Jewish state to exist in its present form.

The fact that 'Zionism' rather than specific Israeli policies generally bears the brunt of their antagonism is at first sight puzzling and certainly not without significance. It is surprising to the extent that since 1948 the Zionist movement has scarcely played a decisive role in the formulation of Israeli policy and its *raison d'être* is by no means clear to many Israelis. On the other hand, opposition to Zionism as a political ideology may appear more easy to justify in terms of world opinion than the openly declared intention to destroy a sovereign, independent nation-state recognised by the United Nations. The negation of Zionism has the further advantage of appearing to be theoretically distinct from hatred of Jews on racial or religious grounds, which since the Holocaust has been officially less than respectable in most countries of the world.

Nevertheless, as this book clearly demonstrates, the image of Zionism and Israel projected in more recent years by many of its opponents has more than a passing resemblance to the literature of classical antisemitism. The origins, motivations and implications of this development provide therefore one of the central motifs in this book, which focuses in particular on contemporary manifestations of anti-Zionism and their link to historical modes of anti-Jewishness.

Since the early 1970s it has become increasingly apparent that this trend in anti-Zionism has gained in importance and has at times even pushed some specifically 'Palestinian' dimensions of the problem into the background. The fate of the Palestinian Arabs (whether we mean those within the Green Line, under Israeli control in the occupied territories or outside the state) remains an unresolved and seemingly intractable political issue, one which will undoubtedly continue to provide anti-Zionism with a powerful lever and a genuine cause. The uprising of Palestinians in Gaza and the West Bank, which began in December 1987, has once more graphically illustrated that truth. But anyone at all familiar with the *global*

1

dimension of contemporary anti-Zionist literature can hardly fail to be struck by the disparity between the reality of Palestinian grievances and the irrationality of certain accusations brought against Zionism on behalf of the Palestinian cause. Whether these charges originated in the Arabo-Islamic world, within the Soviet bloc nations or in the West they frequently have little to do with the undeniable abuses and discrimination against Palestinian Arabs in the territories conquered by Israel in 1967.

In some cases (notably in the Soviet Union or Eastern Europe) attacks on 'Zionism' have been related to domestic political issues such as internal power struggles in the Communist Party, the status of the Jewish minority, national tensions, the discouragement of emigration or the use of popular antisemitism to undermine dissent and liberalisation. Among Arab and Third World radical leaders, 'anti-Zionism' frequently becomes a ritual device for discrediting rivals, asserting legitimacy and political credentials in the 'anti-imperialist' camp or else diverting the masses from more serious issues.

For Islamic fundamentalists, Zionism has long been a symbol of the contemporary crisis of Muslim identity and the erosion of religious values in the Muslim world. As two contributors to this volume show (Emmanuel Sivan and Ronald Nettler), for Muslim fundamentalists the threat represented by Zionism is as much internal as external, a barometer of Western undermining of their society. Traditional anti-Jewish stereotypes often coalesce here with the more contemporary challenge of Israel as a successful modernising society to create a caricatural image of the imagined Judaic–Zionist 'conspiracy' to subvert and destroy Islam. On another level, within Israel itself, Islamic fundamentalism can provide a unifying theme for resistance to Israeli occupation as the 1987/88 events in Gaza have demonstrated. Thus real as well as imaginary motifs interact and coalesce.

In Western societies, too, anti-Zionism can fulfil multiple social, ideological and political needs. These are not always related directly to the Palestinian question or to inter-state conflicts in the Near East. Thus for the Christian Churches support for or opposition to Zionism is frequently linked to major theological issues involving Christian self-identity, attitudes to the Holocaust and the whole complex of Jewish–Christian relations in the contemporary world. For some liberals and social democrats in the West, anti-Zionism has become a touchstone of their sensitivity to the underprivileged Third World and their resentment of American policy, in which Israel is seen to play a particularly nefarious role. For some radical American blacks, as Earl Raab points out, antagonism to Zionism became a way of asserting their adhesion to Third World ideology and their rejection of a white Western capitalist system perceived as discriminating against them. In this case, as among many radical groups influenced by New Left or neo-Marxist modes of thought, anti-Zionism emerged as an integral part of a counter-culture directed in the first instance against racism and imperialism at home.

The connection with the Middle East is not infrequently vicarious, though in an age of instant electronic communications around the globe, the illusion of a single, over-arching union of the oppressed may be more easily sustained. Moreover, the prominence of Israel and the Middle East in the televisual media has tended for a variety of reasons to reinforce the impact of a kind of vague, floating anti-Zionism even among ideologically uncommitted persons in democratic Western societies. At the time of the Lebanon War, when this media effect was most strongly felt, anti-Israeli feeling seemed to slide with alarming ease into a visceral anti-Zionism that was not above trading on traditional anti-Jewish stereotypes. More recently, during the Palestinian rioting in the West Bank and Gaza, one has seen a further example of the same syndrome.

The relationship between anti-Zionism and antisemitism which forms the core of the essays in this book is in reality notoriously difficult to define in objective terms. Clearly the link is not a uniform one either in intensity, scope or political significance in different parts of the globe. It may range from charges of bias and double standards in the Western media's treatment of the Arab–Israeli conflict (which are taken to discriminate subtly against Jews) to the satanisation of visibly Jewish Zionists in Arab and Soviet media. It may embrace such fundamentally divergent phenomena as periodic resentment against the Israeli lobby in the United States (or occasional aspersions about Jewish loyalties in other Western countries) and the sustained, orchestrated governmental campaigns against Zionism in the Soviet bloc. In democratic societies, anti-Zionism in the ideological sense, as a systematised defamation of the Jewish nation, is still confined mainly to the radical right and left though it has more recently made considerable gains in the liberal centre. In totalitarian societies it fuses much more readily with age-old antagonisms to Jews and Judaism, creating a fully-fledged system of social and political Satanism. As Yehuda Bauer suggests, the reification of Zionism as an absolute evil cannot ultimately be disconnected from the historic antagonism to Jews through the ages.

Some of the examples provided by Ted Friedgut concerning pre-Gorbachev Soviet anti-Zionism further illustrate this point. As in the Arab–Islamic world (and even in some Third World countries) Zionism is stigmatised as a spectre threatening peace, progress and prosperity throughout the world. It is pictured as a vast, mysterious, dark and omnipotent power manipulating world imperialism behind the scenes through its alleged control of the media, the banks, the multinationals and a multitude of other transnational organisations. The connection between such notions of the Zionist 'corporation' and 'Mafia', and older stereotypes concerning the international Jewish conspiracy to dominate the Gentiles is strikingly obvious. The *Protocols of the Elders of Zion*, the classic antisemitic fantasy fabricated by the Tsarist Okhrana and taken up with such deadly effect by Hitler and the Nazis, acquired a new lease of life thanks to Soviet, Arab and Muslim fundamentalist propaganda against Zionism. Israel is the geopolitical centre of this evil conspiracy in the revamped anti-Zionist version of the *Protocols*, but it represents no more than an instrument of the far wider ramifications of the global power-network organised by 'World Jewry'. Needless to say such a paranoid vision of contemporary history is fully shared by neo-Nazis, fascists and right-wing antisemites in the West and Latin America for whom (as Natan Lerner points out) anti-Zionism is a convenient fig-leaf under which to hide their visceral hatred of Jews.

The Manichean notion that Zionism is engaged in a deadly, occult kind of conspiracy against the forces of light, feeds on some of the oldest anti-Jewish superstitions in Western culture. One of the most repellent contemporary manifestations of this lie is the Soviet-inspired myth that Zionists collaborated with the Nazis in bringing about the Holocaust. As David Cesarani reminds us in his analysis of the *Perdition* affair in Great Britain, this kind of fabrication serves a calculated political purpose – namely to undermine the moral legitimacy of Israel by rewriting the Holocaust as an episode in the 'criminal' history of Zionism. In Jim Allen's play, Israel is depicted as a nation built upon a pillar of unjustified Western feelings of guilt. Supposedly, it was Zionism that was guilty of sacrificing millions of Diaspora Jews for the future glory of Israel. Zionists, we are asked to believe, either massacred or abetted the murder of the Jews of Europe because they had ideological affinities with Hitlerite Nazism, because they refused to fight antisemitism (even welcoming it or encouraging it) in the belief that 'the spilling of Jewish blood would strengthen their demand for a Jewish state after the war'.

This mode of dehumanising Zionism as a form of demonic neo-Nazism is, whatever its intentions, clearly bound to encourage the emergence and diffusion of new antisemitic stereotypes. The image of an inhuman, repulsive, treacherous and ruthless movement animated by an evil essence and a remorseless drive for power, deprives Jewish nationalism of any moral basis. For Jews to support such a movement (as they predominantly do) means that they are objectively accomplices of a new racism and Nazism, partners in a terrible 'crime against humanity'. It is not only the Soviet and Arab media which have routinely engaged in such wild hyperbole and political obscenities. During the Lebanon war, sections of the Western media also spoke of a 'war of extermination' or an Israeli 'genocide' of the Palestinian people, comparing Begin with Hitler, the Israel Defence Forces with the Wehrmacht and the Zionists with the SS.

During 1986 and 1987 (until the uprising in Gaza and the West Bank) there was a temporary lull in this kind of hate propaganda. Arab efforts to ostracise Israel from the family of nations and to blacken the reputation of

Zionism did not cease, but there have been some signs of a greater willingness to come to terms with the reality of a Jewish state according to the path taken by Egypt nearly ten years ago. The international environment, though still receptive in moments of crisis to anti-Zionist rhetoric, may provide part of the explanation for this change. With the end of the oil crises and the decline of Arab financial power some of the steam seemed to go out of the Arab campaign. The Arab states have never seemed so divided as they do today, their fragmentation having been glaringly exposed during the Iran-Iraq war. (Iran's own extremist anti-Zionism has taken second place to its hatred of the heretical Iraqi enemy.) The PLO, for its part, has increasingly abandoned the military option and come to declare its willingness to negotiate with Israel while still stopping short of full unequivocal acknowledgement of its right to exist. However, on the fringes of the PLO and among its radical factions like Abu Nidal and the Abu Mussa group or Jibril's Popular Democratic Front for the Liberation of Palestine, extremist anti-Zionism continues to flourish. These groups despise Arafat's 'diplomatic' strategy and openly proclaim their desire to destroy Israel. Their intransigence is reinforced by the *intifada* and the consequences of Israeli repression in the territories which has helped to unite the Palestinians and to substantially bolster their cause in the eyes of world opinion.

Cracks have however appeared in the long-standing alliance between the Soviet Union, the Arabs and parts of the Third World which anti-Zionism traditionally helped to cement. The Soviet Union under Gorbachev appears to be reconsidering many of its commitments to the Third World. It may also come to reassess the value of its support for the PLO and some of the radical Arab states. Moreover, the rise of Islamic fundamentalism constitutes a palpable threat to Soviet interests and may be a further reason to revise its Middle Eastern policies and to regard Israel in a more benign light. Furthermore, Moscow's anti-Zionist and antisemitic strategy has brought no obvious gains either in domestic or foreign policy in the past few years, and the harm done to its international image by the harassment of its own Jewish minority has been only too obvious. This is already reason enough to explain why a younger and more pragmatic leader should want to tone down some of the more extreme official manifestations of anti-Zionism in the Soviet Union. These do not sit well with the new slogans coming out of Moscow – *perestroika, glasnost* and democratisation. Gorbachev's eagerness to improve relations with the United States and Western Europe, to obtain Western trade and technology in order to modernise Soviet society, create their own dynamic towards encouraging more Jewish emigration and greater flexibility towards Jews remaining in the USSR. By allowing the most prominent Jewish activists to leave, Gorbachev has taken some of the heat out of charges of Soviet antisemitism, without encouraging any major ideological change of line towards

Zionism. By carefully chosen signals towards Israel he has also helped ease the Soviet Union back into the peace process in the Middle East.

But it is unlikely that Soviet antisemitism and anti-Zionism will fade away in the immediate future. Opposition to Gorbachev's reforms both at the level of the bureaucracy and among the masses is already expressing itself through antisemitic channels in a society which is thoroughly permeated by ethnic tensions. Moreover, liberalisation has permitted the emergence of a Russian nationalist type of antisemitism, closely parallel to the Nazi variety, which has found public expression through the well-connected Pamyat organisation. This group has admittedly been roundly condemned in some official Soviet publications and this might be interpreted as an encouraging development. The outcome of Gorbachev's efforts to transform the Soviet system from within may, however, simply accelerate the shift from the older Stalinist variety of 'anti-Zionism' to a full-blown populist antisemitism whose inspiration comes from below.

In the Western world, too, especially in the wake of the Palestinian uprising, there are no signs of any significant abatement in anti-Zionist activity or of a toning down of the more virulent modes of anti-Israeli incitement. The associations of Zionism with racism (reinforced by the notorious 1975 UN resolution), imperialism and reaction remain strong in many circles that regard themselves as liberal, progressive and enlightened. The younger generation, especially those on the left, continues to view Israel through a Third Worldist prism as too militarist, Western and powerful for its taste – above all, as too reminiscent of past Western colonisers. The link with South Africa, much exaggerated by anti-Zionist propagandists, reinforces these perceptions. Moreover, in many European countries where antisemitism was traditionally strong, such as Germany, Austria, Poland or France, there are signs that it is far from being a spent force even if its hold has considerably declined in comparison with the pre-war era. As the impact of the Holocaust recedes with time (or produces its own backlash and 'revisionist' travesties) the moratorium on Jew-baiting may well be lifted. A future historian might be forced to conclude that since the Six Day War, anti-Zionism has provided the ideological framework in which a new antisemitism could be incubated, only to discard this protective shield in the late 1980s and revert back to one of the oldest traditions of European Christian culture.

In the Arab world the outlook is much more discouraging in spite of signs that the more moderate Arab states might move towards a peace settlement with Israel. In a widely reviewed recent book, *Semites and Anti-Semites*, the distinguished historian Bernard Lewis observed that the extent of open antisemitism in the Arabic mass media and in educational materials in the Arab world is scarcely inferior to that of Nazi Germany. This finding is confirmed in recent monographs by Rafi Israeli and Rivka Yadlin dealing with antisemitism in Egypt since the Peace Treaty. Similar trends can be documented in Syria, Khomeini's Iran, Ghaddafi's Libya and above all in the various Muslim fundamentalist movements. For these fanatics, the fight against Israel is first and foremost a battle against the Jews. Fusing their age-old Koranic image of the Jews as a perfidious and permanent enemy of Islam with more modern notions of a Jewish cabal seeking to control the world, their *Jihad* against Israel has an ominously apocalyptic flavour. Thus, the leading fundamentalist organisation among the Palestinians in Israel's occupied territories, Hamas, did not hesitate to speak in its official covenant (August 1988) of 'world Zionism' and the 'warmongering Jews' as having caused two World Wars 'through which they made huge financial gains by trading in armaments, and paved the way for the establishment of their state' (Article 22). For Hamas, the revival of some of the hoariest myths of European racist antisemitism is a natural corollary to its call for Israel's extinction.

As the essays in this book demonstrate, anti-Zionism is not therefore simply another manifestation of disagreement with certain policies of the Israeli government, or an expression of real or vicarious sympathy for the Palestinian Arabs as a dispersed or oppressed people. Ever since the creation of the Jewish state (and indeed long before then) it has been the major ideological weapon of Israel's most implacable and determined Arab enemies. Subsequently it acquired a global dimension through its adoption by the Soviet Union and the Communist countries, spreading to parts of the Third World and extending its influence in many Western countries. In the United Nations during the 1970s (under the stewardship of a former Nazi, President Kurt Waldheim of Austria) it achieved further respectability as an article of faith adhered to by the most disparate and heterogeneous political groupings. More recently, as Antony Lerman points out in his article 'Fictive anti-Zionism', has extended its inroads into the most unlikely corners of the globe, making its own unique contribution to the linguistic, ethical and political corruption of the age. The 'Palestinian question' is intractable enough without having to bear the burden of this particular incubus of irrational hatred.

One might be tempted to abandon the morass of lies, distortions and half-truths embedded in much of contemporary anti-Zionist ideology to the attentions of political psychopathology. Experience teaches us, however, that this response would be decidedly unwise, given that anti-Zionism grafts itself so easily on to the much older root of classical antisemitism providing it with new sources of nourishment and revival. As these essays reveal, contemporary anti-Zionism and antisemitism often resemble Siamese twins, sharing a common attraction to extremism, bigotry, fictional constructs and satanic conspiracy theories. This alone would be sufficient reason to expose their malevolent influence.

*Hebrew University of Jerusalem*                              ROBERT S. WISTRICH

# Part I
# Communist and Left
# Anti-Zionism

# 1 The Evolution of Soviet Anti-Zionism: From Principle to Pragmatism

Zvi Gitelman

Soviet ideology and practice have been consistently hostile to Zionism, though that hostility has varied somewhat in form and intensity over the course of the past 80 years. No government in Russia could ignore Zionism, since it emerged a century ago as a major ideological and political force among a Jewish population that was then the largest in the world, and which remains today the world's third largest Jewish community.

Several decades before Theodor Herzl convened the first Zionist Congress in 1897, modern Zionist ideas were being discussed among the 'enlightened' Russian Jewish intelligentsia. By the 1880s Zionist circles were found in several Russian, Belorussian, Lithuanian and Ukrainian cities, all then part of the Russian Empire, and a few hardy souls had even emigrated to Palestine where they established the first agricultural colonies. Zionism struck a more responsive chord among the Jews of the Russian Empire than it did among their West European brethren. Indeed, in the light of the different conditions of Eastern and Western Jewry it could hardly have been otherwise. Western European Jews had been politically emancipated by the beginning of the nineteenth century, whereas Russian Jewry was still legally inferior to most of the rest of the Empire's inhabitants, none of whom enjoyed the civil liberties and democratic freedoms of French or English citizens. Moreover, successive Tsarist regimes held out little hope for the amelioration of the Jewish position.

In the 1860s there had been faint glimmerings of such hopes, only to be snuffed out by political reaction which, throughout Russian history, seems to follow close on the heels of any attempt at reform. Therefore, it was hard to imagine Russian Jews developing long-term loyalties toward the Tsarist regime. They might have been more tolerant of their political disabilities had their economic situation made up for these handicaps in some way. But, partially because of the political restrictions that confined the Jews to the Pale of Settlement and barred them from the professions and civil service as well as from owning land, the economic situation of the Jews was generally miserable. This compounded their feelings of political alienation and prevented most Jews from developing deep attachments to the system. An ideology which held out the promise of migration to a better economic situation and the abolition of political disabilities was, therefore, highly attractive. It did not arouse the fears and ambivalences seen among West European and American Jews who were troubled by the spectre of 'dual loyalties' or even by the very notion that the Jews constituted a nation and that individual Jews were not 'true' Frenchmen, Englishmen or Americans.

Indeed, most Russian Jews did not wait for the realisation of the Zionist dream in order to achieve economic improvement and political liberation. They sought both by emigrating to America, Western Europe and Latin America. In principle, however, Zionist ideas made more sense to Jews in the Russian Empire than to any other European Jewish community. There were, of course, Russian Jews who opposed Zionism. Some did so on the same grounds that Jews did elsewhere – on religious grounds (though some of the greatest Russian–Lithuanian rabbis were sympathetic to Zionism), out of assimilationist convictions, on practical grounds or because of their commitment to socialist universalism. But there was broader, undifferentiated support for Zionism among the Jews of the Russian Empire than among any of the other large Jewish communities of the time.

There is no logical or actual connection between Tsarist and Communist attitudes toward Zionism. Communist spokesmen have been consistently hostile to Zionism, but not necessarily from antisemitic motives. Some antisemitic Tsarist officials, on the other hand, were more ambiguous towards Zionism. Its positive feature, in their view, was that it promised to rid Russia of the Jews. In 1903, the year of the notorious Kishinev pogrom, the Russian Minister of the Interior, Count von Plehve, wrote a confidential memorandum to fellow officials in which he explained that Zionist activity should be opposed and stopped because it sought to prevent the assimilation (and hence the disappearance) of the Jews. Zionist activities that were not aimed at removing the Jews immediately from the Russian Empire were to be closed down. Zionist activity had been illegal, but tolerated, until von Plehve discovered that Zionism was not simply an emigration movement but one aimed at raising – or even creating – the national consciousness of the Jews.

In August 1903, Theodor Herzl was granted an audience with von Plehve. The minister told Herzl that he would support 'pure Zionism' – getting the Jews to Palestine as soon as possible – but would oppose educational activities in Russia which retarded the process of assimilation.[1] This is perhaps an eerie foreshadowing of the short-lived Nazi willingness to allow German Jews to go to Palestine in the 1930s, not because they were 'collaborating with the Zionists', as contemporary Soviet propaganda would have it, but because at that stage they were eager to make Germany *Judenrein*. Only later did they expand their ambitions and set their goal as getting rid of the Jews from all of Europe, not by emigration but by wholesale annihilation.

After the abortive 1905 revolution, the 'years of reaction' set in and Zionist activity declined. Whereas in 1914 there had been 26 000 people who purchased the symbolic shekel and thus qualified for membership in the Zionist movement, a year later there were only 18 000. However, the fall of the Tsarist regime, removed all the political and ethnic disabilities which had impeded Jewish activity. A period of unparalleled cultural and political activity began. A recent arrival from the United States commented: 'It is impossible to describe the exhilaration and the holiday atmosphere in the Jewish world immediately after the fall of tsarism . . . There were no differences of opinion in the Jewish world. Class interests disappeared. The only desire of the Jewish bourgeoisie and the Jewish workers was to support the Provisional Government.'[2]

On 2 April 1917 the Provisional Government abolished all restrictions which had been placed on national and religious groups. This permitted a flurry of political activity among the Jews. By May 1917 there were 140 000 shekel holders in nearly 700 communities, and by October their ranks had swelled to 300 000 in 1200 branches.[3] Though the Bolsheviks seized power that month, Zionist activity grew quite unimpeded for most of the next year. Despite the decision of the Zionists in 1906 to involve themselves in Diaspora affairs and not to restrict themselves to the ultimate aim of settling in Palestine, Russian Zionists remained largely neutral in the Russian Revolution, except for the left-wing of Poalei Zion and other socialist–Zionist groupings who had to confront the disputes between the Mensheviks and Bolsheviks as well as the ideological issues of the day. Struggling to establish their power and fend off the counter-revolutionary attacks of the various White restorationist forces, as well as the separatist efforts of several nationalities, the Bolsheviks did not pay much attention to the seemingly quixotic and somewhat uninvolved Zionists. However, by mid-1918 activists in the Jewish Commissariats and the Jewish sections of the Communist Party (*Evsektsii*) began to attack Zionism as part of their attempt to secure a monopoly of power and 'make the revolution on the Jewish street'.

The Jewish Commissariat, part of the Commissariat of Nationalities, tried to address the immediate economic and social needs of the Jewish population, much of which had been ruined by war and revolution. They also tried to establish an organisational monopoly within the Jewish community. The Jewish sections were even more determined to establish a political monopoly. Therefore, beginning in 1918, attempts were made to either eliminate or take over all Jewish political, cultural, social and welfare organisations, since almost none were under Bolshevik control. Because of the weakness of the Bolsheviks among the Jewish population – contrary to popular belief, there were fewer than a thousand Jewish Bolsheviks before 1917 and only about 1200 joined in 1917 itself[4] – the takeover of Jewish life was not easily accomplished. It took about five years to eliminate the Jewish parties (particularly the socialist, anti-Zionist Bund), drive the religious schools underground, defeat the Zionists and take over the cultural, social and welfare organisations which had flourished in 1917.

The Jewish Communists realised that the Zionists, who were not as well organised nor as militant as the Bund, were the numerically dominant group among politically conscious Jews. The local *kehillas*, illegal since the mid-nineteenth century but revived in 1917, broadened their former purview from purely religious to broadly communal concerns. In most areas the elections to the *kehillas* left the Zionists in control. Elections to a national Jewish Congress, which was designed to chart the future course of post-revolutionary Jewry, showed a strong Zionist predominance. The Zionist parties received about 60 per cent of the vote, the socialist parties about 25 per cent and the Orthodox about 12 per cent.[5] In the Ukrainian Provisional Jewish National Congress the Zionists got nearly twice as many delegates as their nearest competitors. Though the National Congress was never held because the Bolshevik Revolution intervened, the elections to it highlighted Zionist popularity. Finally, in the election to the Constituent Assembly, dismissed by the Bolsheviks in early 1918, the Zionists scored a huge victory. Out of nearly half a million votes cast for Jewish parties, the Zionist and religious parties got over 417 000.[6]

These elections were rendered meaningless by the October Revolution. By July 1919 most Zionist organisations in Kiev were ordered to cease their activities. At the same time, the Central Committee of the Zionist Organisation appealed to the Soviet government to certify the legality of Zionist activity. The government resolved that the Zionist party had not yet been declared counter-revolutionary and that its cultural and educational activities did not contradict the decisions of the Communist Party, so all Soviet organisations could be instructed not to hamper Zionist activity.[7] However, a month later all Hebrew instruction was declared illegal,[8] and sporadic harassment of Zionist leaders and activities began. The Jewish sections, now strengthened immeasurably by the influx of veteran politicians from the left wings of Jewish socialist parties which had been forced to merge with the Bolsheviks, pressed for sterner measures against the Zionists. The former Bundists and others brought with them a long standing animus against Zionism, one which they shared with both the Bolsheviks and Mensheviks. Zionism was now the main political enemy of the sections and the latter urged the mobilisation of state power for the defeat of what they perceived of as the 'class enemy'. Zionism represented to them the ideology of the Jewish middle class and the clericals.

The efforts of the Jewish sections were only partly successful. In some localities Zionists were arrested and Zionist activity came to a halt; in other areas, particularly in small towns, such activity went on well into the mid-1920s. A few Zionist groups, such as the agriculturally oriented *Hehalutz* and the EKP (Poalei Zion Party) – which tried to synthesise Communism and Zionism – were permitted to operate legally until 1928 when they were dissolved. On the whole, however, Zionism was effectively outlawed by the early 1920s. In September 1924, 3000 Zionists were arrested in 150 localities, with most getting sentences of from three to ten years at hard labour camps. Some Zionists were offered the choice of 'exile' to Palestine but most were sent to the Far North, Central Asia and Siberia. Between 1919 and 1924, 20 000 Soviet Jews had succeeded in emigrating to Palestine, but in the following decade only 12 500 succeeded in doing so. In all, between 1919 and 1936, about 30 000 Jews left the Soviet Union for Palestine. After that date for over 30 years hardly any were able to go on *aliyah* (to emigrate to Palestine).

THE BASES OF SOVIET ANTI-ZIONISM

The origins of Soviet anti-Zionism lie in Leninist ideology. The Soviets have remained consistently opposed to Zionism as an ideology for over 80 years, though this has not prevented them from supporting the Zionist state when *realpolitik* considerations indicated such a policy. For the most part, however, in the last 30 years ideological and practical considerations have meshed quite well, both pointing in anti-Zionist as well as anti-Israel directions. Some have attributed the hostility displayed by the Bolsheviks to Zionist activity largely to the Jewish sections of the Party. Guido Goldmann, for example, writes: 'It was the . . . Jewish sections of the Communist Party who spearheaded the fight against Zionism from the start, and . . . these sections possessed considerable freedom of action in their first years, which accounted for the extreme harassment of Zionism during the very early years of Soviet rule . . . This is not to deny that the regime would very likely have liquidated the movement anyway.'[9] It is probably true that were it not for the sections, the drive against Zionism might have been somewhat delayed and perhaps milder (though had it taken place in the 1930s rather than the 1920s the fate of the Zionists would have been much worse). This is because the Bolshevik Party as a whole had greater and more dangerous enemies than Zionism; the activity of the sections may have nudged the anti-Zionist campaign higher in the list of priorities, but the only difference might have been in timing.

Soviet anti-Zionism was not a creation of the sections but derived directly from Lenin's insistence that the class struggle took priority over the national one. In the Marxist world view, the fundamental cleavage in society is between social classes. Ethnic or national differences are merely transitory phenomenon of the capitalist era. These differences are exaggerated by the capitalists for their own ends – for example, to keep workers of different nationalities from uniting – but under socialism they will disappear. Lenin's main argument about what he saw as Jewish nationalism and separatism was with the Bund, not the Zionists. It was the Bund which had played a major role in founding the Russian Social Democratic Labour Party and which at the turn of the century proposed that the party be constructed along federal lines, with the Bund enjoying autonomy within the RSDLP in all matters concerning the Jewish proletariat.

Lenin argued that this would weaken the revolutionary unity and drive of the Social Democrats, establishing a dangerous precedent for the organisation of socialist society. But the arguments he used against the Bund could be turned even more sharply against the Zionists. As early as 1903 he attacked the 'Zionist fable about antisemitism being eternal' and thereby justifying the need for a separate Jewish homeland, since Jews would never be accepted in any kind of society, not even a socialist one.[10] Lenin mocked the Bund for coming perilously close to the 'Zionist idea of a Jewish *nation*', one which he considered absurd.[11] 'This Zionist idea is absolutely false and essentially reactionary', he writes, approvingly quoting both Karl Kautsky and Alfred Naquet's rejection of the idea that Jews are a nation.[12] Lenin's anti-Zionism involved an unequivocal rejection of the idea that the Jews form a separate nation. It was 'reactionary' in political terms and scientifically untenable.

> Irrefutable practical proof of that is furnished by generally known facts of recent history and of present-day political realities . . . That is precisely what the Jewish problem amounts to: assimilation or isolation – and the idea of a Jewish 'nationality' is definitely reactionary not only when expounded by its consistent advocates (the Zionists), but likewise on the lips of those who try to combine it with the ideas of Social-Democracy (the Bundists). The idea of a Jewish nationality runs counter to the interests of the Jewish proletariat, for it fosters among them . . . a spirit of hostility to assimilationism, the spirit of the 'ghetto.'[13]

Stalin echoed and amplified these ideas in his first theoretical work, *Marxism and the National Question*, written in 1913. Defining a nation as a 'historically evolved, stable community of language, territory, economic life, and psychological make-up manifested in a community of culture', he declared that 'it is sufficient for a single one of these characteristics to be absent and the nation ceases to be a nation'.[14] Since Jews have neither a common language nor territory nor economic life, they cannot possibly be a nation. Thus, the fundamental Zionist premise of Jewish nationhood, from which the desire for a sovereign state and the development of a modern culture logically flow, is rejected unequivocally.

However, the reality of several million unassimilated Jews, the great majority of whom had Yiddish as their mother tongue, forced Lenin and

Stalin to compromise their principles. While they never acknowledged the existence of a Jewish *nation*, the Bolsheviks categorised the Jews as a 'nationality', thus affording them a status similar to over 110 other such ethnic groups in the USSR. But the Jews have not enjoyed the same privileges (e.g. native language schools) as other nationalities – even non-territorial ones – in recent decades. In the late 1920s, when agricultural settlement schemes for the Jews were promoted by the Soviet government (culminating in the abortive Birobijan project) it was hinted that should these projects attract large masses of Jews and if a flourishing Yiddish cultural life evolved, it might be possible to declare the Jews a nation even by Stalinist criteria. This was probably not meant seriously, but conceived as a way of promoting the Birobijan project among Soviet Jews and their co-religionists abroad. In any case, the conditions never came close to fulfilment and the Jews have not attained the status of a nation, even under the more flexible standards evoked in Soviet discussion of the 1960s.[15]

In sum, Bolshevik–Communist ideological objections to Zionism are based on the rejection of the assertion that Jews constitute a nation and that the 'Jewish problem' is insoluble in the Diaspora because antisemitism is an incurable malady. The Soviet assumption is that socialism will solve all ethnic problems, including that of the Jews. It does this by bringing about the non-coercive assimilation of peoples. While Lenin's expectations that this assimilation would occur with the advent of socialism has proved unrealistic, according to Soviet commentators the vision of assimilation and 'fusion' (*sliianie*) of nations will eventually be fulfilled. What Lenin did not foresee, they say, is that the intermediate step of the 'drawing together' (*sblizhenie*) of nations would take as long as it has under socialism. On the other hand, the rapid acculturation of Soviet Jews into the Russian and other non-Jewish cultures proves that the Leninist idea is essentially sound and that the 'Jewish problem' has been solved fundamentally in the USSR. In fact, Jews are to be lauded for being in the vanguard of the assimilators. They offer a good example to the other peoples.

## ZIONISM AND ANTI-ZIONISM IN THE STALINIST PERIOD

By the time the first five-year plan was launched in 1928 and Stalin's formula for the rapid modernisation of the USSR was being implemented, Zionist activity had been forced deep underground or had ceased altogether. The repressions of the Great Purges swept up many formerly active Zionists, or even nominal members of parties which were Zionist or were construed as such by the overworked imaginations of the NKVD. It was during this period that the appellation 'Zionist' was broadened to include all kinds of people the regime wished to identify as political deviants, even those who were militantly opposed to Zionism. Propagandists and secret police operatives took Lenin's rhetoric one step further and accused former Bundists not merely of verging dangerously close to some elements of Zionism, but of actually being Zionists themselves. This tactic was later used in the show trial of Rudolf Slansky in Czechoslovakia in 1952, when the official announcement stated: 'The court is trying Trotskyite–Titoist Zionists, bourgeois–nationalist traitors and enemies of the Czechoslovak people, of Peoples' Democracy and of socialism . . .' Slansky confessed under torture to being supported by Zionists and to having 'filled important sectors of the government, economic and Party apparatuses with Zionists . . . These Zionists placed other Zionists in those sectors, and through them I maintained contact with Zionist organisations.'[16]

Ironically, shortly after the term 'Zionist' first began to be used in the late 1930s with deliberate imprecision, to describe supposed enemies of the system, large numbers of genuine Zionists entered the Soviet Union. This was one of the unintended consequences of the Soviet annexation of eastern Poland (West Ukraine and West Belorussia), the Baltic states, and parts of Rumania (now Soviet Moldavia) in 1939–40. These were areas in which Jewish political and cultural life had flourished, so that among the more than a million Jews who came under Soviet administration there were many Zionists. The Soviet authorities attempted, usually successfully, to identify and arrest those who had been Zionist activists. The jails and labour camps were quickly populated by these people, and their impact on Soviet Jewry was considerable, as a substantial number of memoirs attest. The *Zapadniki* (Westerners) re-connected Soviet Jewry to Jewish culture and to the events of the previous twenty years in the Jewish world. Several of the leaders of the Zionist revival of the 1960s and 1970s have testified that it was the *Zapadniki* who first educated them to the existence of a modern Jewish political culture and explained the meaning of Zionism to them. It is not by chance that one of the first areas in which the Jewish national revival of the 1960s appeared was the Baltic, incorporated into the USSR only twenty years or so before young Jews would rediscover the significance and attractions of Zionism.

The sudden influx of the *Zapadniki* was followed almost immediately by the Holocaust. The death and destruction wrought by the Nazi invasion and occupation of the USSR also shattered many of the illusions Soviet Jews had entertained about their position in modern society. Perhaps the majority had been seduced by the Soviet insistence that socialism had solved the 'Jewish problem', as well as all other ethnic problems. The 1930s were painted as a period of rapidly increasing *sblizhenie*, an era suffused with the spirit of 'proletarian internationalism'. Mass migration from the old Pale of Settlement areas to the rapidly expanding industrial cities of the Soviet heartland led to rapid linguistic acculturation, as Jews abandoned

Yiddish for Russian and other languages. It was characterised by steeply rising rates of intermarriage. Recent émigrés who came to maturity in the 1930s have described their feelings at that time that all ethnic barriers had been torn down. Jews were rising to the heights of the Soviet political system; they were playing a leading role in the emerging socialist economy and in Soviet culture; their highly visible and prominent place in academic life was in sharp contrast to the restrictions which had barred them from higher education under the Tsars. Pogroms seemed to be a thing of the past. As the Soviet population moved rapidly into literacy and education, it was widely held that the traditional bases of antisemitic feeling would disappear. Would not enlightenment do away with all forms of irrationality and superstition, including religion, fear of the unknown and hostility toward people different from oneself?

These beliefs were cruelly destroyed not only by what the Nazis did, but by the reactions of segments of the Soviet population as well as the Soviet authorities to the German atrocities. There was significant collaboration with the Nazi invaders, especially in the Baltic and the Ukraine. German propaganda, which argued that the war and the sufferings of the Soviet people were the fault of the Jews, seemed to strike a responsive chord in much of the population. Jews in the Red Army, where many served with great distinction, reported antisemitic sentiments expressed in the ranks. The authorities did nothing to counteract these beliefs and sentiments. Moreover, the special fate of the Jews was played down or ignored altogether, embittering many Jews who had put their faith in the fairness of the Soviet system. The shock of recognition, seeing the old wine of antisemitism in new bottles, drove many who would have been appalled by the notion that they were Zionists to the same conclusions some Russian and Western Jews had reached nearly a century before: no matter what the form of government and the espoused values of the society, Jews living as minorities in lands of others would never be safe from antisemitism. Without having read a line of Zionist theory, never having attended a Zionist meeting or having been a member of a Zionist organisation, many Soviet Jews were nevertheless forced to come to Zionist conclusions.

During the war there were some official Soviet contacts with leaders of the Jewish population in Palestine. The Soviets apparently wanted to gauge the strength of pro-Soviet sentiment in the Yishuv and hoped to mobilise some support for the Soviet war effort. Between 1945 and 1949 the USSR took a forthright position in favour of the establishment of a national Jewish home in Palestine, one which would open its gates to mass immigration (though not, of course, from the USSR). The Soviet Union supported the idea of partitioning Palestine to create Jewish and Arab states there. The Soviet delegate to the United Nations Special Committee on Palestine, Semion Tsarapkin, made a speech which could have been understood by the naive listener as an endorsement of Zionist goals. 'The

Jewish people were . . . striving to create a state of their own and it would be unjust to deny them that right. The problem was urgent . . . Every people – and that included the Jewish people – had full right to demand that their fate should not depend on the mercy or good will of a particular state. The Members of the United Nations could help the Jewish people by acting in accordance with the principles of the Charter, which called for the guaranteeing to every people their right to independence and self-deter-mination.'[17] Lenin was apparently forgotten as the Jews were designated a 'people' with the right to an independent state. Tsarapkin's colleague, the then-Deputy Foreign Minister of the USSR Andrei Gromyko, addressed the General Assembly exactly one year before the State of Israel came into being and made poignant reference to the fact that

> During the last war, the Jewish people underwent exceptional sorrow and suffering. Without any exaggeration, this sorrow and suffering are indescribable. It is difficult to express them in dry statistics . . . The fact that no western European State has been able to ensure the defence of the elementary rights of the Jewish people . . . explains the aspirations of the Jews to establish their own State. It would be unjust not to take this into consideration and to deny the right of the Jewish people to realize this aspiration. It would be unjustifiable to deny this right to the Jewish people . . .[18]

The Soviet Union supported the establishment of Israel, approved the sale of Czechoslovak arms to the Haganah and voted for admitting the Jewish state to the UN. Did this signal a fundamental shift in the USSR's attitude toward Zionism? Benjamin Pinkus convincingly argues that it did not.

> A rigorous examination of Soviet speeches on the Palestinian question in international forums, of Soviet press reports and of the more academic political publications reveals that this shift, so important in itself, failed to bring with it a parallel change in policy towards Zionism . . . The positive Soviet attitude towards the establishment of the State of Israel and towards its War of Independence ameliorated the Soviet leader-ship's attitude towards Zionism only insofar as, for the space of a year until August 1948, the term was ignored rather than attacked. More-over, this amelioration did not lead to the granting of permission for Soviet Jews to emigrate to Israel. Indeed, there was instead an inverse correlation between the authorities' attitude towards Israel and that towards Soviet Jewry: the *pro-Israel* policy led to an increasingly *anti-Jewish* policy . . .[19]

It was precisely in 1948 that the most explicitly antisemitic policies in Soviet history were implemented. Jews were systematically eliminated from leading positions in the state, party and economic apparatuses; they were removed from high positions in academic life and the number of Jews admitted to higher education was cut drastically; leading Jewish cultural figures were arrested, many of them eventually killed; public antisemitism increased and went unpunished; the media were full of derogatory references to Jews; Jewish cultural activity was brought to a total halt.[20] The 'Doctors Plot', in which Jewish physicians were accused of collaborating with the Joint Distribution Committee and Western intelligence services, and attempting to murder medically some Soviet leaders, may well have been a prelude to a massive purge of Jews, possibly including their mass deportation to Siberia. Stalin's death, however, ended these plans and the physicians involved in the plot were officially declared innocent a month after Stalin died.

## ANTI-ZIONISM AFTER STALIN

Just as the campaign against the Jews abated after Stalin died, so too did anti-Zionist rhetoric. To be sure, there was no change in the fundamental hostility of Soviet Communism toward Zionism. But the frequency and virulence of attacks on Zionism diminished. However by the end of the 1950s the anti-Zionist campaign had begun to pick up again. 'During 1959–63, this policy reached peaks that in some ways even recalled the years 1949–53. That campaign was waged simultaneously on two fronts . . . the arrest and penal exile of Jews who expressed any manner of sympathy for, and a desire to emigrate to, Israel; the other, loud and unrestrained, took the form of a propaganda campaign conducted in all the Soviet media. It brought with it the renewed output of anti-Zionist books and pamphlets, after a ten-year hiatus in such publications, as well as many articles in the central and local press . . .'[21]

According to Pinkus, the anti-Zionist themes of the time included the portrayal of Israel as a 'base and bridgehead of imperialism'; attacks on foreigners, including Israeli diplomats, who spread Zionist ideas; attacks on Zionism as linked to capitalism, world reaction and even fascism; and the disappointment of Soviet citizens who had emigrated to Israel. These themes were continued even after the fall of Khrushchev in October 1964. Still, there was some easing of the campaign in 1965 and 1966. A crucial turning point was reached with the June 1967 war in the Middle East.

The Soviet Union and all its East European allies (except Rumania) broke diplomatic relations with Israel in 1967, and none has fully restored them to date. The Soviet Union also launched an intensive anti-Zionist campaign of such proportions that one might conclude that Zionism was one of the greatest dangers posed to the world in general and the Soviet Union in particular. If this campaign was intended to dampen the interest in, and sympathy for, Israel, displayed by Soviet Jews in 1967 – and by certain segments of the non-Jewish population in Poland and Czechoslovakia – then it backfired. Latent Zionist proclivities were activated by the stimulus provided by the war as well as by Soviet reaction to it. Groups of people demanding emigration to Israel emerged all over the USSR – in Georgia, the Baltic, the Russian heartland, the Ukraine, Moldavia, Belorussia and Central Asia. In the 1970s around half a million Jews applied for invitations to leave the USSR, and about half that number succeeded, most of them going to Israel. Perhaps this movement had something to do with the unprecedented volume of anti-Zionist publications and television programmes attacking Zionism. While this article does not focus on contemporary Soviet anti-Zionism, some remarks are in order which will attempt to place it in historical perspective.

## SOVIET ANTI-ZIONISM: PAST AND PRESENT

There is both continuity and change in Soviet attitudes toward Zionism when viewed from the perspective of the last 80 years. Zionism has been treated negatively from Lenin to the present, even during those brief periods when the USSR supported the state of Israel, the embodiment of the Zionist vision. Zionism has always been seen as a diversion from the class struggle and as weakening the cause of the working class, even when it has been combined with Marxist socialism. Despite the considerable support it has received in many countries, including among the 'toiling masses' of pre-revolutionary Russia, the Bolsheviks and Soviets have always insisted on identifying Zionism with the Jewish bourgeoisie and its 'clerical allies'. Moreover, Zionism is constantly accused of promoting the separatism of the Jews. This is an accusation strangely reminiscent of the antisemitic canard that Jews are 'clannish' – a charge often made by precisely the kinds of people who exclude Jews from their society and then complain that they have special characteristics which make them a group apart.

Furthermore, the Soviets have consistently linked antisemitism and Zionism. Ever since Lenin they have claimed that these are two sides of the same chauvinistic coin – both ideologies insisting that the Jews are different and separate. While antisemites make the mistake of thinking that Jews are inferior to others, Zionists err in asserting the superiority of the Jews (what the Jewish Communists used to condemn as the 'Chosen People mentality'). Communists have indeed always argued that Zionists and antisemites feed off each other. Antisemitism drives Jews into the hands of Zionists who claim to offer them a 'solution' to their problem by accentuating their distinctive characteristics as a group. But this blind alley prevents Jews from being a part of the only truly universal solution (that is, socialism) to problems of ethnic and racial hatred including that of anti-semitism. During the Brezhnev years this anti-Zionist logic was driven to the point of obscene historical falsification. The Soviets gave great prominence to the myth that the Zionists were 'allies' of the Nazis during the Second World War and that Zionists actively co-operated in the destruction of the Jewish people.

This last theme is a reflection of the major change that has taken place in Soviet attitudes towards Zionism. Anti-Zionism has always been legitimate in Leninist thought and policy. But this was not the case with antisemitism. Lenin explicitly denounced Judeophobia in his theoretical writings. During the Civil War (1918–21), at a time when it was impolitic for him to do so, Lenin made a number of speeches condemning antisemitism and these were even recorded for wide distribution. During Lenin's lifetime the Bolsheviks actively fought both Zionism and antisemitism.

However, for the last half-century or so they have fought only on the anti-Zionist front. Condemnation of antisemitism delivered *en passant* by Kosygin and once or twice by Leonid Brezhnev – invariably linked to a simultaneous condemnation of Zionism – pales into nothingness when set against the mountains of material attacking Zionism. It looks derisory even when compared to the party and government efforts to combat antisemitism which were made in books, films and lectures during the 1920s. Not only is antisemitism no longer condemned but anti-Zionism has the effect of promoting it. The anti-Zionist campaigns have become a legitimising cover for a growing antisemitism which is still officially said to be illegitimate. Since many Jewish and non-Jewish people as well as organisations which are not Zionist (some of them are even opposed to Zionism) are nonetheless labelled as such in Soviet publications, one is forced to the conclusion that 'Zionist' is being used as a code word for 'Jews' or for one who sympathises with Jews and their causes. How else can one explain condemnation of the anti-Zionist Bund as 'Zionist'? Or of American or European Jews and non-Jews who have no Zionist affiliations at all being tagged with the same label?

This shift in Soviet anti-Zionism has been accompanied by other changes as well. The target of Lenin's polemics was an institutionalised movement, with an ideology, programme and party membership. The Zionist movement, however, was driven out of existence in the Soviet Union, so that within the country the targets of anti-Zionist vituperation are individuals or small groups, unable to respond publicly and deprived of access to the media or to publishing outlets where they could answer the charges made against them. A movement is far better able to defend itself in political combat than an individual who is singled out for condemnation. Furthermore, in the 1920s the struggle against Zionism was carried out in the main by Jews, and most often was conducted in Yiddish. Thus, it remained largely within the Jewish population. It could still be seen as primarily a debate among Jews. Today, the anti-Zionist campaign involves more non-Jews than Jews and is carried out largely in non-Jewish languages, thus making anti-Zionist material easily accessible to the entire Soviet population. Given the distorted and misleading presentations of Zionism and Zionists which characterise much of the genre, this material cannot but have a widespread and negative effect on the standing of Jews in Soviet society.

Thus, one might conclude that the Soviet Union has been consistently anti-Zionist but it has not been consistent in its opposition to Zionism. What began as an ideological disagreement based on the logic of certain Marxist–Leninist assumptions turned into a crude political tool that could be used for purposes altogether different from what Lenin had in mind. Nevertheless, Lenin's anti-Zionism was itself based on an enormously presumptive and erroneous belief that he understood the social processes by which the world seemed to be 'governed'. Both Lenin and Stalin decided, *ex cathedra*, that the Jews are not a nation; that the best thing for them to do would be to assimilate; that socialism would solve the 'Jewish problem'. What the Jews themselves thought and desired was simply irrelevant. For how could one compare the subjective illusions of a people with the 'objective scientific truth' of a theory? With the benefits of both hindsight and freedom from any particular dogma it would appear that Lenin erred seriously in his assessment of both Zionism and the solution to the Jewish problem. For his errors the Jews have been paying ever since.

**Notes**

1. Yitshak Maor, *Hatnuah hatsionit berusia* (Jerusalem: Hasifria hatsionit, 1973) pp. 220–2.
2. 'Ben Khaim' [S. Aguskii], 'Di role fun di idishe arbeiter in der rusisher revolutsie', *Funken* (New York), vol. 1, no. 8, 25 March 1920.
3. See Arie Tsentsifer (Refaeli), *Eser shnot redifot* (Tel Aviv: Brit 'Kibutz Galuyot', 1930) p. 20. See also Joseph B. Schechtman, 'The USSR, Zionism and Israel', in Lionel Kochan, (ed.) *The Jews in the Soviet Union since 1917* (London: 1970) p. 101.
4. Zvi Gitelman, *Jewish Nationality and Soviet Politics* (Princeton, NJ: Princeton University Press, 1972) pp. 105 and 116.
5. Ibid., p. 79.
6. Ibid., p. 80.
7. Schechtman, p. 104.
8. Maor, p. 506.
9. Guido Goldmann, *Zionism Under Soviet Rule* (New York: Herzl Press, 1960).
10. V. I. Lenin, 'Does the Jewish proletariat need an "independent political organization"?', *Collected Works*, vol. 6 (Moscow: Foreign Language Publishing House, 1961) p. 334.

11. Lenin, 'Maximum brazenness and minimum logic', in ibid., vol. 7, p. 63.
12. Lenin, 'The position of the Bund in the party', in ibid., p. 99.
13. Ibid., pp. 100–101.
14. Joseph Stalin, *Marxism and the National and Colonial Question* (New York: International Publishers, nd) p. 8.
15. See Grey Hodnett, 'What's in a nation?' in *Problems of Communism*, vol. 16, no. 5, September-October 1967.
16. Quoted in Peter Meyer *et al*, *The Jews in the Soviet Satellites* (Syracuse: Syracuse University Press, 1953) pp. 167, 178.
17. The text of the speech is in Yaacov Ro'i, *From Encroachment to Involvement* (Jerusalem: Israel Universities Press, 1974) p. 49.
18. Quoted in Ibid., pp. 38–9.
19. Benjamin Pinkus, *The Soviet Government and the Jews 1948–1967* (New York: Cambridge University Press, 1984) pp. 233, 235. On Soviet–Israeli relations, see Yaacov Ro'i, *Soviet Decision Making in Practice* (New Brunswick, N.J.: Transaction Books, 1980). On Soviet policy toward Israel in the period under discussion, see Arnold Krammer, *The Forgotten Friendship* (Urbana, Ill.: University of Illinois Press, 1974) and Robert S. Wistrich (ed.) *The Left Against Zion* (London: Frank Cass, 1979).
20. For documentation and analysis of this period, see Yehoshua Gilboa, *The Black Years of Soviet Jewry* (Boston: Little, Brown, 1971).
21. Pinkus, p. 240.
22. Ibid.

# 2 Soviet Anti-Zionism: Origins, Forms and Development
## Theodore H. Friedgut

The violent antipathy to all aspects of Zionism expressed in the Soviet media over many years has deep historical roots and numerous motivations. Opposition to Zionism originated before the Bolshevik revolution and has been a relative constant throughout all periods of Soviet history. At the same time, Soviet political practice, both domestic and external, with relation to Zionism, has varied greatly, subordinated to broader policy considerations. In addition, the saliency of each particular type of objection to Zionism has varied sharply over the years, as has the prominence of the entire question of Zionism. Even today it is not hard to distinguish very different depictions of Zionism in the Soviet press, leading to different conclusions regarding both Israel and Soviet Jews.

The original objections of Russian Marxists to the Zionist movement derived from their adherence to Marx's social analysis. Marx declared that the proletariat has no fatherland and proceeded to sketch a world-wide social structure based on class rather than on nation. He regarded the blossoming of national states in Europe as an ephemeral phenomenon of the period of capitalism, weakening as trans-national capitalist empires grew and disappearing entirely with the founding of a universal socialist society. In such a scheme there was no logic to the development of a specifically Jewish national entity. The Jews, a stateless minority wherever they existed, were the litmus test of all social schemes of the time. Karl Kautsky, the ideologist of German social democracy proposed that the Jews should assimilate into the nations among whom they lived, thus removing the Jewish question from the political agenda. This view became the dominant socialist prescription for the Jews, although other solutions (in particular non-territorial cultural autonomy) were put forward.

For the Russian social democrats the question of national minorities was particularly prominent since the Russian Empire – 'the prison house of nations' – was a ferment of national animosities and repressed aspirations. Lenin, who at the beginning of this century fully accepted Kautsky as an ideological authority, embraced assimilation as a solution to the Jewish question in Russia. He firmly opposed separate Jewish political organisation within Russia, denying the existence of a Jewish nation that transcended geographical and historical boundaries.[1] From the outset Lenin's view was controversial. Written in the wake of the Kishinev pogrom, Lenin's proposal for Jewish assimilation grated on the sharpened sensibilities of some Jewish members of his party. One of these, replying to Lenin, raised the question as to why only Jewish cultural and national identity should be obliterated in the process of solving the national question in the Russian empire?[2]

The multiplicity of solutions for the Jews of Russia was not simply a matter of ideology. The turn of the century was a period of great ferment in Russia, both ideological and organisational. Within a few years of each other, latent tendencies of Marxist and populist revolution, liberal enlightenment and Zionist nationalism had coalesced into distinct, though largely illegal or semi-legal organisations, contending within themselves for definition of their outlook, but even more sharply competing among themselves for the support of Russia's Jews and nascent Russian public opinion.[3] Within this context, Lenin and the Russian social democrats found themselves in political competition with the young Russian Zionist movement. These two movements were diametrically opposed. The Marxists were class-based, oriented towards immediate action and focused on transforming Russia into a socialist state. The Russian Zionists embraced a national concept of Jewishness which included both secular and religious, employer and worker, and looked to eventual territorial concentration in Palestine as the basis for a solution of the Jewish problem.

The two movements inevitably clashed owing to their competition for support in the Jewish Pale of Settlement. A new element of friction between Marxism and Jewishness was added when Lenin's centralist model of party organisation led to the Jewish Bund leaving the party and continuing as an autonomous organisation. Despite the ferocity with which the Bund and the Zionists competed against each other, Lenin, Plekhanov and the other Social Democrats lumped both together as Jewish national deviations, providing a simplistic condemnation of any proposal for Jewish national identity or particularity. This trend of thought, combining the authoritarian exclusivity of Lenin's organisational theory with the rough and tumble of political competition in turn-of-the-century Russia's revolutionary underground, remains to this day one of the bases for Soviet anti-Zionism.[4]

The advent of Lenin's Bolsheviks to power in 1917 added several new dimensions to Soviet–Zionist relations. Despite the continuing opposition of the Bolsheviks to Zionist ideology and the suppression by the Soviet state of Jewish religion and the Hebrew language, groups of the Socialist–Zionist Poalei Tsion and training farms of the Hehalutz movement continued to operate in the USSR until the late 1920s. Then the total mobilisation of Soviet society under Stalin's heavy hand ended the existence of virtually all autonomous organisations, including the Jewish sections of the Soviet Communist Party (the *Evsektsiia*) which had been in charge of mobilising support for communism in the Russian Jewish community and had led the Soviet regime's fight against the Jewish religion and Zionism.[5]

Once the Soviet Union had been established, the Zionist attempt to mobilise Jewish support for settlement in Palestine was considered counter-revolutionary, diverting the Jews from the tasks of building Soviet socialism. At the same time, the pressure of national minorities and the need of the Bolsheviks to obtain public support led to the deferring of the Marxist dream of universal human homogeneity. Assimilation was shelved and replaced by the slogan of 'national in form, socialist in content' – adopted as the guideline for the Jews as well as for other nationalities. This campaign reached its apex with the establishment of the Jewish Autonomous Region in Birobijan, hailed by the Soviet authorities as the realisation of Jewish national statehood within the boundaries of the Soviet Union. While remaining constant in their rejection of the concept of a single nation embracing all of world Jewry, the Soviet authorities affirmed Jewish 'nationality' and territorial nationhood within the USSR, gaining support and generating enthusiasm in both the Soviet Union and in the Jewish world at large.

Throughout this period an active fight against Zionism (especially against Jewish settlement in Palestine) was carried on in the Comintern, the international organisation of the Communist movement. The British Empire held the Mandate over Palestine and was still dominant in the Middle East. The British had issued the Balfour Declaration and were implementing its terms within a general context of Anglo–Zionist cooperation. The growth of an Arab national movement, both in Palestine and elsewhere in the Middle East, presented the Comintern with a prospect of anti-colonial uprisings which might offer the chance of establishing socialist influence among the rebellious populations. In Palestine this meant seeking Arab support against the British and the Zionists through the intermediary of a local communist party to be dominated by Arabs, a concept which remains in effect to this day. The equation of Zionism and imperialism has meant that in Soviet terms a Zionist state of Israel is indelibly tainted by the 'original sin' of imperialism and it can therefore never live at peace with its Arab neighbours nor deal justly with its native Arab minority. This has served as the *leitmotif* to justify communist support for the Arab side of the conflict in Palestine from the massacre in Hebron in 1929 to the *Fatah* terror activities of the 1980s. Only when Soviet state interests have dictated otherwise, most notably during the years 1947–49, has the Soviet Union silenced its condemnations of Zionism and turned away from seeking influence among the Arabs. Thus, with the development of Soviet activity abroad, and particularly in the Middle East, a new dimension was added to the two original forms of Soviet anti-Zionism.

An additional element entered Soviet anti-Zionism in the aftermath of the Second World War. Ostensibly anti-Zionist writings began to be characterised by inclusion of all the crudest antisemitic legends about a world Jewish conspiracy seeking universal domination. These accusations, altered only minimally, and barely disguised by the use of such terms as 'bourgeois' and 'cosmopolitan', were the same as had been circulated by the most reactionary antisemitic circles of Russia in Tsarist times.[6] A number of factors appear to have come into play here. In the course of Stalin's purges the Old Bolshevik intelligentsia had been virtually exterminated. In the policy-making levels of the Soviet Communist Party and the Soviet government, Jews had been virtually eliminated. Both of these elements, steeped in the traditions of the revolutionary movement, eschewed recourse to antisemitism. In their place, Stalin had installed parvenus of inferior moral and intellectual stature who had not participated in those early debates, and had no inhibitions about mixing anti-Zionism and antisemitism. Drawn largely from social strata in which antisemitism had been an accepted commonplace, they made their careers through complete and unquestioning subservience to the supreme leader. One facet of Stalin's paranoia in his last years, was a pathological hatred and mistrust of the Jews as individuals and as a group, to the point of seeking their mass exile to Siberia and most probably their physical destruction.[7]

Compounding these human factors was the post-war Soviet domestic policy dilemma of how best to rebuild Soviet power in such areas as the Baltic republics and those parts of the Ukraine annexed by the Soviet Union from Poland in 1939. These had always been areas with a high incidence of antisemitism and had in addition been exposed to Nazi propaganda during the war. This propaganda had created an identification between Jews and communists, taking advantage of the fact that many Jews were active in the communist movements in the Western areas of the USSR and had played a prominent part in their Sovietisation. To seek public acceptance by not interfering too vigorously to punish antisemitism was simply a path of least resistance for a regime burdened beyond its strength.

The utilisation of antisemitism as a mobilisation tool did not however originate at this time. In the Russian revolutionary movement, frustrated by its inability to gain mass support, there had been debates among both Populists and Social Democrats as to whether the movement should try to harness the mass energies of antisemitic *pogromschiki*, gaining control of them and turning them against the Tsarist autocracy and its supporters. At no point, however, did any part of the Russian revolutionary movement join antisemitism to anti-Zionism, or sponsor any anti-Jewish actions *per se*.

The so-called 'Doctors' Plot' was the culmination of the most brutal antisemitic campaign in Soviet history. Only Stalin's death in March 1953 stopped it from turning into a new wave of blood purges. In an atmosphere of Cold War and a hysterical press campaign against enemies from within and without, the accusation that a group of prominent Jewish physicians working as 'agents' of the American Joint Distribution Committee, and directed by 'the infamous Jewish bourgeois nationalist' Solomon Mikhoels, had already murdered several Soviet leaders and were planning further murders, had precisely the public effect that accusations of ritual murder enjoyed in earlier times.[8]

In addition to the domestic factors mentioned earlier, international factors also played a part in the intensification of anti-Zionism during these years. The forthright and uncompromising support of the USSR for the establishment of Israel had achieved its policy goal. The British Empire had been pushed back in the Middle East and nationalist feelings inflamed in the Arab World. The Soviet Union, now more capable of helping to realise the potential of the colonial peoples as a destabilising factor in international politics became more actively supportive of the Arabs and progressively more antagonistic to the Zionist state which it had helped to establish.

Soviet antagonism to Israel in the early 1950s was not solely a function of the situation in the Middle East. The Cold War between the United States and the USSR was focused in Europe but extended across the entire world. The Berlin blockade, the communist coup in Czechoslovakia, the creation of NATO and the Korean War brought the world to a state of polarisation little short of a new world war. In this context, Israel was clearly a part of the West. Israel had entered into the reparations agreements with Konrad Adenauer's government in the German Federal Republic which was one of the Soviet Union's main propaganda targets. The Soviet propaganda campaign against West Germany was broadened to include Israel and the accusations of 'revanchism' and neo-Nazism lumped Adenauer with Ben-Gurion. Here we have the first nascent buds of the equating of Zionism with Nazism that was to become one of the main themes of Soviet anti-Zionist propaganda in the 1980s.

While international politics and the geopolitical aspirations of the USSR provide background motivations for antagonism to Israel and for the depiction of Zionism as a subversive anti-Soviet force, this analysis cannot be complete without consideration of the factor of Bolshevik–Zionist competition for the loyalty of Soviet Jews – a throwback to pre-revolutionary problems of the communist movement. Let us remember at this point the situation of Soviet Jews after the Second World War. First and foremost there was the trauma of the Nazi Holocaust. Its impact on Jewish self-consciousness cannot be overstated. Together with this came the shock of wartime and post-war antisemitism felt by a generation that had grown up after the revolution and felt itself a part of the Soviet cultural and scientific intelligentsia. The wave of Jewish refugees from Poland and the Baltic states brought to Soviet Jews an infusion of persons bearing with them direct knowledge of Jewish tradition and of Zionism. Many of them were indeed activists of various Zionist movements.

The news of the establishment of Israel, and Soviet support for the new Jewish state, acted like a detonator upon this already unstable emotional mixture. Not only did the Soviet Union support Israel diplomatically but it also sanctioned the supply of arms as well as the training and emigration of Jews from Eastern Europe, many of whom had been in the Red Army during the Second World War and had later been repatriated to their lands of birth, particularly to Poland.[9] The best-known result of this situation was the massive public demonstration which greeted Golda Meir, Israel's first ambassador to the Soviet Union, at the Moscow synagogue in the autumn of 1948. As the historic photograph of this occasion shows, a large proportion of those in the crowd were Georgian Jews for whom the occasion must have seemed like a fulfilment of Messianic prophecy. There can be little doubt, however, that the enthusiasm expressed so openly at the synagogue in Moscow was felt in some degree by virtually all Soviet Jews.

This public display, seen by the authorities as an expression of sympathy for Zionism (and for a foreign state) served as confirmation of the regime's deep-seated doubts about Jewish loyalties. Moreover, as a spontaneous public expression of heterodox opinion the demonstration by the synagogue violated the most fundamental rules of Stalin's society. At every level of activity the regime intensified the already existing campaign against Soviet–Jewish symbols of national identity.[10] It should be remembered that the 'anti-cosmopolitan' campaign dated from the end of 1947, and that the same Solomon Mikhoels who was accused as the central figure of the 'Doctors' Plot' in January of 1953, had been murdered by Soviet secret police agents in Minsk in January 1948.

It is possible that some or all of the subsequent developments might have taken place even without the demonstration at the synagogue. Anti-nationalist campaigns involving purges, arrests and executions had taken place in Georgia and in the Ukraine in the same period. But none had been accompanied by such strident accusations of international conspiracy and preparations for mass deportation of a national group. A similar connection between the autonomous expression of Jewish feelings and the intensification of anti-Zionism by the Soviet authorities is to be found in the public emergence of the Jewish exodus movement at the end of 1969 and through 1970.[11]

The 'Black Years of Soviet Jewry', from the end of 1947 to Stalin's demise in March 1953, appear to be the apogee of everything anti-Jewish and anti-Zionist in Soviet policy. Nonetheless there would appear to exist a trend of thought in Soviet historiography which even today sees this period not as too harsh, but rather as lacking in consistent opposition to Zionism. While Gromyko and his associates in the Soviet UN delegation studiously avoided linking their support of a Jewish state with recognition of Zionism, or even with acknowledgement of the existence of a single worldwide Jewish nation, there were several months in early 1948 when full political and material aid to Israel by the Soviet Union was accompanied by an easing of domestic anti-Jewish pressures.[12]

V. V. Bol'shakov, currently a *Pravda* correspondent, and well known for his periodic attacks on Zionism in the Soviet press, has criticised Soviet historians in that between 1932 and 1956 they showed a 'neglect of the criticism of Zionism, affecting negatively the struggle against bourgeois ideology, and in particular against Jewish bourgeois nationalism . . . Any weakening or deviation from such criticism results in the strengthening of the Zionist ideology'.[13] When these words were published in 1973 general criticisms of Stalin's regime were quite out of style, but even in the heyday of Khrushchev's anti-Stalin campaigns, 'soft on Zionism' was not one of the charges levelled against the former tyrant. Bol'shakov also criticises anti-Zionist writings of the late 1950s (during the Khrushchev period) for underestimating the dangers posed by Zionism, because the historians failed to expose fully 'contemporary international Zionism's global (and not merely local) resources, goals, undertakings and links'.[14] Here we have a return to the sinister descriptions of the Cold War years. Zionism is not merely the local Middle Eastern pawn of imperialism, as it had been described by the Comintern in the 1920s – a model to which Soviet writers of the mid-1950s were returning. Bol'shakov had revived the Soviet version of the *Protocols of the Elders of Zion*, in which 'international Zionism' becomes the moving force of all that is evil in the world, using world-wide Jewish networks and riches to manipulate imperialism against the Soviet Union, seeking to forestall or overthrow revolutions in the developing world.

Together with the theme of identifying Zionism with Nazism, this revival of the demon of a worldwide Jewish conspiracy represents the extremist position of Soviet anti-Zionism. With its roots in concepts created by Russian antisemites of the Tsarist period it undoubtedly constitutes a threat to all Soviet Jews. The theme of a world Jewish conspiracy embraced by antisemites of Tsarist times had no necessary relation to modern Zionism. Its roots were in religion and in Russian social and political problems rather than in the area of international relations. It was anti-Jewish, pure and simple. In adopting these concepts, Soviet antisemites have laid at the door of Zionism all the same evils, often tracing their roots back into Jewish religion and culture. The claim of attacking modern political Zionism thus became a cloak for plain anti-Jewish prejudice. Trofim Kichko, whose antisemitic tract, *Judaism Unembellished*, evoked protests from many European communists and criticisms within the USSR in the mid 1960s, later published *Judaism and Zionism*, purporting to demonstrate both the evil of Zionism and the identity of Zionist goals with those of the Jewish religion. Such attacks label the entire Jewish past as antithetical to Soviet values. They thereby impugn the legitimacy and loyalty of Jews, individually or as a community, within the Soviet Union. Although such explicit argumentation is less frequent today than are purely political accusations against Zionism, it returns periodically to the pages of the Soviet press.[15] This mingling of antisemitism and anti-Zionism is thus part of each recurring anti-Zionist campaign. It underlines what is probably the fundamental problem of Soviet Jews – the mistrust with which both influential sectors of the authorities and a large part of the public regard the Jews.

As can be seen from the foregoing analysis, Soviet anti-Zionism is a complex phenomenon touching on both domestic and external affairs, and involving both contemporary Soviet society and past Russian history. It is therefore not surprising that the different interpretations of Zionism found in the Soviet press today may serve as weapons to be used by various groups in the factional disputes within the Soviet leadership. Such usage has been suggested in connection with the prolonged jockeying for position in the interregnum between Brezhnev's illness in mid-1983 and Gorbachev's accession to power in March 1985.[16] Certainly the sudden changes in the balance with which Zionism and the Jews were presented in the Soviet media during this period are hard to explain without reference to competing factional pressures. In the Soviet press, the prominence to be given to any subject, and the way in which that subject is to be presented are subject to continuous central control and review. As we have noted, Bol'shakov criticised the weakness of Soviet anti-Zionism during the Stalin period, implicitly questioning Soviet support for the creation of Israel, and by extension, the conduct of Soviet foreign policy. This critique was published only a few months after the promotion of then Soviet Foreign Minister Gromyko (most prominent remaining representative of Stalin's foreign policy team) to the Politburo in an extensive leadership shuffle linked to disputes over Brezhnev's policy of détente. Bol'shakov, in the same article, specifically attacked the journal *World Economy and International Relations* for ideological errors regarding the relation between Zionism and antisemitism.[17] At the time of this publication, this journal was prominent in the propagandising of Brezhnev's view of détente. Accusations of this sort, allegedly relating to one issue, but in actuality growing out of a very different policy dispute, are not uncommon in Soviet politics.

In the early 1980s the activities of the Anti-Zionist Committee of the Soviet Public (AKSO in its Soviet acronym) seemed to support the view that different factions have different views on how to present anti-Zionism, contending with each other for influence. AKSO was set up in April 1983 as a propaganda tool in the anti-Zionist campaign which flared up in the wake of the June 1982 Israeli invasion of Lebanon. More immediately, it is thought to have been a Soviet reaction to the convening in Jerusalem (in March 1983) of the Third World Conference on Soviet Jewry.[18] At AKSO's first press conference its members differed openly over the publication of clearly antisemitic propaganda in the guise of anti-Zionism, and the argument appears to have continued behind the scenes ever since.[19]

Following its founding in April 1983, AKSO began to swing between two orientations. Some of its press conferences were devoted to attacks on 'international Zionism' as a prime evil in the contemporary world, focusing both on the situation in the Middle East and on the entire development of international politics since 1917. This trend reached its zenith in October 1984 with a press conference devoted entirely to the theme that the Zionist movement had cooperated with the Nazis from the early 1930s and throughout the war; it was claimed that Israel today was using policies copied from the Nazis.[20] The historical references, replete with presentation of documents, were presented by Iulian Shulmeister and other veteran Soviet–Jewish spokesmen of anti-Zionism. They were supplemented by declarations of non-Soviet participants who denounced Israel's actions in Lebanon. Particularly significant in this context were the extreme (and often fantastic) charges of Nazi–Zionist collaboration brought by Samuel Zivs and by Shulmeister, both of whom had previously shown some measure of principled discrimination in their attacks on Zionism.[21] It appeared that the extreme antisemitic versions of anti-Zionism which not only deny the legitimacy of Zionism as a Jewish national movement, but dehumanise the state of Israel and all its agencies, presenting them as contemptible, pernicious and unworthy of life itself, had been freed from all restraints. They had swept aside the less virulent school of anti-Zionist propaganda which seemed to be aimed at discouraging the Soviet–Jewish emigration movement and any sympathy or vicarious pride which Soviet Jews might harbour towards Israel.[22]

This second trend of AKSO's activities has emphasised a concern for the well-being of Soviet Jews and their legitimacy as an integral part of Soviet society, clearly and repeatedly stating that emigration on the basis of family reunification has been virtually completed and should be considered a thing of the past. This group of themes, subordinate in the early declarations of AKSO, emerged as dominant in May 1984, but faded towards the end of that year.[23] Although statements of AKSO spokesmen and newspaper articles have repeated the domestic theme of the end of the family unification process, the emphasis of AKSO activity has been international, dwelling on the Zionist–Nazi theme and attacking the United States for alleged antisemitism.

An important barometer by which the strength of the radical antisemitic faction in the anti-Zionist campaign could be judged was the prominence given to the writings of Lev Aleksandrovich Korneev. Korneev, in his middle fifties, is of the same generation as Gorbachev, born and raised under Soviet rule, his education and career having taken place almost entirely in the post-Second World War years. Originally a linguist, he has generally been presented in the Soviet media as a historian. From the end of the 1970s he began to spew forth a stream of works ostensibly attacking Zionism, but in fact portraying Jews and everything Jewish in terms indistinguishable from those employed by Hitler or Goebbels. He even embraced the neo-Nazi denial that the Holocaust ever took place. Korneev characterised Soviet Jews who have emigrated as being purely motivated by greed. He recreated the genre of ritual murder by luridly portraying a religious Israeli soldier who cold-bloodedly murders a pregnant Arab woman to win a hundred shekel bet – a calumny which was repeated and enlarged upon by later Soviet writers.[24]

At the height of the anti-Zionist campaign of 1982–83, Korneev's work was published in all parts of the Soviet press. Then through 1984 he appeared very infrequently and the few articles published were of comparatively moderate tone. It has been suggested that the extremity and crudity of Korneev's attacks on the Jews and on Jewish history in the guise of anti-Zionism proved to be an embarrassment to the Soviet authorities. Perhaps the protests of a Leningrad scientist, Ivan Martynov, sent to various Soviet officials, helped to arouse some reaction.[25] Martynov himself was arrested and brought to trial in Leningrad in early 1985 because of his persistent criticisms.

At the same time, Korneev made a brief re-appearance. A multi-part article repeating and enlarging upon all the charges made regarding Nazi–Zionist contacts, appeared in a Soviet newspaper.[26] In his series, Korneev changed the year of the dynamiting of the King David Hotel by the Irgun from 1946 to 1944 – thus showing the Irgun as fighting on the side of the Nazis, rather than portraying the act as anti-imperialist. He also invented a new character, a Palestinian Zionist known as 'Moishe the Redhead', who supposedly was chief of Hitler's espionage services in the late 1930s. A radio interview with Korneev, broadcast both in Russian and in English for audiences abroad, recited the now-familiar litany of how Jewish bankers financed Hitler, and of Zionist guilt for the deaths of European Jews. The only new element in this broadcast was the admission that Jewish fighters from the Minsk and Warsaw ghettoes participated in the anti-Nazi struggle, but Korneev added: 'the Zionists, partners of the Nazis, had nothing to do with this sacred struggle'.[27] But this renewed exposure seems to have been short-lived. One version is that at the same time that Martynov was tried in Leningrad, an order was issued banning Korneev from the Soviet press. Whether or not a formal ban was issued, Korneev's four articles in *Sotsialisticheskaia industriia* were not listed in the gazette of newspaper articles published weekly as a research aid in the USSR. They simply vanished down the memory hole. At the same time, the Soviet armed forces ideological journal, approved for printing by the censors on

18 January 1985, carried an article almost certainly written by Korneev, but published under the pseudonym L. Aleksandrov (Korneev's first name and patronymic are Lev Aleksandrovich).[28]

A ban on Korneev, and the advent to power of Mikhail Gorbachev, a young, energetic and sophisticated leader who placed the reinstitution of détente high on his list of policy priorities, quickly raised expectations that the attacks on Jews, Zionism and Israel might be moderated. Immediately following Gorbachev's installation as General Secretary of the CPSU there was a flurry of emigration. The number of Jews leaving the USSR rose from 61 in January to 88 in February, 98 in March and 166 in April – only to fall back to 51 and 36 in the following two months, rising to 174 in July and then plummeting to an all-time low of only 11 in August 1985. In the past few years, of course, there has been a sharp increase in Jewish emigration from the Soviet Union. Meanwhile Gorbachev's efforts to consolidate his personal power resulted in the removal of two of the highest Soviet officials thought to espouse violent anti-Jewish views – Politburo member Grigorii Romanov and head of the armed forces Political Administration General Alexei Epishev. Their antisemitism had nothing to do with the removal of either man. Nevertheless, the dismissals appear in retrospect to have been a good omen for the implementation of more liberal policies under Gorbachev.

The question as to whether the accession of a new leadership in the USSR has presaged a change in the attitude to Zionism, Israel or to Soviet Jews, has obvious importance. It affects both the present daily life of Soviet Jews and their future as Jews, whether through the revival of some measure of Jewish culture and community life within the USSR or through renewed emigration. Beyond this, the Soviet Union, as a great power actively involved in all areas of international relations, has a considerable capacity to influence the images in the world of Jews, Israel and Zionism as a national movement. This has been forcefully demonstrated by the persistent Soviet initiatives to spread the slogan 'Zionism is Racism', which still finds a place on the agenda of virtually every international gathering held today.

The concluding portion of this essay will therefore be devoted to an examination of the Soviet media in the first year after Gorbachev's accession, to determine: (a) how Soviet Jews were presented? (b) how the state of Israel was portrayed? (c) how Zionism was characterised? As has been the case in the past, the three categories are often intertwined, and it is clear that some Soviet writers still use Jew, Zionist and Israel with a high degree of interchangeability.

In articles dealing with Soviet Jews as Jews, the most prominent theme during the first eight months of 1985 was the condemnation of emigration and the characterisation of the emigrants either as renegades or as victims of their own poor judgement. At no time was it even hinted to the Soviet reader that a Soviet Jew might have emigrated even for such a justifiable reason as family reunification, and that in his new place of residence he might lead a life equal in worth to that he left behind. But first and foremost the emigrants were characterised as unpatriotic. As one article in the Soviet press put it: 'Friends often ask me what I think of those people who, under the pretext of family reunification, leave for permanent residence in Israel. . . . They have abandoned their homeland.'[29] The theme of the Soviet Union as the sole homeland of Soviet Jews appeared frequently and with great emphasis, emphasising that emigration had ended.

Repeatedly the Soviet press carried accusations that the emigrants were renegades working against the Soviet Union 'on behalf of the CIA, using material sent by Zionist friends in New York . . .'[30] The negotiations to set up Voice of America transmitters in Israel were attacked for providing 'employment for renegades of Jewish nationality who left the USSR and who propagate aggressive Zionist ideas and militant anti-communism'.[31]

Alongside these negative depictions of Jews who emigrated, one could find positive descriptions of the Jew's place in the USSR. Letters to the Soviet papers depicted the peaceful respected lives led by Jewish scientists, workers, artists and Communist Party members.[32] This was in stark contrast to the tragedies and troubles in Israel which were said to drive many Soviet Jews to suicide.[33] The result, according to the Soviet press, was that there are no more emigration requests coming to the state institutions of the Lithuanian republic. The 'vyzovi' – affidavits promising sponsorship to a would-be immigrant – which nevertheless continue to arrive, were described as unsolicited and as having been sent as provocations by strangers.[34]

Reinforcing statements made by Jews regarding their own status in Soviet society were interviews depicting persons with names or associations of a clearly Jewish nature, showing them as contributing patriotically to various aspects of Soviet life. These interviews, appearing in central party and government publications could be understood as an attempt by the authorities to portray for the general public an authoritative image of the Jews who remain in the Soviet Union as an honourable and integral part of Soviet society. It is as though an attempt were being made to compartmentalise antisemitism, restricting all the lurid descriptions of subversive allies of the CIA and of neo-Nazis to those Jews who have left the Soviet Union, while depicting those who remain as respectable and loyal.

During a session of the USSR Supreme Soviet in 1985 an interview with one of the deputies, R. Geller, was published. Identified as a worker in the Birobijan transformer plant she spoke with enthusiasm of the outstanding work groups in her factory, some led by workers with Jewish names, others by workers with Russian names.[35] She thus drew a picture of idyllic proletarian internationalism. Among the many articles devoted to the fortieth anniversary of the victory over Nazi Germany, facts of Jewish participation were often included, particularly in the newspapers of areas with a relatively active Jewish population.[36] Most remarkable among such articles is 'Recalling the Lessons of Tankograd', by I. Zaltsman and G. Edel'gauz, which appeared in the Communist Party's central ideological journal. In addition to establishing that the director and chief engineer of the Soviet Union's most successful Second World War tank factory were Jews, the article specifically mentioned Jews among the nationalities represented in the work force, rather than obscuring them in the anonymous category of 'and others'.[37] On rare occasions, a newspaper even went out of its way to suggest the Jewishness of a high official. Towards the end of an interview with the head of the KGB in the Moldavian republic, the journalist addressed him as Gavriil Moiseevich, a name and patronymic suggesting Jewish antecedents, rather than by his family name Volkov, a common Russian name.[38]

With all such positive characterisations, it is clear that the Jew is considered a good Soviet citizen only in as much as he is primarily Soviet, and willing to restrict his Jewishness to the narrow limits of a history which begins with Shalom Aleichem and does not stray beyond the borders of the Soviet Union. As Gavriil Moiseevich Volkov put it, the Zionists, having failed in their attempt to organise a mass exodus of Soviet Jews from the USSR, now resort to tactics of 'ideological sabotage'. The demand of Jews for promotion of Jewish culture becomes, in Volkov's analysis, a primary instrument of such ideological sabotage.[39] Within the narrow bounds of such deracinated Jewishness, the Soviet Jew is, on balance, depicted as a positive and loyal element. However, towards the end of the period surveyed, one jarringly discordant article appeared. Loaded with such code words as 'cosmopolitan' and 'bourgeois nationalist', it raised the spectre that 'international Zionism' was capable of reaching any and every Jew, turning him against his native land.[40] The theme of the Jew as essentially alien and a potential traitor has not been fully exorcised as yet from the Soviet press under Gorbachev.

Israel is, with some exceptions, still painted in predominantly dark colours. Nevertheless, shades of difference may be discerned even within such a bleak presentation. One trend of articles is written in pity and in sorrow for the unfortunate Israelis who are sinking in a bog of economic, social and military difficulties, imposed upon them by the pernicious policies of their Zionist leaders. The other trend sparks with anger and contempt for Israel as a centre of ultra-chauvinism, aggression and subversion on an international scale. The first trend has been dominant under Gorbachev, but is far from holding a monopoly. It is clearly connected to the campaign to discourage pressures for emigration by Jews (a parallel campaign emphasising unemployment and social injustice blackens the United States as well). Since the economic situation is truly difficult in Israel, these reports are often merely factual recitals of external debt, budget cuts, price rises and anticipated unemployment.[41] Where commentary is added, it usually blames the 'aggressive, expansionist course of Israel's ruling Zionist elite'.[42] Here we may point out that in this type of article a distinction is sometimes made between the Israeli people and the Zionist leadership of Israel. Such a distinction is often used in constructing a model in which Israel is only a small regional cog in the global plans of imperialism.

The harsher depictions of Israel are exemplified in an article headlined 'Israel Trains Murderers'.[43] The article attacks Israel's entire educational system for teaching 'the reactionary ideas of Zionism', and giving Israeli youth 'military-Zionist training'. It sums up: 'Brought up on Zionist ideals, the young settlers destroy Arab mosques, blow up houses, kill peaceful inhabitants and forcefully expropriate Arab lands'. In this version, Zionism is fundamental to the character of Israel and of its people, and is not simply the ideology of a ruling clique. The only attempt at mitigating this condemnation is the mention of 'thousands of healthy youth, led by communists', who are said to oppose the Zionist educational system of Israel. Here the Soviet Union has taken a plank from the platform of the Israeli Communist Party, according to which only de-Zionisation can cleanse Israel's soul.

Not even this slim hope of redemption can be found in the pages of *Komsomol'skaia pravda*, the Soviet youth newspaper. In the mid 1980s this paper was most strident in its hostility to Zionism. Throughout 1983 and 1984 it ran a periodical series under the heading 'Zionism is Fascism'. In 1985 it was by far the most extreme in its formulations. 'The Tel Aviv ideologists have a name – well known for its anti-human ideology . . . and whose crimes have a specific goal – the confirming of the supremacy of the Jewish race.'[44] Israel, Zionism and the Jewish 'race' were woven into a single strand and the reader warned of the danger which Zionism (and by implication Israel and the Jews) posed to the whole world, and to the existence of mankind. Even when the texts of *Komsomol'skaia pravda* do not include characterisations of Zionism, or even the word 'Zionist', the headlines of the articles do so.[45] The interchangeable use of Israel and Zionist has been prominent in this paper's reportage, with such passages as 'the long chain of crimes of the Israeli Zionists . . . the inhuman nature of the Zionist war machine . . . the Zionists who are worthy heirs of the Nazis' concentration camps and punitive expeditions'.[46]

In these extreme versions, Israel and Zionism are not only stripped of any legitimacy in the international arena, but are totally dehumanised. Israel and Zionism are portrayed as irredeemable, bestial and dangerous. This dehumanisation is clearly an advance justification for the killing of Zionists (that is, Jews or Israelis) and even the destruction of their state, despite official Soviet policy statements to the contrary.[47]

In surveying the portrayal of Jews and of Zionism in the Soviet press of the 1980s, we have already established the persistent continuity of Soviet hostility to Zionism, and noted the spillover of this category into vilification of Jews and of Israel as a state. Only in part can this be explained on the basis of competition for the loyalty of Soviet Jews. The extreme portrayals of Zionism betray an almost mystical fear of the power and influence of Jews, reaching back through the *Protocols of the Elders of Zion* and into medieval demonologies.

Here is one example, published in a journal in 1985 that appeared in major Western languages as well as in Russian. 'The cosmopolitan big bourgeoisie adopted Zionism as a form of bourgeois nationalism. . . . The Jewish state was not an end in itself but a means for securing global objectives.'[48] The article then continues in familiar patterns, presenting the 'fact' of Zionist–Nazi collaboration, the continuation of Nazi policies by Israel today, and the 'evident hand' in Czechoslovakia in 1968 and in Poland in 1980–81, of Zionists, who demand the loyalty of all Jews everywhere, even against the interests of their own country. This diatribe, clearly intended to spread Soviet anti-Zionism and suspicion of the Jews among audiences throughout the Western world, could almost have been written by Korneev himself. Another article in the same journal creates a new and different image of Zionism as embracing all Jews by naming as Zionist both the anti-Zionist 'Rav Tov' of the Satmar hassidim, and the non-Zionist HIAS – its initials given a sinister bend by the author who renders them as 'Hebrew International Aid Society'.[49]

The Soviet press is still far from speaking with a single voice. In this same period of 1985 in which *Komsomol'skaia pravda* and *New Times* carried their luridly antisemitic characterisations of Zionism, *Pravda*, the leading Communist Party daily, virtually ignored the subject of Zionism, though it attacked Israel and Israeli–American ties ferociously. In addition, *Literaturnaia gazeta* used the same technique as was noticed in *Komsomol'skaia pravda* of publishing a headline incongruent with the content of the article, catching the readers' eyes with lurid anti-Zionism, while delivering much more moderate information. One heading read: 'Evidence of Crimes: New Facts, Testimony, Documents on Zionism as an Ideology, its Policies and Practices.'[50] The article was a review of a new edition of AKSO's 'White Book', much of it devoted to denunciations of Israel's conduct in Lebanon and in the occupied territories of the West Bank, and replete with denunciations of Israel as heir to the Nazis, in the spirit of AKSO's October 1984 press conference. The review published under the extremist headline ignored all these aspects and dealt only with the domestic aspect of the end of Jewish emigration, claiming that the USSR had fulfilled its obligations under the Helsinki agreements in a humane and positive manner. Virtually the same phrasing was used by Gorbachev in his press conference in Paris at the beginning of October 1985. Significantly, all attempts to reopen the emigration issue are now characterised as American (not even Zionist) anti-Soviet plotting. The impression created was of a directive from a central authority calling for moderation in attacks on Jews and Zionism. Meanwhile, the editor gave free rein to his prejudices through the headline and the accompanying pictures of an Israeli prison, Israeli soldiers patrolling an Arab town, violence by soldiers against civilians, and the corpse of an Arab youth – none of which were connected to anything in the article.

Even before his accession to power, Gorbachev had been running the Secretariat of the Soviet Communist Party's Central Committee, the key executive organ of the Soviet regime. In this capacity he was in a position to control the agenda and the approach of the Soviet press. Certainly after his formal election to the post of General Secretary in mid-March 1985 and his reshuffling of the Politburo at the start of July, Gorbachev was clearly dominant, if not yet an absolute ruler. Yet much of the material of an inflammatory and antisemitic nature appeared after these events, and after the dismissals of Romanov and Epishev. Thus the accession of a new leader and a young generation of leading officials did not instantly cause major changes in the expression of anti-Zionism in the Soviet media, nor have the differences of approach in various sections of the media lessened. Though changes have undoubtedly occurred under Gorbachev, some have even been negative, such as the emergence of *New Times*, a weekly aimed at foreign audiences which generally presented a moderate, respectable and reasonable image, as one of the vehicles of extremist anti-Zionist invective. It has unashamedly used antisemitism in its attacks on Israel and on Zionism, reviving such code words of the Stalinist era as 'cosmopolitan', 'bourgeois nationalist', and so on. Even more significantly, the free rein given to openly racist organisations like Pamyat – despite the criticisms in the official Soviet press – suggest that levels of antisemitism may actually have risen in Soviet society in the last few years.

Whatever the modification of the regime's expressions regarding the reliability of Jews as Soviet citizens, it is clear that the slogan 'Neither antisemitism nor Zionism', coined by Brezhnev at the party congress in 1981 and adopted by AKSO, is applied only in part. The clear emphasis has been on stamping out Zionism and interpreting any elements of Jewishness drawn from beyond the geographical and temporal borders of the Russian revolution, as 'Zionist ideological sabotage'. The mainstream of the Soviet battle against Zionism has always been the attempt to isolate the remaining Jews of the Soviet Union from other Jews as part of the traditional communist denial of a single world-wide Jewish people. Today, this is a more difficult task than ever before, since about 300 000 Soviet Jews have emigrated since 1966, with the majority settled in Israel. Direct familiar communication has thus reinforced the already existing metaphysical links which bound Soviet Jews to the fate of the Jewish people the world over.

The denial of a single Jewish people takes its most extreme form among those who evince the greatest fear and hatred of the Jew as a person and of

Zionism as a movement. In Korneev's writings it even included a denial of the existence of a Jewish nation in Israel where, in his view, 'the Jews are part of a potentially possible Israeli nation'.[51] The same rejection of Jewish national community is evident in Soviet presentations of Ethiopian Jews' immigration to Israel. This has been invariably presented as 'the illegal transport of Ethiopian citizens of Jewish faith to Israel by the Zionists'.[52] Such a refusal by Soviet ideologists to regard various Jewish communities around the world as part of a single people, limiting the description of them to being of the 'Jewish faith' (whether or not the individuals profess any religious belief) appears incongruous against the background of the Soviet regime's registration of its Jews as being of 'Jewish nationality'. There is in fact no official registration of religious beliefs in the USSR. An even more blatant contradiction appears in the rejection of the concept of any 'Alliance Israelite Universelle' in a national sense by precisely those persons who most loudly proclaim the existence of an international Zionist conspiracy for the benefit of the Jewish 'race', one commanding the potential obedience of Jews everywhere in the world.

Despite early signs that there had been only a minor relaxation of anti-Zionism and no elimination of antisemitism under Gorbachev, more recent evidence suggests a turn for the better motivated both by Soviet *raison d'état* and the dynamics of change engendered by the policy of *glasnost*. Gorbachev's desire to use détente to ease the difficulties his economy faces has been clearly expressed. The priority of this tactic appears to override other domestic and international considerations, thereby renewing the option of emigration. Nevertheless it is prudent to remember that anti-Zionism remains an immanent element in the Soviet world-view. Moreover, antagonism to Israel remains a prominent if more muted feature of Soviet foreign policy, partly derived from the close cooperation of the United States and Israel in regional and global political affairs. Neither of these phenomena need necessarily be moderated in conjunction with the renewal of Jewish emigration. It should be remembered that the anti-Zionist campaign of 1969–1970 accompanied the revival of open emigration after the Six Day War and was in large measure an instrument to discourage Jews from joining the emigration movement. In addition, though both anti-Zionism and opposition to Israel may have been somewhat attenuated and are operationally distinct from antisemitism, the persistent injection of blatant anti-Jewish expressions into anti-Zionist and anti-Israel campaigns over many years have left their residues and call for caution in dealings with the Soviet Union.

## Notes

1. See Lenin's article citing Kautsky in *Iskra*, no. 51, 22 October 1903, reprinted in V. I. Lenin, *Complete Collected Works* (5th edn.; Moscow: 1959), vol. 8, p. 74. For a discussion of Lenin's views on nationalism see Demetrio Boersner, *The Bolsheviks and the National and Colonial Question* (Geneva: Librairie E. Droz, 1957).
2. V. B–v, 'On anti-Semitism, assimilation, and proletarian struggle', *Iskra*, no. 55, 15 December 1903.
3. The Jewish Bund held its founding congress in 1897, as did the Zionist movement. The Russian Social Democratic Labour Party, which at its founding included the Bund, was formed in 1898, the populist Socialist Revolutionary Party was officially formed in 1901, and the Russian liberal movement *Osvobozhdenie* (Liberation) which later became the Constitutional Democratic Party began its activities in 1902.
4. See, for instance, the opening paragraph in V. V. Bol'shakov, 'Criticism of Zionism in Soviet historiography', *Voprosy istorii*, no. 9, 1973, p. 78, or Lev A. Korneev, 'Who profits?', *Neva*, no. 5, May 1982, p. 148, which quotes the same articles by Lenin.
5. A detailed analysis of the rise and fall of the *Evsektsiia* and its activities against Zionism, will be found in Zvi Y. Gitelman, *Jewish Nationality and Soviet Politics: the Jewish Sections of the CPSU, 1917–1930* (Princeton: Princeton University Press, 1972).
6. For an instance of nearly verbatim copying of Tsarist antisemitic material by Soviet sources in the 1970s, see G. Svirsky, *Hostages* (New York, Knopf, 1976).
7. For Stalin's antisemitism see S. Allilueva, *Only One Year* (Harmondsworth: Penguin, 1971), pp. 138–141, and N. S. Khrushchev, *Khrushchev Remembers* (Boston: Little, Brown and Co., 1970), pp. 259–69.
8. This entire period is analysed in detail in Yehoshua Gilboa, *The Black Years of Soviet Jewry* (Boston: Little, Brown and Co., 1971). For a classic fictional account of the period see Ilya Ehrenburg, *The Thaw* (New York, Knopf, 1962).
9. This aid, proudly cited by Jewish Communists in various countries as proof of Soviet benevolence towards Israel, is categorically denied in a recent Soviet military-ideological journal. See L. Alexandrov, 'Israel's other war', *Kommunist vooruzhenykh sil*, no. 3, February 1985, p. 85.
10. For examples of public warnings that Jews should distinguish between Soviet support of Israel and a condoning of Zionism or Zionist sympathies within the USSR see Ilya Ehrenburg's article in *Pravda*, 21 September 1948, and the account of Paul Robeson's concert in Moscow, in Arieh L. Eliav, *Between Hammer and Sickle* (New York, Signet, 1969), pp. 40–3. See also Israel A. Genin's public lectures on 'The Palestine problem', published later in Moscow as a brochure. In these 1948 lectures Genin denounces Zionism for its links with monopoly capital in the world.
11. Analysis of this campaign will be found in Jonathan Frankel, 'The anti-Zionist press campaigns in the USSR, 1969–71; an internal dialogue?', *Soviet Jewish Affairs*, no. 3, May 1972, pp. 3–26.
12. For details of this period see Jonathan Frankel, 'The Soviet regime and anti-Zionism: an analysis' (Jerusalem, Soviet and East European Research Centre, Hebrew University, Research Paper no. 55), pp. 14–15.
13. Bol'shakov, 'Criticism of Zionism . . .', pp. 79–80.

14. Ibid., p. 80.
15. See B. Kravtsov, *Leningradskaia pravda*, 19 and 20 April 1983, and M. Gol'denberg, 'Genocide in the name of Jehovah', *Nauka i Religiia*, no. 6, 1983. Gol'denberg is also the author of *Myths of Zionism* (Kishinev, 1972).
16. See Theodore H. Friedgut, 'Soviet anti-Zionism and anti-Semitism – another
17. Bol'shakov, 'Criticism of Zionism. . . .'
    cycle', *Soviet Jewish Affairs*, vol. 14, no. 1, 1984, pp. 18–20, and Theodore H. Friedgut, 'Neither Zionism nor anti-Semitism: the Jews in the Soviet media during Chernenko's first six months', in D. Pri-Tal, (ed.) *The Jews of the Soviet Union: Immigration and Struggle in the 1980s* (Hebrew), vol. 8, no. 2, Jerusalem, 1984, pp. 27–36.
18. See Frankel, 'The Soviet Regime . . .', note 66, p. 78.
19. Discussion of this incident is to be found in Friedgut, 'Soviet Anti-Zionism. . . .', pp. 11–16. For a *samizdat* account of an open and bitter discussion of this topic in the Institute of Oriental Studies of the Soviet Academy of Sciences in February 1976, see E. L. Smolar, 'The Protocols of the Elders of anti-Zionism', in *Evreiskii samizdat*, no. 16, Jerusalem, Hebrew University, the Centre for Research and Documentation of East European Jewry, 1978. This material is cited extensively in English by Frankel, 'The Soviet Regime . . .', pp. 50–3.
20. An official Soviet report of the press conference in English is to be found in *New Times*, no. 44, October 1984, pp. 26–32.
21. For the report of Zivs' criticism of 'erroneous presentations' of anti-Zionism see the *New York Times'* report on the AKSO press conference, 7 June 1983. For Shulmeister's criticism of Vladimir Begun's anti-Zionist tract *Invasion Without Arms*, see R. M. Brodsky and Iu. A. Shulmeister, *Sovetish heymland*, March 1980. For an earlier work by this same pair of Jewish anti-Zionists see *Zionism – Weapon of Reaction* (Lvov, 1976).
22. For a striking example of the two totally different presentations of Zionism by a single author, see S. Fridmanas, 'Danger, Zionism!', in *Sovetskaia Litva*, 1 June 1983, and the same journalist's 'Myths and reality – the handwriting of Zionism', *Sovetskaia Litva*, 26 November 1983. The differences between the two articles are analysed in Friedgut, 'Soviet Anti-Zionism . . .', pp. 18–19.
23. Family reunion as a basis for Jewish emigration was established by a December 1966 statement by the then-premier of the USSR, Alexei Kosygin. For statements by AKSO members regarding completion of the family reunification process see the report of the AKSO press conference in *Literaturnaia gazeta*, 23 May 1984, and interviews with Samuel Zivs and Tsezar Solodar in *Izvestiia*, 3 November 1984.
24. For some details of Korneev's writings see Friedgut, 'Soviet Anti-Zionism. . . .', pp. 8–10 and note 33. For the repetition of his blood libel see the report of Doctor of Historical Sciences K. Khachaturov on his visit as part of a Soviet delegation to Israel. He writes: 'Zionist thinking about the Arab *untermenschen* allows the murder of Arab mayors . . . disembowelling of pregnant women and systematic annihilation of the population of Lebanon.' *Izvestiia*, 13 January 1985.
25. The bulk of Martynov's extensive correspondence against Korneev reached the West and was translated into English. See Ivan F. Martynov, 'Documentary evidence of anti-Semitism in the Soviet Union today', Highland Park, Illinois, Chicago Action for Soviet Jewry, 1983.
26. See Korneev's articles in *Sotsialisticheskaia industriia*, 10, 11, 12, 13 January, 1985.
27. See *BBC Summary of World Broadcasts*, Part 1, USSR, SU/7885/A1/11,

17 January 1985. For the origins of the lie regarding alleged Jewish financing of Hitler, see C. C. Aronsfeld, 'The myth of Zionist–Nazi collaboration: some sources of Soviet propaganda', *IJA Research Reports* (London: Institute of Jewish Affairs), no. 2, April 1985.

28. See L. Alexandrov, 'Israel's other war', *Kommunist vooruzhenykh sil*, no. 3, February 1985, pp. 81–6. This article is virtually a word for word repetition of Korneev's other works in its treatment of the historical appearance of the Jews (tribes from Arabia which in the twelfth century BCE conquered Canaan with fire and sword-cf. Korneev, *Neva*, no. 5, May 1982, p. 148.) as well as in his definition of the aims of international Zionism – 'the achieving of maximum control in the capitalist system for the super-enrichment of the Jewish bourgeoisie' – cf. Korneev, *Sovetskaia Rossiia*, 17 May 1983. I am indebted to Dr Mikhail Agurskii who first suggested that L. Aleksandrov was a pseudonym for Korneev.

29. *Sovetskaia Litva*, 1 March 1985. See also S. Fridmanas in ibid., 17 January 1985, and *Sovetskaia Belorussia*, 9 July 1985.

30. *Komsomolskaia pravda*, 12, 13, 14 July 1985. See also *Sovetskaia Litva*, 17 July 1985 which adds Nazi war criminals to the list of agents of evil.

31. *BBC Summary of World Broadcasts*, Part 1, USSR, SU/7838/A1/11, 2 January 1985.

32. *Sovetskaia Litva*, 1 March 1985.

33. Boris Antonov, 'Zionist promises: a mirage', *New Times*, no. 27, July 1985.

34. *Literaturnaia gazeta*, 21 August 1985. This latter claim is repeated in *Sovetskaia Belorussia*, 9 July 1985.

35. *Izvestiia*, 2 July 1985. Ms Geller is among the signatories of an AKSO telegram to the US Congress deploring the fact that there were 715 antisemitic incidents in the United States during 1984. *Pravda*, 27 February 1985.

36. See, for instance *Sovetskaia Belorussia*, 4 July 1985.

37. I. Saltzman and G. Edel'gauz, 'Recalling the Lessons of Tankograd', *Kommunist*, no. 16, 1984, pp. 76–87.

38. *Sovetskaia Moldavia*, 20 December 1984.

39. Ibid.

40. Y. Borin, 'Zionism: its roots and consequences', *New Times*, no. 32, August 1985, pp. 18–21.

41. See *Sovetskaia Litva*, 16 July 1985; *Pravda*, 20 January 1985; and *Sovetskaia Rossiia*, 9 July 1985.

42. *Sovetskaia Litva*, 13 July 1985.

43. *Sovetskaia Litva*, 9 July 1985. The article was syndicated through the Novosti News Agency.

44. *Komsomolskaia pravda*, 18 May 1985.

45. See 'I Accuse Zionism', *Komsomolskaia pravda*, 16 August 1985, and 'A bomb for the Zionists', *Komsomolskaia pravda*, 21 August 1985.

46. *Komsomolskaia pravda*, 6 June 1985.

47. For a full discussion of this concept see Ehud Sprinzak, 'From Delegitimization to Dehumanization', *Forum*, no. 53, Fall 1984.

48. Y. Borin, 'Zionism: its roots and objectives', *New Times*, no. 32, August 1985, pp. 18–21.

49. Boris Antonov, 'Zionist promises: a mirage', *New Times*, no. 27, July 1985.

50. *Literaturnaia gazeta*, 21 August 1985.

51. Lev A. Korneev, 'Who profits?', p. 148.

52. See *Komsomolskaia pravda*, 17 January 1985, *Izvestiia*, 18 February 1985, and sub-headings of articles listed in *Letopis gazetnykh statei*, no. 13, 1985, entry no. 8595, and no. 14, 1985, entries no. 7838 and no. 7973.

# 3 Left-wing Anti-Zionism in Western Societies
## Robert S. Wistrich

Ever since political Zionism first emerged on the stage of history at the end of the nineteenth century, it has had its opponents as well as its advocates on the left. In the golden era of the Second International – that is, before 1914 – it was generally the Marxist as opposed to the 'revisionist' wing of social democracy, especially in Central and Eastern Europe, that stood in the forefront of opposition to Zionism as a political ideology and movement. Frequently, too, it was Jewish intellectuals, especially in Eastern Europe, who were most vehement in their rejection of Zionism, branding it as a clerical, obscurantist attempt to return the Jews to the ghetto or as a design to subjugate the Jewish masses to the retrograde nationalism of the Jewish bourgeoisie. Both Jews and non-Jews in the revolutionary Marxist movement tended to see Jewish nationalism in Lenin's terms (derived from a polemic against the anti-Zionist Bund rather than against the Zionists!) as an absolutely 'un-scientific' and 'reactionary' idea whose purpose was to divert the Jewish masses from the class struggle. As Karl Kautsky and the Austro–Marxist Otto Bauer emphasised at the turn of the century, Zionism and Jewish nationalism stood in contradiction to the only truly progressive solution of the 'Jewish question' – namely, assimilation of the Jews in the classless society of the future to be created by socialist revolution.

By seeking to revive a fossilised ghetto Judaism, the Zionists, so the argument ran, were perpetuating a reactionary caste, a relic of the Middle Ages and creating an obstacle in the common struggle against antisemitism. The Russian Marxists, Lenin, Trotsky and Julius Martov, also shared this view, as did an entire generation of internationalist revolutionaries – many of whom were, in Isaac Deutscher's phrase, 'non-Jewish Jews' seeking to cast off their ethnic identity and escape into the utopia of universalist socialism. Already this first phase of Marxist anti-Zionism showed a curious characteristic that has persisted to the present day – namely, that individuals and ideological tendencies with little else in common (and sometimes even bitter enemies *within* the left,) such as the centrist Kautsky, the reformist Social Democrat Otto Bauer, the ultra-leftist Rosa Luxemburg, the Bolsheviks Lenin and Stalin, the Menshevik Martov, and the internationalist wanderer between the worlds, Trotsky – could unite on at least one issue: their opposition to Jewish nationalism.

The arguments of this classical Marxist left against Zionism are still frequently quoted in the ideological anti-Zionist literature of the contemporary left, but it is crucial to note some very important differences. In the first place, before 1914 and indeed until the post-Holocaust period and the creation of the state of Israel, the subject of Zionism never assumed *major* importance on the left. Although there are a number of basic doctrinal texts, even these possess an ad hoc character and have only in retrospect been invested with a quasi-sacral quality. Thus modern Soviet propaganda will endlessly refer to Lenin's so-called polemics against the 'Zionists' without revealing that he barely discussed the subject and reserved most of his polemical efforts on the 'Jewish Question' for denouncing the Bund or condemning antisemitism. Similarly, the Western New Left as well as the Communists will resuscitate texts on the *Judenfrage* as ancient as Karl Marx's young Hegelian polemic of 1844 against Bruno Bauer to justify an entirely different political purpose – namely the Soviet political war against 'international Zionism'. Neither Marx, Engels, Kautsky, Lenin, Trotsky nor Rosa Luxemburg would ever have dreamed that Zionism could become a *major world problem*, an ideological issue of the first importance for the Socialist bloc on a par with the struggle against capitalism or imperialism, or that it could become a code word for the forces of reaction in general.

For the traditional Marxist left such a proposition would have been incomprehensible, and to admit it would have implied that something had gone radically wrong with the entire Marxist view of the historical process, in which ethnic and national antagonisms are inevitably to be superseded by class polarisation on a universal scale. For if one thing united traditional left-wing thinking on the Jews (in both East and West) it was the assumption that Judaism was bound to disappear according to the laws of historical development, that the final emancipation of the Jews implied the dissolution of any Jewish group identity. The total failure of this historical prognosis or prediction is, in my opinion, itself one of the reasons for the extraordinary antipathy of many Marxists toward Zionism today – for the state of Israel, the offspring of the Zionist movement, by its very existence calls into question the whole Marxist tradition of theorising on the Jewish question.

As we have pointed out, Marxism did from the outset relate to the ideological content of Zionism but rejected it on principle as incompatible with the doctrines of proletarian internationalism. In particular, it denied that the Jews were a nation, that they had a common history, language, culture, and so on – arguments that frequently recur in the extreme-left polemics against Zionism today. But here, too, the context is very different, as are the modes of debate, the tone of the argument, and its underlying meaning or deep structure. No one familiar with the older 'anti-Zionist' texts could, for example, mistake the fact that they were motivated by a pro-Jewish attitude or, rather, sympathy for the Jews as the object of persecution through the centuries; that in opposing Jewish nationalism, socialists believed in all sincerity that they were serving the *best interests* of the Jews, whose salvation, so they thought, depended on the creation of a classless society in which all differences of race, religion, ethnicity and caste would become irrelevant.

This anti-antisemitic anti-Zionism may still exist in some quarters on the left, but it is hardly the dominant mode of discourse. For the extreme left in Western societies not only denigrates Israel and Zionism in a systematic manner, but its irrational hostility frequently spills over into contempt or antipathy towards Jews and Judaism as such. True, this contemporary anti-Zionist left – whether it be orthodox Communist, Trotskyist, Maoist, gauchiste or anarchist – will invariably claim that it is anti-racist and rejects antisemitism. Yet the stereotypes of Jews that are found in the literature of the political left are extremely negative, reflecting as they do a built-in visceral hatred of Israel and Zionism. Thus the Israelis are invariably militarist, aggressive, expansionist, fascist oppressors; colonisers who ruthlessly confiscate other people's lands; blackmailers who try to silence criticism by playing on the Holocaust; and, worst of all, modern practitioners of 'genocide' against the Palestinian people. Those in the Jewish Diaspora who support such devils are themselves accomplices of war criminals, aiding and abetting the oppression of defenceless people, financing and whitewashing a military machine that is a threat not only to the Palestinians or the Arabs but to all of humanity and to world peace as a whole.

Nor should it be thought that this type of rhetoric is merely Israelophobic or that it remains at the level of an abstract 'anti-Zionism' with no practical consequences or implications for the perception of Jews in general. True, the extreme left will often bracket Israel with other ultra-reactionary regimes like South Africa or the 'fascist' military Junta in Chile – or, as in the past, with governments like white Rhodesia, Peron's Argentina or the Shah's Iran – and then claim that its hostility derives from the racist colonialist *policies* of the Israeli government. But if this were really the case, there would be no need for the far left to expend such enormous polemical energy in vilifying 'Zionism' and arguing that the ideological basis of the state of Israel is *a priori* pernicious, malevolent and inherently racist. Moreover, by insisting on dismantling the Jewish state and 'de-Zionising' Israel so that it can then be replaced by the 'secular democratic state' of Palestine – one in which the Jews would at best be reduced to their traditional status under Islam (that of a 'protected' minority) – the left makes itself the accomplice of a radically discriminatory, *politicidal* formula invented by the PLO. Thus on the extreme left, sanction is given to the destruction of an existing state – one that is based on the democratic will of its Jewish majority – if necessary by the use of terror and in any case by the method of armed struggle and a popular war of liberation. In these respects, the extreme left in Western societies is in fact more radical than the Soviet Union, which has been careful, even as it infects the bloodstream of its own population and that of the Third World with the antisemitic virus, to proclaim its respect for the 1948 borders of Israel.

Admittedly, the Soviet position on this issue is also ambiguous at times, yet it has never *officially* embraced the PLO thesis on the need to physically destroy the Zionist 'entity'. For Soviet purposes it would appear sufficient to weaken Israel significantly, isolate it and cut it off from its Diasporic hinterland and its main protector, the United States. A completely successful Arab campaign against the Jewish state might after all have the unfortunate effect of rendering the USSR superfluous in the Middle East, given that apart from its armaments and ideological warfare against Israel it can offer little else to its client states. Not surprisingly, the position of communists in Western societies tends to reflect this Soviet ambivalence and to be less virulent than that of the far left as a whole toward Israel. This is particularly the case given that Western communists in general do not share the endemic antisemitism of their Soviet counterparts and, of necessity, seek to adapt to the ethos and norms of their surrounding democratic and pluralist environment. Not that the French or Italian or any other Western communists are anything but militant anti-Zionists and Israelophobes, ready to denounce the new 'fascism' as the occasion demands – but they are rarely to be found disseminating the occult theory of the 'World Jewish Conspiracy' and other such made-in-Russia concoctions. Unlike the Soviet or East European communists, they generally reject Zionism not as the sinister manipulating force *behind* Western imperialism but rather as its agent. Nor on the whole do they characterise Israel as a 'settler colonialist state' implanted as an alien entity in the heart of the Arab East – this is the militant Trotskyist theory – inasmuch as such a characterisation would undermine their recognition of the Jewish state's right to exist. But if Western communists can at times sound *relatively moderate* in their anti-Zionism, that is a sign of just how far things have gone on the left.

The origins of this development go back to the rise of a militant 'gauchisme' in most Western societies in the late 1960s, the emergence of a radical generation for whom the Palestinians were depicted as belonging to the wave of the future. The new prophets of the left all came from the Third World – Ho Chi Minh, Che Guevara, Fidel Castro, Franz Fanon, Mao Tse-Tung and, last but not least, Yasser Arafat – a fact that has by now brought forth its bitter fruit. Although the fringe politics of the radical left may at that time have seemed a marginal issue in many Western countries, 'anti-Zionism' has since become an integral part of the political culture of the left *as a whole* – contaminating the mainstream social democratic parties, the trade unions, the liberal-left intelligentsia as well as the traditionally receptive student milieu, the Trotskyist sects and the anarchist subculture. Even beyond the organised political left, the influence of this diffuse, almost instinctive anti-Zionism reaches into related sectors like the peace movements, women's liberation movements, black power, Green movements and so on. At first sight, this development may seem puzzling as well as disconcerting. Why should the Green parties, feminists, black militants or the peaceniks feel the need to ritually denounce 'Zionists'? Could it be that they are all puppets of the KGB, naive fools manipulated by His Master's Voice in Moscow, whose role is simply to destabilise and demoralise the Western democratic countries from within? In the East–West confrontation, anti-Zionism does undoubtedly play an important role, but is it credible that all these diverse radical groups, in the West often led by politically sophisticated people with minds of their own, far from enamoured of the Soviet system, are themselves mere tools of an expansionist superpower? It would be tempting to believe as much, and it would greatly simplify our task of understanding and combatting the phenomenon, but I do not think it is really the case.

The Western radical left's progressive alienation from Zionism and its love affair with the Palestinians partly stems, I believe, from deep inner changes in its composition, outlook, and *modus operandi* as well as from its radically altered perception of the nature of the conflict in the Middle East. Since the stunning Israeli victory of 1967 it has gradually ceased to believe in the picture of an embattled, tiny Jewish state surrounded by bellicose enemies intent on its destruction. It has increasingly accepted the Arab view that the real confrontation is between an oppressive militarist state of Israel and the oppressed Palestinians under its occupation, deprived of national and human rights and subjected to racist discrimination. Israel, the idol of the social democratic left in the 1950s and early 1960s with its kibbutzim, its constructivist socialism, its secularism and its egalitarian ethos, has for many on the left progressively turned into the nightmarish vision of a ruthless Sparta busy expropriating occupied land, threatening its neighbours, adopting an exclusivist, theocratic tone of self-righteousness and the posture of a *Herrenvolk vis-à-vis* the Arabs under its rule. As with many caricatures, one may reject the exaggeration in this picture yet recognise the grain of truth without which it would be inconceivable that people who are by no means antisemites could come to believe in such simplistic notions. Even many dovish Israelis, confronting their own government's policies in recent years – especially during the *intifada* – might find themselves agreeing with the left-wing critique on specific issues while rejecting any blanket condemnation of Zionism *per se*.

For it is undeniable that Israel has steadily moved to the right during the past decade at a time when the main thrust for *delegitimising* Zionism was being developed on the international left. Equally important, the fact remains that Israel is technically an 'occupying' power in an age when for states that are not superpowers, such a position is bound to evoke criticism. Moreover, most of the original socialist, pioneering ethos has withered and in its place has come a narrow, integral nationalism with a strong religious messianism sometimes underpinning it – one that for the secularist left inside (let alone outside) Israel is difficult to digest. Furthermore, as Israel has gained in military strength and increasingly radiated an image of self-confident, coldly efficient power – not in itself guaranteed to evoke the enthusiasm of the left, especially its neutralist and pacifist wings in the West – identification has naturally tended to shift to the weaker party in the conflict, namely, to the Palestinian Arabs. That many of these people should be landless, homeless and abandoned was already enough to win them sympathy on the left. That they are non-white and non-Western, technologically backward and until recently politically disorganised has not exactly weakened this tie of sympathy.

The rise of Palestinian terror, moreover, was bound to win the applause of the new left, given its romantic cult of *guerilleros*, its attraction for direct action and political extremism, its belief in simple slogans and its studied indifference to gradualism, old-fashioned socialist programmes and liberal democracy. Leftist anti-Zionism over the past twenty years has built on these affinities, which extend beyond ideology and have led to the establishment of organisational links between radical Palestinian and Arab terror groups from Syria, Iraq and Libya on the one hand and militant extremists in the West on the other. It is no accident that groups like the Red Army Faction in West Germany, the Red Brigades in Italy, the IRA and the neo-fascist extremists in Europe have co-operated in the past with the PLO or Libya's Qaddafi, just as they have maintained contact with Soviet and East European security services. For all these terrorist organisations, 'anti-Zionism' is an important link in a larger pattern of seeking to undermine the very fabric of Western democracies by a campaign of terror, intimidation and disinformation. The fact that among the targets of such violent groups are Jewish as much as Israeli institutions in the Diaspora, is a reminder of the way in which the struggle to destabilise Israel requires that the position of the Jews as a whole be undermined. For extreme left anti-Zionism does not ultimately distinguish between the Israelis and 'Zionist' Jewry in the Diasporic hinterland any more than do the Palestinians, the Iranians or radical Arabs – and the weakening of the civil position of Jews who support Israel is regarded by many militant groups as an important strategic task.

Does this mean that we should therefore regard the anti-Zionist attitudes and actions of the extreme left in Western society and the gradual permeation of the more moderate left by the same virus as unequivocally antisemitic in motivation and character? Has the systematic defamation of Israel and Zionism, and the turning of Israelis into 'Nazis' and Palestinians into 'Jews' created or invented a new form of antisemitism? Are the dangerous new stereotypes first promoted on the left but no longer its exclusive property (e.g. those of the 'imperialist, racist and genocidal' state of Israel) themselves the continuation in the post-Holocaust world of Hitler's legacy, or are they perhaps something different for which we have yet to find an adequate category or meaning?

My own inclination would be to see this phenomenon as a continuation, albeit in a novel form, of some radical left and even radical right traditions and, at the same time, also as a break from the mainstream of pristine Marxist ideology. The internationalism of the founding fathers of Marxism is dead, and in its place have emerged all kinds of hybrid and bastard forms of national socialism, especially in the Third World. Within this pantheon, Zionism has never really found its place as a legitimate national-liberation movement, although in theory there are no overriding reasons for this, beyond the classic Marxist dogma of the disappearance of the Jews and Judaism as a necessary prerequisite of human progress. The older Marxism did not, however, denounce Zionism as a *colonialist* movement (at least not before the 1920s); nor did it brand Zionism as racist, even though the charge was frequently made that it represented a mirror image of antisemitism. On the other hand, the newer and more eclectic offshoots of Marxism have turned not only Zionism but also Judaism into prototypes of 'racism' thereby reviving in contemporary language the old radical stereotype of the bloodthirsty, tribal, Moloch-like character of the religion of Jehovah and his people.

Such anti-Judaic images and stereotypes have begun to gain wider currency in circles far beyond the leftist lunatic fringe, and when they are picked up by the mass media – as in the wake of the Lebanon war – they inevitably inflame public opinion. This is particularly the case now that the taboos against post-Holocaust antisemitism have begun to fade and repressed passions in the collective unconscious of the West are reasserting themselves. After 1945 racism became the unpardonable sin and crime against humanity, yet this very charge is turned at times in a quasi-racist manner against its ultimate victims by the children and grandchildren of the perpetrators, by the accomplices and bystanders in Western Christian civilisation who only 45 years ago were responsible for genocide against the Jewish people. The irony is compounded in that the finger is also pointed in the name and on the behalf of that Third World which also suffered directly in the flesh from the original sin of Western racism. The psychological ramifications and the buried guilt complexes in this complicated intellectual manoeuvre are profoundly disturbing, yet they are also part of the total *gestalt* of contemporary anti-Zionism in its leftist and other incarnations. The negation of Israel and the related assault on Judaism have their latent as well as their manifest content, their deep structure as well as their transparent functions and motivation. To decode their buried message must be one of the primary tasks of any analysis of contemporary anti-Zionism, of which we are only at the beginning.

# 4 The Perdition Affair
## David Cesarani

Until the early 1980s the myth of Nazi–Zionist collaboration had not figured greatly in anti-Zionist propaganda emanating from British sources. During the intense wave of anti-Zionism which swept British campuses in the late 1970s, the main attack stemmed from the equation of Zionism with racism and the association of Israel with South Africa. The invasion of Lebanon in 1982, however, triggered an avalanche of anti-Zionism which saw major innovations in the British context. One of the most significant was the introduction on a large scale of the myth of Nazi–Zionist collaboration.

A catalyst in this process was the publication in England of Lenni Brenner's *Zionism in the Age of the Dictators* and the subsequent promotional tour.[1] The brunt of the assault again fell mainly on Jewish students, but within three years this strain of propaganda moved from the periphery to the centre of public debate about Israel and Zionism. As so often before, what started as a mêlée on campus developed into a war of attrition along a line that ran the gamut of the country's media. The controversy surrounding Jim Allen's play *Perdition*, based on the Kastner case and the extermination of Hungarian Jewry in 1944, showed how far the association of Nazism and Zionism had infiltrated literary and cultural circles and the strong sympathetic response it was capable of evoking amongst the educated, reading public in Britain.

Jim Allen was born into an Irish–Catholic working-class family in Manchester in 1925. After leaving school, he worked in a variety of manual jobs, including a period underground as a miner. During his National Service he spent time in Occupied Germany. Allen joined the Labour Party, but was expelled in 1962 for membership of a Trotskyist group. He has constantly been involved with this far-left tendency, most recently in the Workers Revolutionary Party. Allen's Marxist–Trotskyist ideals inform his dramatic work: he has written consistently about the struggle of the working classes, the oppressive nature of capitalism and of the capitalist ruling class. He has also shown a preoccupation with the failure of leadership on the left and the way that time and again the working classes have been betrayed by their own representatives. His TV dramas *Spongers*, *Days of Hope*, *The Lump* and *The Big Flame*, all dealing with British working-class history and experiences, have enjoyed critical acclaim and popular success.

According to Allen, the idea for a play dealing with the Holocaust stemmed from his involvement ten years ago in a BBC TV play dealing with the Ardentine Caves massacre in 1944. Later he says that he spent eighteen months researching the play that eventually became *Perdition*.[2] Allen prefaces the published version of the play with a bibliography of the books he consulted.[3] However, by his own admission, he relied heavily on Brenner's *Zionism in the Age of the Dictators* which he calls 'a goldmine source'.[4] Many of his 'facts' and 'quotations' had been pre-selected and edited by Brenner to fit the well-established anti-Zionist argument that Israel is a 'racist' state governed by a fascist (Yitzhak Shamir), the origins of which can be explicated by reference to parallels between Nazi and Zionist ideology and instances of concrete collaboration.[5]

*Perdition* itself is a court-room drama based on the libel case brought by Rudolf Kastner against Malkiel Grunwald in Israel in 1953–54. Kastner, a Hungarian Jew, had been a member of the wartime Rescue Committee in Budapest which sought ways of aiding Jews from Slovakia and, after the German occupation of Hungary in March 1944, managed the efforts to save Hungarian Jewry. Grunwald accused Kastner of collaborating with the Nazis and saving himself, his family and certain Zionist leaders while deserting the Jewish community. The case was complicated when it was turned into an attack on the Mapai (Israel Labour Party) government and its leader, Moshe Shertok. Kastner had close links with Mapai; Shertok had been at the Palestine end of his unsuccessful rescue schemes. Kastner faced a hostile anti-Mapai lawyer and a similarly antipathetic judge. Eventually, the judge ruled that the majority of the charges brought by Grunwald were correct and awarded derisory damages to Kastner. Kastner appealed, but without success. He was assassinated before a higher court finally cleared his name four years later.

Allen's version of the horrendous events in Hungary and the subsequent Kastner affair was overdetermined by his anti-Zionism. Michael Hastings, Head of the Literary Department at the Royal Court Theatre where the play was to be staged, made no bones about this when he said 'it does provide a subtext acutely aimed at discrediting Zionism . . .'[6] In an interview with *Time Out* magazine, Allen described his play as 'the most lethal attack on Zionism ever written, because it touches at the heart of the most abiding myth of modern history, the Holocaust. Because it says quite plainly that privileged Jewish leaders collaborated in the extermination of their own kind in order to help bring about a Zionist state, Israel, a state which is itself racist.'[7]

This statement locates the play squarely in the category of anti-Zionist propaganda which regards the accepted history of the Holocaust essentially as an ideological prop for Israel's survival. In such polemics, Israel and Zionism are thought to derive their strength and legitimacy from the torment of the Jews in 1933–45 and from Western guilt that the massacres continued unhindered. Anti-Zionists bent on undermining this supposed prop do not deny that the Holocaust occurred, in the manner of extreme right-wing revisionists. But they utilise certain historical events like the Kastner case to argue that the Jews were accomplices in their own destruction. Furthermore, Zionism is discredited and anathematised by its alleged association with national socialism.[8]

The assertion that Zionism and Nazism share an identity of ideology and concrete interests lies at the heart of *Perdition*. According to the hostile lawyer, Scott, 'the act of collaboration did not happen all at once, as the defence will show. It's roots lay in the pre-war efforts of some Zionists to effect an alliance with the Nazis.' The tormentor of Yaron, the fictionalised Kastner figure, states that, 'what he did flowed logically from the Zionist policy of making deals with the Nazis both before and during World War Two, and that to him this act of collaboration was justified in terms of building the Jewish homeland'.[9]

Yaron is even cast as a tragic figure, a weak man dominated by a malevolent doctrine, an example of the sort of abject leadership which is targetted in much of Allen's writing. In her testimony, Ruth, Yaron's accuser, says that 'politics shapes the man and this tells us more about Zionism than it does about Yaron'.[10] Yaron is a double fall-guy: a front man for the Nazis and a stooge for the Zionists. In the end, guilt gets the better of him and the play is as much a drama of expiation as it is an indictment of an ideology. But if Yaron gains a measure of sympathy because he at least seeks 'absolution', Zionism remains unrepentant, its crimes of collaboration with the Nazis unconfessed, with all its evils concretely embodied in the 'racist' state of Israel. This form of anti-Zionist propaganda is not new. As Robert S. Wistrich and others have shown, it has existed for many years in the Soviet Union before being popularised in the West in polemics like Brenner's *Zionism in the Age of the Dictators*. And just as commentators have noted that Soviet anti-Zionism has drawn widely on anti-Jewish stereotypes, so too does Allen. *Perdition* is singular for the range of anti-Jewish imagery and for the Jewish conspiracy theory which lies at its heart.

The revelation of the conspiracy begins with the reading of the indictment.[11] The fictional author of a pamphlet entitled 'I Accuse', Ruth Kaplan, is quoted as follows: 'I accuse certain Jewish leaders of collaborating with the Nazis in 1944. Among them was Doctor Yaron. He knew what was happening in the extermination camps, and bought his own life and the lives of others with the price of silence.' It is claimed by Scott, the defence lawyer, that Yaron 'lied' to the Jews of Budapest: 'You did everything in your power to mislead your people in order to save your own neck.'

The network of conspiracy spreads wider. It is stated that after the Nazis came to power, the Zionists in Germany had 'secret meetings' with them. When the American Jewish leadership learned of the extermination of the Jews, it is alleged that they remained 'silent'. Their leader, Rabbi Stephen Wise, 'agreed to remain silent . . . acting as an accomplice of . . . antisemites in the State Department'. Weizmann is also part of the conspiracy. The Prosecution summarises part of the testimony of Ruth Kaplan: 'Are you seriously suggesting that Chaim Weizmann . . . was . . . part of a cover up?' Ruth answers 'Yes'.

This conspiracy is juxtaposed with the power attributed to the Jews. Had they so desired, they could have resisted the Nazis, in Berlin, Budapest or in Washington. Wise is accused of refusing to mobilise 'all-powerful American Jewry'. Jewish leaders in Germany refused to lead 'Jewish workers [who] went out on to the streets' to fight the Brownshirts. Yaron refused to mobilise 'one million Jews who had nothing to lose. A formidable force.' Instead, the Zionists betrayed the Jews of Europe.

As the play progresses, the act of betrayal becomes the black centre of the conspiracy and the cover-up. Scott makes the accusation that Yaron and the Zionists in Budapest were 'hired functionaries who secretly crept out of Hungary at the height of the Deportations . . . First you placed a noose around the neck of every Jew in Hungary, then you tightened the knot and legged it to Palestine'. He adds: 'To save your hides you practically led them to the gas chambers of Auschwitz. You offered them soothing assurances while the gas ovens were made ready . . .' According to the play's indictment: 'A curtain of silence, prompted by shame, has shielded this dark page of Jewish history', but the trial has now exposed this conspiracy to betray.

The theme of a covert plot and betrayal resonates with the story of Judas. This is reinforced by ascriptions of Jewish cruelty, callousness, expediency and ruthlessness. The purpose of this is personal gain or the achievement of a greater good – Zionism. Explaining Zionist behaviour, Ruth alleges that 'in return for keeping the peace in the camps, they would be allowed to select certain Jews for rescue'. She claims that 'their goal was the creation of the Jewish Homeland, and to achieve this they were prepared if necessary to sacrifice the Jews of the diaspora'. This was the 'cruel criteria' of Zionism.

Zionists are invariably driven by the desire for personal gain and more ominously still, are willing to justify any means, no matter how terrible to achieve their goal of Jewish statehood. They are characterised as heartless traffickers in human lives: 'Israel was coined in the blood and tears of Hungarian Jewry.' These references to blood connect with a plethora of Christological references in the last twenty pages of the play. Yaron mentions Pontius Pilate and Golgotha; he describes the trial, which it turns out was his devising, as a 'confessional' in which he was hoping for 'absolution'. There are also several metaphors relating to the Crucifixion. The juniour counsel for the defence gleefully exclaims to Scott: 'You crucified him.' Yaron congratulates Ruth on her pamphlet with its 'words hard as nails'. He approves of Scott too: 'I like him. Merciless. I felt that he was ramming spears into my body.'

*Perdition* virtually ends with references to 'polluted wells' and once again to crucifixion – both major themes in traditional Christian antisemitism. There are also parallels between Allen's writing and the antisemitic image of the Jew found in *The Merchant of Venice*. Yaron and his accomplices are described as 'the Zionist knife in the Nazi fist'. The *Merchant* abounds in cutting imagery. It also builds a picture of the Jews as a cold people without sentiment, willing to sacrifice life for abstract higher principles. If Yaron delights in the 'spears' which Scott thrusts into him, Shylock in Act 3, Sc. 2 of *The Merchant* exclaims: 'Thou sticks't a dagger in me . . .' and like Yaron he ends up grovelling for absolution.

To alleviate Western guilt for the Holocaust and to subvert its utility to Zionism, Allen reconstructs it as a conspiracy of evil in which the Jews themselves collaborated. Allen also overcomes the problem of Jewish powerlessness which the events of 1933–1945 appeared to exemplify and which is often held to vindicate the necessity of a Jewish state. Instead of being powerless and doomed to extermination, the Jews are implicated in a vast conspiracy as allies of the mighty Nazi Empire. The claim of Zionists and others that the Holocaust revealed the helplessness of Jews in the era preceeding the creation of Israel is thereby neutralised.

If Allen's play had been simply another piece of anti-Zionist propaganda it would have been painful but unexceptional. However, Allen went further and slid into antisemitism. *Perdition* incorporates the myth of the Jewish conspiracy, the myth of Jewish power as well as numerous anti-Jewish stereotypes that have to do with betrayal, cruelty, double-dealing and a host of emblems resonating with imagery from the death of Christ. Nor is there any defence in the fact that the play is about the suffering of the Jews and portrays some of them in a heroic mode. The only Jews to appear in a positive light are left-wing Jews, anti-Zionist Jews or assimilated Jews – none of whom would find ready acceptance in an average Jewish community and who have no obvious commitment to Jewish continuity. In the words of the writer Frederic Raphael, Jim Allen 'equates all specifically Jewish allegiance with aberration'.[12]

The play was sent to the Royal Court Theatre, London's most prestigious venue for the presentation of new work, in mid-1985. Max Stafford-Clark, the theatre's Artistic Director, and Michael Hastings, the Head of the Literary Department, were aware that it was controversial and therefore sought the opinion of historians and experts. During the winter of 1985/86, the play was scrutinised by the Institute of Jewish Affairs and myself. In May 1986 plans to put on the play at the Library Theatre, Manchester were dropped after consultations with the historian Martin Gilbert. The play then entered a limbo which was partly due to a dispute between the author and the theatre over the choice of auditorium.

Despite the adverse comments, the Royal Court resolved its internal dispute with Allen and proceeded to production in the late autumn of 1986.

Though the Anglo–Jewish communal establishment was aware of this development, there was no action to forestall the play's opening or to prepare a coherent communal response until the eleventh hour. Ultimately the press picked up hints of a brewing controversy – partly through rumblings of discontent within the theatre – and on 14 January the *Guardian* published a 2000 word story by David Rose on the play, its author and circumstances surrounding its production. The Rose article led to a storm of correspondence about *Perdition* and immediately attracted media coverage. In the midst of the controversy, Dr Stephen Roth, Director of the IJA, and Martin Gilbert went to the Royal Court to explain Jewish misgivings about the play. They tried to show that the Royal Court was in danger of putting on a play which posed as 'faction', but was full of errors of fact as well as tendentious interpretations of history and negative stereotypes of Jews. At the same time, Jewish student organisations, Holocaust survivors and right-wing Zionist groups prepared to protest against the play – raising the spectre of Frankfurt Jewry's response to Fassbinder's play *Garbage, the City and Death* in October 1985.

On 20 January 1987, after a four hour meeting of the Royal Court's council and on the eve of the press preview, Max Stafford-Clark decided to cancel the play. As he later stated in the press, this was because he felt that it was bound to offend Jewish people. He no longer had sufficient faith in its validity or veracity to be ready to defend it. This was Stafford-Clark's autonomous decision; but the all-enveloping clamour made it appear as if he had been bullied into censoring the play.[13] The cancellation attracted massive media coverage – on TV, radio and in newspapers, including editorials in the *Guardian* and the *Daily Telegraph*. The play's author and director, Ken Loach, (a longstanding collaborator with Allen and a fellow-Trotskyist) immediately claimed that it had been 'banned' as a result of 'pressure from a political group'. The debate about the facticity and artistic merits of *Perdition* were conflated with a debate about censorship which placed the Jewish community and the play's detractors in an invidious situation, damned if they contested the play and damned if it went on. The row over the cancellation raged on for two months, conducted mainly in the pages of the *Guardian*. More than 150 letters and articles appeared in the daily and weekly press; the play was discussed on two TV programmes (one, a noisy round-table debate with Jim Allen, Lenni Brenner and Marion Woolfson pitted against Stephen Roth, Martin Gilbert and Rabbi Hugo Gryn) and several radio arts programmes.[14]

Despite the fact that Stafford-Clark had publicly stated that absolutely no political or financial pressure had been brought to bear on the theatre, Allen and Loach claimed repeatedly that the play was 'banned' as a result of 'pressure' on the Royal Court by prominent Jews and 'the Zionist lobby'. Loach alleged that a 'clique' comprising Lord Weidenfeld, Lord Goodman and Stephen Roth – men who can 'buy their own way' – were responsible for the suppression of *Perdition*. He insisted that 'there was a heavy and effective piece of lobbying by a very small group' which forced its cancellation.[15] Allen has suggested that theatres which showed any interest, even school halls, were leaned on to prevent performances of his work.[16]

The far-left press defended the play and protested loudly about Zionist censorship. *Socialist Worker* (Trotskyist) and *Tribune* (left-wing Labour) published articles in support of Allen and alleging the existence of a powerful Zionist lobby. The centre-left press was more judicious: *New Socialist* gave space to David Rosenberg of the Jewish Socialist Group and the *New Statesman* ran several pieces in a to-and-fro debate between its theatre critic Victoria Radin, Ken Loach and David Rose, with a selection of letters for and against either side.

The dispute was broadened still further when the Directors Guild of Great Britain made a declaration condemning the 'banning'. This led to a retort by Michael Winner and another wave of correspondence with several major directors, including Richard Attenborough, Karel Reisz, John Schlesinger, Clive Donner and Bryan Forbes associating themselves with Winner's position. Actors were divided, too. Left-wingers in Equity, the actors' Union – in which Vanessa Redgrave and Andrew Faulds, the anti-Zionist Labour MP, are prominent members – tried unsuccessfully to get its annual conference to adopt a resolution supporting Allen.

The recent publication of *Perdition* in book form provides still more evidence, if it were needed, of the true nature of the whole enterprise. The publishers, Ithaca Press, already boast the fullest possible range of anti-Zionist authors on its list. The play has been brought out by Ithaca 'in collaboration with' Jerusalem Peace Services, the anti-Israel organisation run by Uri Davis. It is part of a series to be produced by Ithaca Press and will take its place alongside books and pamphlets by Uri Davis, Moshe Machover, Akiva Orr and other long-standing opponents of Zionism. The book includes historical background material by Lenni Brenner and Akiva Orr. Brenner runs through his now familiar interpretation of history, suggesting that the Zionists collaborated with the Nazis while Orr presents material from the transcripts of Kastner's actual trial and appeal. Yet the trial and conviction of Zionism are in reality the central axis of the play. This is further underlined by the letters of support by Maxime Rodinson and Noam Chomsky specially written to accompany the published text. Chomsky's contribution is particularly revealing since in 1980, in almost identical circumstances (and in almost the same words), he wrote a preface for Robert Faurrison's notorious book *Testimony in Defence* which denies that the Holocaust took place!

Jim Allen is an almost paradigmatic exponent of Trotskyist anti-Zionism. Although his anti-fascist and anti-racist credentials are impeccable, he enunciates a doctrine about the Jews which denies them the choice of their own self-definition and self-determination. The uproar stimulated by his play signified the extent to which these inimical assumptions and ideas about Jews have penetrated literate society in Britain. In a TV arts programme, shortly after *Perdition* was withdrawn, the author and critic Michael Ignatieff commented that the defenders of the play who had made constant reference to a Zionist lobby were 'pandering to the latent anti-semitism which is still a factor in the modern world'. He also wondered how it was possible, politically and aesthetically, for the Royal Court to have taken on such a play and not surprisingly attributed it to the kind of leftist anti-Zionism which had become firmly established in literary and artistic circles in Britain during the past decade.[17]

**Notes**

1. Lenni Brenner, *Zionism in the Age of the Dictators* (London: Zed Books, 1983). On the book and the tour, see Bryan Cheyette's review in *Patterns of Prejudice*, vol. 17, no. 3, July 1983, pp. 49–51.
2. *Time Out*, 21–28 January 1987.
3. Jim Allen, *Perdition, A Play in Two Acts* (London: Ithaca Press, 1987).
4. *Guardian*, 14 January 1987.
5. See Cheyette, *Patterns of Prejudice*; Robert S. Wistrich, *Hitler's Apocalypse: Jews and the Nazi Legacy* (London: Weidenfeld and Nicolson, 1985), chapters 10, 11; Gill Seidel, *The Holocaust Denial: Anti-Semitism, Racism and the New Right* (Leeds: Beyond the Pale Collective/Turnaround Distribution, 1986), pp. 85–92.
6. *Time Out*, 7–14 January 1987.
7. *Time Out*, 21–28 January 1987.
8. See Wistrich, *Hitler's Apocalypse*, chapters 10, 11.
9. Jim Allen, *Perdition*, pp. 21, 25. The published version of the play differed significantly from the version that went into rehearsal at the Royal Court Theatre. Quotations from the play, unless attributed to the published text, refer to earlier versions each of which was, at the time, declared 'final'. For a speculative explanation of these changes, my review of *Perdition* in *Jewish Chronicle*, 3 July 1987.
10. *Perdition*, p. 45.
11. The following quotations are taken from the rehearsal version. This analysis was first published in *The Jewish Quarterly*, vol. 34, no. 1 (125), 1987, pp. 6–9.
12. *Listener*, 2 April 1987.
13. For the definitive version of the affair by Max Stafford-Clark, see his account in the *Guardian*, 13 March 1987.
14. See *Perdition* for a comprehensive list of articles and letters published in the British press between 10 January and 21 May.
15. The Brian Hayes Show, (a phone-in programme), London Broadcasting Company, 26 January 1987. See also Loach's interview in *Newsline*, 31 January 1987.
16. *Stage*, 5 February 1987; *Tribune*, 5 March 1987. See also Allen's comments on *Diverse Reports*, Channel 4, 18 February 1987.
17. *Saturday Arts Review*, BBC 2, 28 January 1987.

# Part II
# Muslim, Arab and Third World Anti-Zionism

# 5 Islamic Archetypes of the Jews: Then and Now
## Ronald L. Nettler

Born in the early years of Islam's self-determination, Islamic archetypes of the Jews and Judaism have, over the ages, remained firmly rooted, if not always vital and active. In recent times their original uncompromising tenacity, buttressed by certain congenial changes in the political milieu, has become stronger than ever. Especially since 1948 and against the background of Islam's centuries of slow decline, the archetypes have in fact attained an intensity comparable to that of their original appearance in Islam's well-known early trials with the Jews. Indeed one might say that Islam has thought about the Jews most intensely, creatively and productively in two main periods: the classical Medinian era and our own mid-to-late twentieth century. Hence contemporary Muslim attitudes, at least in their own perception, can best be understood with reference to the formative period of Islam's encounter with the Jews. At the level of archetypes, history would appear in Muslim terms to be repeating itself.

In both instances Islam itself has been beset by a great existential challenge and Jews have seemed to epitomise and be central to its problems. The first trial produced the Jewish archetypes along with a positive resolution of Islam's Jewish problem in an emerging Islamic self-identity and a defeat of the Jews. The second challenge, in our own time, has seemed for Muslims to recapitulate the original encounter, but has yet to result in any 'positive' Islamic resolution. In seeking such an outcome, Muslims today employ the ancient archetypes as well as modern ideas and experience. This has involved more than simply a crude manipulation of ancient sources. The classical motifs of thought concerning the Jews, fixed centuries ago, have been organically developed and applied to a modern situation. Muslims hope that such efforts will, as part of a general programme of Islam's modern rehabilitation, result in a return to the sort of relationship which the Islamic archetypes of the Jews necessitated and which their religion once had the power to maintain.

Kenneth Cragg has perceptively observed that the early Muslim archetypes of the Jews were 'the most abiding and massive example of an identity discovered out of an antipathy'.[1] He was referring to the indictment of Jewish 'disloyalty' in the Qur'an, the allegations concerning their obduracy against their prophets and their 'invention' of fables – charges intended to disqualify their special status with God. For the history of Muhammad's early conflicts with the Jews, combined with certain features

of Islamic doctrine, created a dark Jewish portrait in the early Islamic
theoretical literature. From Islam's emerging principle of worldly (political
and military) success as proof of its own divine origins to its unfortunate
confrontation with Medina's Jewish tribes who declined the 'reasonable'
act of communally recognising in the new faith something legitimate,
Islamic archetypes of the Jews and Judaism were nurtured. The appearance of these archetypes soon became a permanent impress on Islamic
doctrine. Here was an enumeration of negative traits and images, which
would constitute a fixed portrait of the Jews in subsequent Islamic sources.
The authenticity of the Prophet's early struggle with the Jews in Medina
would itself reinforce the archetypes for subsequent generations.

But Islam's Jewish archetypes were concerned not only with the Jews.
They were also, implicitly, concerned with Islam's own emerging self-
identity in opposition to the perceived Jewish 'obduracy' toward the new
truth. The Jews in Medina did indeed in this way cause the Muslims to
'discover' their own identity. The Islamic archetypes of the Jews were
subsequently to be permanent reminders for Islam of what its mission was
all about. Hence one might argue that Islam's first, and most important,
self-formulation emerged only by virtue of the Jews' very resistance to
Muhammad's revelation. Thus Islamic archetypes, however negative in
their portrayal of the Jews, held a potently positive message of Islam's own
contrasted brilliance. The Jews' place in Islam's early scheme of things
was, consequently, central. Contemporary Islam has similarly perceived
the Jews and Judaism of today in images derived from ancient archetypes –
especially as twentieth-century reality seemed, in Muslim eyes, to bristle
with a 'Jewish threat' reminiscent of the earlier challenge. The archetypes
were less strident in the intervening centuries of Islamic rule mainly
because the Jews had been forced into the place of inferiority designated
for them by Islam. They were objects of contempt (and often of legal and
social discrimination) but not of hatred. The archetypes re-emerged with
full force only in our century when Jews acquired a status of power,
sovereignty and equality which have always been considered by Islam as
illegitimate. Let us now review the basis of this illegitimacy in the ancient
Islamic archetypes of the Jews.

The main portrayal of the Jews in the Qur'an is that of rejectors of
Allah's truth and persecutors of his prophets. This meant, of course, that
the Jews were mortal enemies of Islam. From this motif were derived
other, subsidiary themes. Here the Jews were portrayed as possessors of a
tarnished truth (which they themselves tarnished) who, for the most part,
could not recognise in Muhammad's revelation the most perfect version of
their own. They ought to have welcomed and acknowledged this new
doctrine of completion and fulfilment. Instead they denied and rejected it.
Rather than put their full weight behind Muhammad's people they chose to

oppose him, sometimes even aiding his enemies. Yet it was the Jews, from Islam's point of view who, more than anyone else, were obliged to give such acknowledgement. It is hardly surprising then, that the Qur'an in one well-known condemnation of the Jews described them as 'the most hostile in intent toward the believers' along with the pagans.[2] This already encapsulated, in essence, the Qur'anic view of the Jews.

Such a stubborn denial of truth – part of the 'eternal' Jewish nature, as early Islam conceived it – impelled the Jews to act with conspiratorial malevolence toward Muhammad and his new tradition. Hence the various motifs of Jewish perfidy in early Islamic theoretical and historical literature. The Jews' role as allies of Muhammad's various opponents was, for example, a commonplace in the *hadith*, *sira* and historical literature. One of the most extreme forms of Jewish perfidiousness alleged in the Islamic sources was the portrayal of the Jews as the killers of Muhammad.

In keeping with the Qur'anic portrayal of the Jews as persecutors and even killers of their own prophets, this idea brought the story up to date, as it were, in a sort of *dénouement* of the long drama of Jewish attacks on the prophets and prophecy. The archetypal logic of the tale was flawless: in Islamic terms, this was the final Jewish assault on the apex of prophetic religion. Recounted rather prosaically in the standard story of Muhammad's painful and protracted death from poisoning by a Jewish woman, Zaynab, this assault appeared, for example, in a received biographical text of Muhammad's life, *Kitāb Al-Tabaqāt Al-Kabīr* by Ibn Sa'd:

*Account of the Poison Which Was Given to the Apostle of Allah, May Allah Bless Him*

. . . They say: Verily the Jews poisoned the Apostle of Allah . . . Umar Ibn Hafs informed us on the authority of Malik Ibna Dinar, he on the authority of al-Hasan: Verily, a Jewish woman presented poisoned [meat of] a she-goat to the Apostle of Allah . . . He took a piece from it, put it into his mouth, chewed it and threw it away. Then he said to the Companions: Halt! Verily its leg tells me that it is poisoned. Then he sent for the Jewish woman and asked her: What induced you to do what you have done? She replied 'I wanted to know if you are true; in that case Allah will surely inform you, and if you are a liar I shall relieve the people of you . . .' . . . The Apostle of Allah, may Allah bless him, got himself cupped in the back of the neck because of what he had eaten . . . The Apostle of Allah, may Allah bless him, lived after this three years, till in consequence of his pain he passed away. During his illness he used to say: I did not cease to find the effect of the [poisoned] morsel I took as Khaybar . . . The Apostle of Allah, may Allah bless him, died a martyr . . .[3]

Another early archetype of Jewish perfidy and destructiveness toward Islam was the story of 'Abd Allah b.Saba', the man held responsible, in the main Sunni historiographical accounts, for the first serious internal rebellion suffered by Islam. Culminating in the assassination of Islam's third caliph, Uthman, this rebellion was traditionally perceived as the first, and fateful, breach in Muslim unity; the breach that adumbrated the subsequent long period of harsh internal strife and dangerous disunity which marked the permanent loss of Islam's political innocence. Described in the sources as an uprising in which the putative Jew and alleged founder of the heterodox Shi'ite sect 'Abd Allah b.Saba' played the key role, the portrayal of this major Islamic catastrophe exuded resonances of Jewish and Jewish-inspired heterodox Muslim elements conspiring to wreck the political stability and security of Islam; indeed to wreck Islam itself. Thus did the great historian Tabari recite received traditions of 'Abd Allah b.Saba's' proselytising his Islamic heterodox doctrines, vilifying Uthman, and calling for revolt:

'Abd Allah b.Saba' was a Yemenite Jew . . . He later converted to Islam in the time of Uthman. Then he travelled through the lands of the Muslims trying to lead them into error . . . [For example] in Egypt he promulgated to the people the [heterodox] doctrine of the Return [of Muhammad, as Messiah]. So the Egyptians discussed this idea. Then, after that, he said that there were one thousand prophets, each of whom had an agent; and that Ali was Muhammad's agent. Then he said, Muhammad was the Seal of the Prophets and Ali was the Seal of the Agents. Also, he asked: 'Who is more evil than those who denied Muhammad's designation of Ali as his agent-successor, pounced upon this successor-designate of Ali's messenger and seized (illegitimately) the rulership of the Muslim community?' [In answer to this question as it were,] he then told the Egyptians that Uthman had seized power illegitimately while Ali was, in fact, the agent successor of Allah's messenger. 'Rebel against this illegitimate rule, provoke it, and challenge your rulers . . .' [said Abd Allah b.Saba].[4]

The main issue is not the historicity of these archetypal tales of a Jewish hand in Muhammad's death nor, later, 'Jewish' fomentation of the historic civil strife and Shi'i sectarianism which would subsequently wreak such havoc in the Muslim society. The relationship between such archetypes and history has to do with the general Muslim–Jewish altercation in Medina, Islam's consequent creation of an identity out of 'antipathy' and its ultimate victory over the Jews. That Muhammad was believed to have died at the hands of a Jewess and that a putative Jew (in origin) was claimed to have been the source of sectarian civil strife in Islam, proved to be far more decisive than the facts of the case. The 'historical' authenticity of these sources has indeed little bearing on their mythological component. The archetypes have a life of their own, beyond the 'real' history which may have provoked their initial appearance. Their existence must probably derived from the genuinely troubled relationship between Islam and the Jews in Medina, buttressed by an emerging Islamic doctrine of Islam's own finality and superiority. These ancient archetypes persisted during the long history of Islam's subjugation of the Jews, as a routine part of doctrine and historiography. Devoid of hatred, the archetypes were prosaically re-counted as part of Islam's portrayal of the 'proper' world order where the malevolent, conspiratorial Jews were finally humbled under Muslim rule. The archetypes represent an Islamic victory pageant as well as a reminder of the evil nature of the Jews: they are, in essence, a morality tale in which good conquers evil. But the catastrophic humbling of Muslims themselves in the modern world and the liberation of the Jews, symbolised by their building a successful state, have revivified the archetypes in a most dra-matic manner. The twentieth century has yet to include any tales of Muslim success in curbing 'evil' Jewish proclivities. This has engendered the need to adapt and update ancient archetypes in modern costume.

Particularly since 1948 Muslim writers have been greatly preoccupied with the Jews. More precisely, their concern has been expressed in a way which is highly reminiscent of early Muslim depictions of the Jews. Indeed, Muslim writing on the Jews today has its point of departure in the framework of ancient archetypes detailed above, notwithstanding the distinctly modern anxieties of such writers about that inescapably modern Jewish creation, the state of Israel. Although Zionism and the Jewish state to which it gave rise provoked the Muslim world to renewed and obsessive concern with the Jews and Judaism, this preoccupation has almost in-variably been expressed in terms highly dependent on the ancient arche-types. Nor has this dependency been merely a ritualistic cover of tra-ditional cliches enabling Muslim writers to make a grand new departure in discussing Islam's new 'Jewish problem'. Even when their discussion is couched in the language of certain imported Western antisemitic notions, Muslim writers have been careful to link the most indigenous forms with borrowed motifs through an organic unity of forms which seems a natural component of their approach. In fact, the natural manner in which they do this leaves no doubt that, for the Muslim writers, whatever they have taken from the West is easily combined with ancient Islamic doctrine. If to us, on the outside, this seems at times an awkward combination, for Muslims preoccupied with their own problems it has been wholly natural.

In recent years Muslim writers have adopted two approaches to Jews and Judaism: the general Muslim view and the fundamentalist outlook. Sharing common foundation in their understanding of Israel as a modern form of Islam's ancient Jewish woes, both schools have produced a large new body of literature on the Jews, Judaism and Israel. They part company, however, where the fundamentalists, given their acute general concern with the attrition of Islam's traditional values and institutions, often posit a Jewish dimension to Islam's internal modern problems. The fundamentalists invariably relate this to Islam's major external problems, such as Israel, Western domination of or untoward influence upon Islamic society and Islam's unsuccessful confrontation with modernity. Since fundamentalist literature also embodies the general, all-Islamic modern archetypes of the Jews, I shall use fundamentalist sources in citing examples, in order to have the most comprehensive view.

Jamal Madi is a well-known Muslim fundamentalist writer and editor. Associated with the Egyptian branch of the popular Muslim Brothers organisation his views on the Jews and Judaism may be seen as authoritative versions of typical contemporary fundamentalist archetypes of the Jews. I have chosen for citation Madi's introduction to his small anthology of Sayyid Qutb's writings on Muhammad's struggles with the Jews (*Ghazawāt Ma'a al-Yahūd* – Battles with the Jews).[5] This brief introduction (23 pages) is a rich repository of the types of motifs we are interested in.

Like most Muslim writing on this subject today, Madi juxtaposes past and present in such a way that the latter reflects the former and vice versa. The ultimate source is, of course, the Qur'an:

> Oh Lord of the Worlds Most High! . . . You have most certainly portrayed the Jews well in your masterly Qur'an. You have penetrated so well into their inner nature. You have described them accurately and perfectly. Your words about them have come as an exemplar of Qur'anic inimitability which no refutation from any side can touch . . . Thus today there is no approach to the Jews other than the Noble Qur'an . . .[6]

The Jews today, writes Madi, are themselves astonished and perturbed by the continuing vitality of the Qur'anic archetypes of their people. This has been true, for example, of leading Israelis who, on visiting Egypt – a Muslim country formally at peace with Israel – encountered Muslim literature which reiterated these stereotypes. Madi mentions Hayyim Ben Shahar, a leading Tel Aviv academic, who 'says that on his visit to Egypt he found hundreds of books which maligned the Jews, harking back to Qur'anic allegations against them'.[7] The most prominent example of this, says Madi, was former Prime Minister Menachem Begin on a visit to Egypt, reported by the Jordanian newspaper *al-Ra'y*: 'On his visit to Egypt in 1981 [Begin] looked for some change in history books which spoke of the [Zionist] seizure of Palestine, and he also examined books of Islamic culture which contained Qur'anic verses criticising and condemning the Jews . . .'[8] According to Madi, Jews such as Ben Shahar and Begin should not have been surprised by this for they had simply 'forgotten Allah's words concerning the eternal nature of the Qur'anic message: "We revealed the Word and we are its Guardians"'.[9]

The general nature of these sacred Qur'anic teachings on the Jews has mainly to do with their enmity to revealed religion as they heard and knew it before Muhammad and, more particularly, as they encountered and rejected its most perfect manifestation in Muhammad's revelations. The goal of the Jews then was the destruction of Islam; and so it is today – as the result of their newfound release from Islam's political hold on them as *dhimmis*, the parlous condition of modern Islam and the fact of the Jews' new state, Israel. Also to be found here, and in keeping with Madi's fundamentalist proclivities, is the claim that the Jews were somehow involved in opposition to modern Islamic revivalism. Here the Jews are depicted as accomplices of the secular Westernised 'Muslim' rulers who have served as lackeys of Islam's enemies and opponents of their countries' best interest. Politically, culturally and intellectually the Jews and these 'Muslim' rulers have worked together to suppress the healthy Islamic impulses toward revitalisation and success.

In his discussion, Madi's method is to combine the early archetypes with their contemporary forms in the usual fashion of Muslim writers today. Thus, after citing several stories of Muslim–Jewish conflicts in Medina drawn from the classical biographical literature on Muhammad (*Sirah*), Madi writes:

> the evil Jewish role did not end with Khaybar [the Muslims' final classical defeat of the Jews]. Rather, the struggle [with them] continues until this moment, current and fixed. One proof of this is what appeared in the [Arabic] magazine, *al-Majallah*, published in London: Among the disgusting pictures of the destruction wreaked by the Jews in Southern Lebanon is one under which is the following caption: 'Israel was here'.[10]

For Madi this caption tells the whole story. In their execrable behaviour toward the people of Southern Lebanon, modern Israeli Jews exemplify the eternal Jewish propensity to do violence to others, especially Muslims. The caption is for Madi not simply an acerbic journalist commentary on the Lebanese invasion but a reflection of an eternal verity. This 'contemporary' event becomes an archetypal happening which represents a permanent Jewish mode of behaviour and not merely a mundane act of aggression.

In a section entitled 'The Jews . . . and Their Destructive Role Today', which follows a recitation of some of the early tales of Jewish perfidy in Muhammad's time, Madi retells more stories in a similar vein from the early post-Muhammadan period and then from our own time, including the Palestinian problem:

> The Jewish conspiracies did not end with their attempts to murder the Prophet . . . No. they have continued after that to plot and surreptitiously to hatch intrigues. Thus were they behind the conspiracy to kill the Commander of the Faithful, 'Umar Ibn Al-Khattab . . . as well as

the violent social and political upheaval in the time of the third caliph 'Uthman Ibn 'Affan, which was fomented by ['Abd Allah Ibn Saba'] the Jew . . . The Jews followed that with spreading the seeds of revolution, discord, conflict and division of the Community into warring factions, like the Shi'ah, the Kharijites, the Qarmations and others.

The black Jewish conspiracy has continued in secret [Jewish] activity promoted by the notorious Jewish societies all of whom are directed towards one goal: the rejection of Religion, discarding it and, in its place, the preaching of atheism, like Isma'ilism, Ahmadism and Batinism.

As for today . . . The Jews' perfidy has continued through their secret societies dedicated to deviation from Islam through Masonism, Rotarianism and Bahaism. Professor Doctor Muhammad Husayn said [regarding this]: 'As for those destructive proselytizing movements which wear the garb of kindness, humanity, love of peace and human brotherhood, they are numerous . . . like Masonism, Communism, spiritual movements and the proselytizing for reconciliation between [other] religions and Islam, particularly Christianity'.

Thus did the Jews attack the world with glittering slogans, all of them leading to the destruction of Islam.

Shaykh Muhammed Abu Zahrah, may Allah have mercy on him, affirmed the cheating Jewish role, with his words: 'I do not think, nor do most Masons, that their organization is just a mere Zionist plaything and not [also] Jewish . . . For the Jews proceed by penetrating this organization, to restore the "Glory of Zion". The meaning of the Glory of Zion; is, of course, the Palestine conflict and the Judaization of Palestine when it has been an Arab kingdom for thirteen and a half centuries.'

We shall never forget the Jews' role in the toppling of the Islamic Caliphate and their effective deposing of the Sultan Abd al-Hamid . . . And today, the dimensions of this conspiracy have become quite clear, in light of the recently published memoirs of Sultan Abd al-Hamid, as well as the appearance of many historical documents and books which have clarified the realities of this conspiracy.[11]

This classical theme of the Jewish conspiracy against true religion (Islam) is connected here not only with the well-known Islamic stories as related above, but also with a variety of movements and sects, indigenous and alien, ancient, medieval and modern. Thus Communism and Zionism, Masonism, Rotarianism and Baha'ism, like the Islamic heterodoxies of Shi'ah, Kharijites and Qarmatians, are all-Jewish inspired challenges to true religion and its values; as was the downfall and eclipse of the last Muslim Empire of the Ottomans. Indeed, for Madi, the Jewish element is the common strand which ties together the historically and culturally diverse phenomena which are threatening Islam, as well as explaining its decline and failure in modern life. The circle of implication has here widened enormously from its classical dimensions. But its archetypal motifs are the same; only sometimes the names and references have been changed as the circle widens.

In true Muslim fundamentalist fashion Madi sees everything in this complex web of ancient and modern Jewish threats and Islamic trials in one main context: the Jewish propensity to attack and diminish the importance of Islamic values and institutions. The fundamentalist claim is that here, in the realm of belief and practice, Islam's enemies (Jews and others) have set their sights, since they know that a Muslim world which believes and behaves in true Islamic fashion is thereby resistant to even the most massive external physical threat; while 'Muslims' whose commitment to Islam is a mere formality or has lapsed are doomed. If the numbers of such false Muslims should grow larger and if their alien beliefs were to be foisted upon their countries, then all would be lost for true Islam. This is why the Jewish challenge to contemporary Islamic movements and the 'collusion' (whether open or covert) between secular leaders of Muslim states and the Jews has been catastrophic for Islam. Focusing on the Muslim loss of Palestine, as one example, Madi analyses this comprehensive threat:

The Defeat which Egypt suffered in 1967 occurred only because the theatre of Holy War was in dire need of the Muslim brotherhood legions of 1948. Thus in the height of preparedness for the conflict, the gallows fell, killing the men of *Jihad* and intellectual leaders such as our martyr . . . Sayyid Qutb . . .[12]

Madi's claim derives here from a common fundamentalist argument. Islamic values and a true Islamic life are the Muslims' main strength and a guarantee against alien invasion, whether spiritual or physical. Thus the only bright spot in the 1948 debacle inflicted by the Jews in Palestine was the valour of the units of Egyptian Muslim Brothers with their fundamentalist fighters. They knew who they were and what they represented; they therefore acquitted themselves heroically in battle. But in the mid-1960s, the period leading up to the fateful Six-Day War, Nasser, the secular nationalist, was persecuting and executing the Muslim Brothers' leaders in Egypt, notably the great thinker and activist Sayyid Qutb. Thus the very people who held the key to victory in the impending confrontation were eliminated by those false 'Muslims' who represented the Western-style secular nationalism which itself has so weakened Egypt (and the whole Muslim world) that the country now lay prostrate, devoid of true values and fair game for Jewish aggression. But the 'Jewish' aggression of Israel was itself the culmination of a history of Jewish involvement in the internal

Islamic decline of the nineteenth and twentieth centuries, often in collusion with their Muslim lackeys. In this view a Jewish–Zionist conspiracy was directly implicated in the collapse of Ottoman control over the Middle East, and Ataturk, the great destroyer of Islam in Turkey and promoter of Western decadence in all of the Middle East, may himself have been a Jew.[13] Zionism, the Jews, Westernisation, imperialism and Christianity coalesce, with the Jews as the main unifying agent.

Thus Nasser and his colleagues were perceived by Egyptian Muslim fundamentalists as working with the Jewish-imperialist, anti-Islamic forces. Madi, in discussing Sayyid Qutb's views on the problem writes: 'You see him [Qutb] directing the Muslim Community's eyes to the stark realities of their [the secular rulers'] conduct in support of the Jews and their involvement in the Jews' plotting . . .'[14] Madi then cites Qutb's dire predictions of what would happen to Egypt and all Muslims as a result of this: 'Qutb said: "After the blow struck against the Muslim brothers [by Nasser] in [1965] there ensued a wave of moral deterioration and atheistic decadence and an even greater wave of deterioration will follow the recent [1966] blow to the [Muslims] – a shock wave so strong that only Allah can know its magnitude. To whose benefit is this decline?"' Madi answered Qutb's question.

> Is it not to the benefit of the Jews and their allies among the confused [Muslims]? . . . And after the execution of Sayyid Qutb and the consequent blow to the Islamic movement, there most certainly did ensue a shock wave stronger than the preceding one. Was this not the defeat of '67 . . . Sayyid Qutb's prediction of [a further shock wave] . . . will continue, ever lasting. Thus in September 1981 Sadat's blow to the Islamic movement (subsequent to his peace with Israel) was followed in October 1981 by Sadat's murder in a way which nobody before him had been killed . . . The enmity of the Jews to the Islamic movement has [thus] remained constant till our day.[16]

## THEN AND NOW

Muslim writers on the Jews today think about their subject in seventh-century terms. Historically and conceptually they 'live' in the seventh century when addressing the contemporary problem of the Jews. Never having imbibed and absorbed the Enlightenment or the critical historiography of the West, these Muslims can, and do, take much more than inspiration from 'history'. For they accept history and tradition as sacred *living exemplars*, sanctified by the impeccable authority of Revelation. They strive not to document current events, as they confront the Jews today, but rather to fortify themselves at the fount of tradition as the struggle continues; and to clarify for themselves and others the nature of the conflict. Here the fixed conceptions, which I have throughout referred to as 'archetypes', further the process of self-fortification and clarification. Archetypes are concerned not with 'then' and 'now' or 'fact' and 'fiction' but with Reality as a reflection of the eternal. If from our external vantage point it may sometimes seem as if Muslims today take some account of historical change in their writings on subjects such as the Jews, it is clear that many Muslims would not agree. In his *History of Israel*, Howard Sacher discusses the growing Arab hostility to the Jews, Zionism and Israel since 1948. As an example he quotes Muhammed Darwazah, a highly Westernised Palestinian Muslim whose remarks provide a fitting conclusion to this discussion:

The venom and gall directed by the Arab press and even Arab scholars against Zionism and Israel, against the Jews as a 'treacherous race' and Judaism as a 'vipers' nest of cunning' gained momentum in the 1950s as it had not in the pre-Israel period. It was a measure of this animus that Egypt's most respected writer, the former Palestinian Muhammed Izzar Darwazah, could indict Jews for their 'historical' malice, treachery and selfishness. 'How extraordinary it is' he wrote 'that we realize that their characteristics today, although they live in various places are exactly as they were described by the Koran . . . Time does not add to their qualities, but makes them more deeply rooted. . . . The vices pass on from fathers to sons.'[17]

## Notes

1. Kenneth Cragg, *The Event of the Qur'an: Islam in its Scripture* (London: 1971), p. 63.
2. Chapter of the Table, v. 85.
3. Muhammed Ibn Sa'ad, *Kitab Tabaqat al-Kabir*, trans. S. Moinul Hag (Karachi, n.d.) vol. II, pp. 249–52.
4. Al-Tabari, *Ta'rikh al-Rusul wa al-Muluk*, M. J. De Golge (ed.) (Leiden: 1898), vol. I (6), pp. 3941–42.
5. Jamal Madi (ed.), *Ghazawat Ma'a al-Yahud* (Alexandria: 1985).
6. Madi, pp. 5–6.
7. Ibid., pp. 6–7.
8. Ibid.
9. Ibid.
10. Ibid., p. 10.
11. Ibid., pp. 16–17.
12. Ibid., p. 21.
13. This Muslim fundamentalist claim, though never proved by Western historiographical criteria, is held by them as an article of faith.
14. Madi, p. 22.
15. Ibid., pp. 22–3.
16. Ibid, p. 23.
17. H. Sacher, *The History of Israel* (Oxford, 1977), p. 453.

# 6 Islamic Fundamentalism, Antisemitism and Anti-Zionism
## Emmanuel Sivan

The resurgence of Islamic fundamentalism is the most important development that has taken place in the Muslim world over the last fifteen years. It
spread from Pakistan to Morocco, seeping into every corner of society,
especially in towns but increasingly also into the countryside. It is particularly felt among those social strata which are in part modernised, but
traditionalists are also being swept up in its wake. While this movement
seized power in only a number of countries (Pakistan, Iran, Sudan) it holds
cultural hegemony almost everywhere else. It sets the tone of the debate
over public affairs, the terms and concepts according to which they are
conducted, and exerts strong influence over the order of priorities in
Muslim societies. This begins to be true even in faraway Islamic lands such
as Malaysia (as proved by the incident with the New York Philharmonic
Orchestra about playing works by Jewish composers). The fundamentalist
attitude towards Jews, Israel and Zionism is thus of vital import.

### 'WESTOXICATION' AND AUTHENTICITY

This attitude is characterised by a sort of seesaw movement – between
disdainful disregard and obsessive hatred – with a whole gamut of shades
and nuances in between. The two major characteristics of this movement
since its inception in the late 1950s are the cause of this 'seesaw syndrome'.
On the one hand this is a movement almost totally concerned with internal
problems, not with outside enemies. The fundamentalists consider that
Islam is now facing a mortal danger, which in scope and nature is quite
unlike anything it has ever faced before. In this day and age the danger
comes from *within*, from secularist-minded Muslim movements, which
though sincere in their concern for the welfare of their peoples are
nonetheless voluntary prisoners of 'poisonous' Western ideas, be they
nationalism, socialism, liberalism, democracy, economic development-at-
any-price and so on. This 'westoxication' (as Khomeini has called it) is
greatly encouraged by the insidious impact of the audio-visual media which
creep subliminally into the hearts and minds of Muslims and enhance their
infatuation with modernity and its alleged 'good life'. The modern state in

Islamic lands, as purveyor of these values, is thus the ultimate danger. Speedy reform must be attempted but failing that, power must be seized. As against this background foreign forces are deemed much less important than they used to be in the days of the anti-colonialist struggle; the post-colonial Muslim state is enemy number one. As Israel was (at least prior to 1977) very rarely the ally of such Muslim states – the Shah's Iran being, of course, a notable exception – such a frame of mind is certainly not one which should lead to obsession with it. Israel is an execrable force, no doubt, but one which should be dealt with only at a much later stage, well after Islam is purified from within and regimes based on Muslim law are instituted everywhere.

On the other hand Islamic fundamentalism espouses the quest for authenticity – namely a return to the pristine verities of Islam – as its positive response to modernity (mere rejection and expurgation not being enough). This means that the programme it sets forth is to be predicated upon vigorously pure Islamic answers to today's problems; outside (usually Western) criteria are spurned as apologetic. As the Pakistani thinker Maudoodi put it, instead of endeavouring to 'prove' that Islam is truly compatible with reason and science – as the 'westoxicated' try to do – one should simply say that true reason (and 'true science') is inevitably Islamic. Instead of trying to show that Islam is democratic, the fundamentalists claim that since Islam is theocratic, democracy is simply out of the question for a Muslim regime. The same holds true for tolerance. Modern-style tolerance predicated as it is on the relativity and fallibility of all human beliefs is incompatible with the Islamic dogma that Islam is the 'pinnacle of all revelation', the perfect truth, superior to all other partly true revelations (Judaism, Christianity) and other, totally false, religions and creeds.

It follows from this last facet of Islamic authenticity, as interpreted by the fundamentalists, that there is no point (indeed it is a grave sin) in arguing – with the 'westoxicated' – that Islam accepts this kind of tolerance. At most Islam can live with medieval-type tolerance, that is a state of affairs where one religion holds a monopoly of truth and power, yet deigns to grant partial rights to some other religions, on sufferance and not based on equality.

There are, it should be pointed out, three major lines of discrimination in classical Islam: male/female, Muslim/non-Muslim, free man/slave. The first two are now openly espoused by the fundamentalists: and unashamedly so. They no longer feel the need to disculpate Islam from male chauvinism and from discrimination of non-Muslim minorities. As regards the 'better (i.e. monotheistic) non-Muslim religions', as long as Jews and Christians know their place and are content to accept the position of inferiors – with guarantee of rights of worship and internal autonomy – they can be left alone. When they break the sacred hierarchy and 'arrogantly' ask for equality, let alone when they become superior to Muslims

(Jews in Israel, Bahais in Iran, Christians in southern Sudan), they should be fought as dire enemies.

The quest for authenticity – i.e. redefinition of the bounds of Muslim identity – has yet other consequences in this context. It has put an end to all attempts designed to nurture 'ecumenic dialogue' with other religions (especially Christianity and Hinduism; Judaism was never considered a likely candidate). It even revived past diatribes, long-held 'historical accounts' to be settled with other creeds, especially with Islam's two early competitors Judaism and Christianity. Medieval polemical tracts were thus dug out. The 'sins' of non-Muslims against nascent Islam (for example, the struggle of the Jews of Arabia against Muhammad) tend to be stressed, if for no other reason (and there are, as we shall see, such reasons), than as part and parcel of a renewed fundamentalist and *literalist* interest in Muslim history. A good example is the resuscitation of the partly-forgotten Karamic image of Judaism as the 'angry and pedantic religion', the mirror image of a supposedly tolerant and lenient Islam. Muslims thus learn to redefine their true identity by looking at others.

## DISDAINFUL DISREGARD

The combination of these two forces – internal *jihad* (holy war) and authenticity – gave birth in the early days of the movement (before 1967) to a sort of disdainful disregard for Jews and Israel. There were almost no Jews left in Islamic lands (Iran excepted) when the movement arose in the late 1950s and thus non-Muslim native collaborationists with the 'westoxication campaign' were mostly Christians, usually lumped together with heterodox Muslims (such as the Alawites). Israel was excoriated as an extension of Judaism in the Middle East, but being a factor operating outside Muslim society (unlike local Christians and Alawites) was certainly a secondary, perhaps even marginal factor, to be tackled at some later, indeterminate date.

Thus Sayyid Qutb, the founder of fundamentalism in Egypt, did consecrate hostile commentaries to the Jews (who rejected Muhammad out of hand) in his famous exegesis of the Qur'an, written in Nasser's prisons during the 1950s. He gives voice there to the traditional themes of Islamic antisemitism and links them to present day Israel as their ineluctable extension (Jewish wrath and fastidiousness, will for power and domination, exclusivity etc.). Yet once out of prison in the early 1960s his actual activity concentrated on Nasser's so-called *paganism* as the overwhelming danger to Islam. This disregard (hateful, not lenient) of Israel was of course helped by the relative lull in the Arab–Israeli conflict in those days. Yet from time to time an anti-Israel obsession surfaces in Qutb's action, a manifestation of that 'see-saw syndrome' referred to earlier. While preparing, for instance, a series of terrorist attacks against government installations in 1965, Qutb's aides planned to hit power stations and communication centres all over Egypt. Qutb himself long opposed this plan for it 'might enfeeble Egypt *vis-à-vis* the ever alert Israeli enemy'. Yet finally he was prevailed upon: striking Nasser's regime was the over-riding goal (the plan itself failed and led to the arrest of the ringleaders, including Qutb, and their execution a year later).

The Syrian movement, led in those days by Marwen Hadid, paid even less attention to Israel, focusing on the struggle for the liberty of religion and against Ba'th atheism and nationalisation policies (1964–67). The same holds true of Lebanon, Pakistan and Maghreb. Iran, on the other hand, had a large, prosperous and modernised Jewish community as well as a conspicuous Israeli presence in close alliance with the Shah. This is why Khomeini from the early days of his preaching (1963) put Israel on a par with that other 'Great Satan', the United States, harping on this theme continuously with frequent references to Qur'anic anti-Jewish lore. Yet even there, interest in Israel and Zionism knew many ups and downs (depending on the particular facet of 'westoxication' discussed and whether Jews or Israel had much to do with it.) Moreover never were the 'external satans' anything more than a secondary danger, an auxiliary of the enemy *within*, that is the Shah's white revolution with its reliance on modern technology and a return to a pre-Islamic Persian identity. Even the Baha'is, relatively richer and more conspicuous, scored better than the Jews as a scapegoat for popular hostility, and one should also remember that the Israeli presence in Iran was then just beginning to expand.

THE 1967 SHOCK

Disdainful disregard characterised the fundamentalist attitude to the 1967 war. It is quite symptomatic that in the very days preceding the war, in late May 1967, when Islamic militant inmates in Nasser's prison camps were called upon to support the war effort, a hardcore group refused to have anything to do with the 'tyrant's war', arguing that toppling Nasser was more important than fighting outside enemies. No doubt, hatred of the Egyptian rule born out of the torture sessions in his prisons was so powerful as to rule out any collaboration with him even in an emergency. The hard core held out except for those who gave way under the pressures and supplementary tortures. It is from this hard core of the 'prison generation' – whose traumatic experience was persecution by the modern Middle Eastern state – that the leaders of the Islamic groups of the 1970s would come.

However, the 1967 débâcle was a shock even to these inmates. Their joy at the 'defeat of the tyrant' was mingled with a sense of humiliation, [demeaning of the Abode of Islam], the loss of honour and Islamic territory, all the more devastating in that it came at the hands of Jews, a despised minority and one not traditionally known for military valour but rather for meekness and timidity. The oft-recurring argument as to the new-fangled Jewish 'arrogance' (that is, not knowing their true place) exemplified this sense of a world order turned upside down.

The shock was even stronger among fundamentalist sympathisers outside prisons, especially in the young age group. Many of the youngsters who formed the Islamic groups in high schools and universities in the late 1960s were motivated by a sense of confusion and utter despair bred out of the war. Many passed through a long period of wailing and brooding, till they found (thanks to some friend or older mentor) their way to the Muslim Association (*jama'at*). This creed offered them a reasonable explanation for the débâcle – the 'paganism' of Nasserism and the Ba'th – and channelled their energies into a struggle for the revamping of society. It gave them faith that their enemies (first internal, then external) could be overcome and that an Islamic world order could be restored.

The fall of Jerusalem – the third most sacred city of Islam – and the attempted arson of the El-Aqsa mosque in 1969, spread the shock waves further afield to Iraq (where Khomeini had been in exile since 1965), Iran and Pakistan. There were even cases of Muslim militants beginning to pray in the direction of Jerusalem. This had been the custom in the early days of Islam, 622–624, before Muhammad, disenchanted with his erstwhile Jewish allies, instituted the Blackstone of Mecca as *qibla* or direction of prayer.

The upshot of all this was a generational split in the fast spread of the fundamentalist movement of the 1970s. Among the rank and file, particularly those in their twenties, members of the post-1967 generation, hatred of Israel and the demonology of Zionism – a twentieth-century re-incarnation of the insidious and cunning spirit of Judaism – was rampant. It is quite symptomatic that Jerusalem as *qibla* was a practice in this age group. They were also the most avid readers of the anti-Jewish literature put out by fundamentalist publishing houses as part and parcel of the 'authenticity drive' discussed above. Muslim student associations even republished many such medieval treatises and anti-Jewish disputations on their own with introductions linking the 'rotten essence' of Judaism to the misdeeds of Zionism. The defeats of the military regimes at the hands of Israel were not only taken as proof of their overall failure and bankruptcy but sometimes also as the result of outright conspiracy (subjective and not only objective alliance) with Israel. Assad in particular was taken to task by the Syrian Muslim Brethren for failing to use the air force against Israel in 1967 (he was the air force commander then) thus leading to the loss of the Golan Heights.

The leaders of the Islamic resurgence were recruited, however, from the 'prison generation' whose almost exclusive fixation was the 'terror state regimes' as harbingers of secularism. Even superpower allies (the USA in the case of Tunisia, Lebanon and Egypt, the USSR in that of Syria and Iraq) were still not getting much attention, let alone their so-called 'lackey', Israel. An Islamic militant group such as the Muslim Liberation Party (which tried to seize power in Egypt in 1974) although led by a Palestinian, Salah Siriya, a former inmate of Nasser's prison, set as its goal the restoration of the Caliphate and had little to say on Zionism, at least in official declarations. Another major terrorist group, the Takfirwa-Hijra (which kidnapped and assassinated a former minister in 1977) said that Egyptian soldiers killed in the 1973 war were not martyrs of the faith for this was not a *jihad*. The real holy war had to be fought against Sadat himself and his ilk; the 'new Pharaoh' should not be let off the hook and be able to present himself as the paragon of religion. The leader of this group, Shukri Mustafa, as well as his aides, were again men in their thirties whose formative experience had been acquired in Nasser's prisons. Nevertheless among the people there was a greater though somewhat fitful interest in the Israeli danger, when compared to positions taken by the movement in the 1960s. Israel was the close ally of the West which now tried to sell to the Arabs the notion of peaceful coexistence as a precondition for economic development and modern consumption patterns; the latter being the new carrot with which the Middle East was to be further lured into relinquishing its heritage.

The generational split brought about an intense internal debate within the movement, evidenced at times in outbursts of interest in Zionist danger followed by quick decline. One catches a glimpse of that debate in a *samizdat* work, 'The Absent Precept' written by Abd Al-Salam Faraj, leader of the Jihad Organisation (who was to be executed for his role in the assassination of Sadat):

> There are some who say that the Jihad effort should concentrate nowadays on the liberation of Jerusalem. It is true that the liberation of the Holy Land is a legal precept binding upon every Muslim . . . but let us emphasize that the fight against the enemy nearest to you has precedence over the fight against the enemy further away. All the more so as the former is not only corrupted but a lackey of imperialism as well . . . In all Muslim countries the enemy has the reins of power. The enemy is the present rulers. It is hence, a most imperative obligation to fight these rulers. This Islamic Jihad required today the blood and sweat of each Muslim.

Roughly the same position was taken by the leadership of the Muslim Brethren as against impatient young followers still smarting under the 'shameful blow' of the 1967 defeat. The order of priorities set by the older generation was explicitly formulated by the Brethren. The military commander in Aleppo, Husni Abbu, during an exchange with the tribunal in his trial, answered as follows:

*Q.* Don't your terrorist actions serve Israel?
*A.* They serve Islam and the Muslims and not Israel. What we want is to rid this country of impiety.
*Q.* Why don't you fight against Israel?
*A.* Only when we shall have finished purging our country of godlessness shall we turn against Israel.

This was no different from the way Shukri Mustafa (of the Takfir group) responded to his judges' question as to what his followers would do if Israel attacked Egypt: 'If the Jews or others come, our movement would not take part in combat in the ranks of the Egyptian army. We would rather escape to a safe place . . . For by no means can the Arab–Jewish conflict be considered an Islamic warfare.'

Yet at one and the same time, the Islamic fundamentalist press – in these core countries but also in peripheral ones such as the Maghreb, and Sudan – tended to use racialist, *Stürmer*-style caricatures of Jews and of Israel's leader. They gave more space to recounting the historical misdeeds of Jews against Islam (linking them, among others, with the Crusaders, that medieval prefiguration of the state of Israel), resuscitated the Blood Libel and its 'Talmudic origins' and gave vent to the arguments of the *Protocols of the Elders of Zion*. Whether this was done by the leadership out of conviction (bred out of the post-1967 escalation of the Israeli–Arab conflict) or just in order to placate young hothead militants, cannot be determined. Still, the anti-Zionist issue could no more be said to be marginal; it was now significantly growing in strength.


THE WATERSHED

The years 1977–78 constitute a watershed in the evolution of fundamentalist thought on the Arab–Israeli conflict. This was due to the convergence of two events: the Sadat peace initiative and the Iranian revolution. Both events took place against the background of the rise to prominence (and subsequent leadership) of the post-1967 generation (now in its thirties) who had always been particularly sensitive to anti-Zionist themes.

The Sadat initiative, in breaking a long-held taboo, dealt yet another shock, comparable to that of the Six Day War, to this generation now coming to revolutionary maturity. It further highlighted what was only vaguely perceived till then – the intricate relationship between domestic and foreign policy. The 'Coca-Cola, *Dallas* and *Love-Boat* invasion' was linked to the pro-American orientation (not merely in Egypt but in other Middle Eastern countries as well) and this in turn required the price tag of peace with Israel. To fight the one ('Open Door' economic policy, advertising which encouraged consumption), the others must be fought too. Even certain members of the older generation such as the widely popular preachers Sheikhs Kishk and Sharawi came to that conclusion. Their deep antipathy to Judaism as the most ancient foe of Islam, a product of the attachment to authenticity, was reactivated and came to the fore. That Sadat made the particular gesture of a visit to Jerusalem only made things worse. Belief in the sanctity of Jerusalem and the notion of the shame of its fall – an emblematic symbol of the decline of Islam – has long been powerful among fundamentalists. This is despite the fact that the Islamic school from which it borrowed many of its ideas, the neo-Hanbalism (founded in the fourteenth century by the theologian Ibn Taymiyya) had always been sceptical about the sanctity of Jerusalem, as a sort of 'innovation' which might eclipse Mecca and Medina. Jerusalem was indeed one of the very points on which twentieth-century fundamentalists deviated from the dictum of their medieval precursors, a concession no doubt to contemporary sensitivity.

The Iranian revolution fired the imagination of the Arab fundamentalists, even though – as we shall later see – they did not accept its direct authority, the revolution being Shi'ite and they Sunnis. The revolution seemed to prove that the unthinkable can happen – an upheaval may be mustered and a 'pseudo-Muslim' tyrant toppled. The methods and beliefs of the Khomeini movement came to serve as a model to be studied except of course on points which were too evidently Shi'ite. One of the major characteristics of the Khomeini gospel, at least in the years immediately preceding the revolution, was the insistence on the relationship between domestic and foreign policy and particularly on 'the American–Israel satanic connection' as a safety net of the regime. Insistence on Israel's role in Iran grew as it became increasingly prominent in the 1970s, all the more so with regard to its help to the execrated SAVAK security services. Iranian revolutionary anti-Israel propaganda and the flaunting of its alliance with the PLO thus did not fall on deaf ears in the Arab fundamentalist circles which were already sensitised to these issues by Sadat's initiative and the rise to the top of the post-1967 generation. Anti-Zionism came to take pride of place, presented as the modern-day incarnation of the authentically Islamic hostility to the Jews. The alliance between the powers that be (open in the case of Egypt and Lebanon, tacit in the case of Syria and Saudi Arabia) was yet another manifestation of Jewish deviousness and the incessant craving for dominance.

The combined impact of the Israeli–Arab conflict and the Iranian revolution propelled the anti-Zionist theme into greater prominence among the fundamentalists in the early 1980s. Exasperation with the solidity of the Egyptian–Israeli peace treaty and with that of the Sadat–Mubarak regime (despite the 6 October 1981 assassination) brought about stronger verbal violence and a growing tendency to see the foreign supporters of the present Arab regimes (US, Israel) as perhaps no less important enemies than the internal foes of fundamentalism. The Israeli invasion of Lebanon, dubbed by the fundamentalists the 'Tenth crusade against Islam' with its shocking climax – the first siege of an Arab capital by the Jewish army – had shaken the Islamic militants almost as severely as 1967, especially as most Arab states stood idly by, launching empty protests and threats. The shock was much greater than that occasioned by the Russian invasion of Afghanistan. In both cases infidels conquered parts of the land of Islam, but Afghanistan was peripheral while Lebanon lay in the core areas; Russia was a superpower and hence its victory understandable while Israel was tiny and inexplicably strong. The 'cognitive dissonance' involved in this latter phenomenon was, as one could expect, bridged over by conspiratorial explanations – Israel manipulating the US, Israel an ally of the Maronites, and so on.

Conspiratorial explanation, borrowing heavily from Qur'anic vituperations against Jewish crookedness and infidelity, were combined – very early in the summer of 1982 – with the demonic image of the 'Zionist entity': powerful, ruthless, barbarian, albeit technologically advanced. This is of course not a new theme in the annals of the Arab–Israeli conflict, but it was coined here anew in a particularly fundamentalist mould – the image of Israelis as *new Mongols*. The Mongol theme is a central one in fundamentalist mythology and demonology; the state of Islam is now assumed to be as critical as it was in the wake of the destruction of Caliphate by the Mongol hordes in 1258. Thus Assad, Sadat and Saddam Hussein were always defined as new Mongols, this time doing the work of destruction from within. It was no mere chance that the fundamentalists justified their recourse to violence against the powers-that-be by referring to the fourteenth century neo-Hanbalites. The neo-Hanbalites had pondered the situation of Islam after the fall of the Caliphate and had recognised the need to fight even so-called Muslim rulers, as the Mongols had become in the late thirteenth century. Regarding the Jews (or Israelis) as Mongols was thus a way of putting the outside danger almost on a par with the internal danger. It was not only a matter of theology – at the popular experiential level the Mongols (Tartars) always stood for the utmost cruelty and humiliation. Thus the term 'Tartar' was a potent, emotionally charged one of vilification, almost dehumanisation. The Sabra and Shatila massacre, which took place after this evolution in fundamentalist thought had occurred, powerfully vindicated this new image.

Iranian propaganda broadcast to Arab lands was quick to use the Lebanese invasion, but for somewhat different reasons. As early as 1980 the Iranians had found much more difficulty than they had expected in spreading their creed of Islamic revolution to the Arab world. The major reason was the distinctly Shi'ite flavour of their ideology which was quite alien to the Arab radicals, most of whom were Sunnis. Iranian radicalism was messianic, linked to the Shi'ite concept of the Hidden Imam (or Messiah) and Khomeini was taken to be his Vicar (*Na'ib*) on earth. All this was strange, perhaps bordering on the heretical, for Sunni ears, as was the special role given to the men of religion (*mulla*) class in the Shi'ite revolution – a role due to their particularly elevated, near sacred position in Shi'ite lore and their concomitant independent socio-economic basis. In Sunni Islam men of religion were just teachers (much as rabbis are in Judaism) and had usually been dependent on and subservient to the powers-that-be and hence despised by the fundamentalists. No wonder that while Arab radicals were interested in the mechanics of the Iranian revolution they were ready to accept neither its ideology nor its operative leadership, let alone to see in Khomeini, the 'Vicar of the Messiah' the ultimate authority for their non-messianic endeavour.

The Iranians have tried from the beginning to adopt Arab radicals as kindred souls, to create operational links and spread their propaganda. Till 1982 their only successes were in the Shi'ite milieu in Iraq (the Da'wa movement) and Lebanon (the Hizbollah in Beirut and Ba'albek). However much they tried by tortuous verbal acrobatics to explain away the ideological differences and/or to underplay the blatantly Shi'ite themes, Arab fundamentalists remained unconvinced. The Israeli invasion of Lebanon offered them new horizons – initially in Lebanon itself. In the aftermath of the war Islamic radicalism spread in an experiential manner among both Shi'ites and Sunnis. The Shi'ites succeeded in wooing a substantial wing of the Amal movement, now called Islamic Amal whose military wing is the suicidal and hence famous Islamic Jihad outfit. Furthermore, Shi'ite militantly penetrated for the first time the hitherto traditional and backward Lebanese south.

Among the Sunnis an analogous evolution can be discerned: relatively reformist groups such as the Islamic Jama'ca turned into militias, and the Sunni south (for example Sidon) which was always moderate and modernist turned fundamentalist. In both cases the humiliating trauma of the Israel invasion was the primary motivating force of this radicalisation. The Sunni and Shi'ite movements found themselves collaborating in the field and soon enough also attempting to bring about ideological rapprochement whose recurrent theme is: the state of Islam is so dire – as exemplified by Lebanon – that sectarian divergencies between Sunna and Shi'a become immaterial. Let all Muslims consider the Shi'a as yet another school of jurisprudence, in addition to the four Sunni legal schools. That means accepting Khomeini as leader of a legal school (named not Shi'ite but Ja'faite) who can thus exercise political command in the whole of the Islamic world, a command which can pass at some later phase to the leader of another school. It is in any case a temporary command held for the duration of the anti-Zionist struggle. The Beirut-based 'Association of Islamic Ulema' (men of religion), chaired by Sheikh Abat al-Hafiz Qasim, was the driving force of this ideological rapprochement which deepened as a result of the Israeli occupation and as the obsession with it among fundamentalists became paramount.

This grass roots initiative was soon seized upon by the Iranian propaganda apparatus which, much like integral nationalism in early twentieth-century Europe, made the danger of the 'Israeli Mongols' the prime reason for the Arabs laying aside doctrinal controversies and uniting around Khomeini's revolution. Until last year, in propaganda directed towards Iraq, Israel was presented by the Iranians as the devil's disciple – the devil himself being Saddam Hussein. In rhetoric directed at other Arab countries (with the exception of Syria, Iran's ally) Israel was portrayed as the arch enemy. As the Lebanese model of Sunni–Shi'ite collaboration against the 'new Mongols' takes deeper root and, as its 'exploits' are daily celebrated by Iranian Arab-language propaganda organs, a new brand of Islamic antisemitism has slowly spread in the Arab world. This is ecumenical (Shi'ite/Sunni), suffused with traditional themes, yet geared to serve the Khomeini-inspired Islamic revolution. Jews are the ever-present enemies of the Islamic resurgence – indirectly in the US through their impact on foreign policy, directly in Israel. Doing away with them remains a *sine qua non* for the success of the Islamic revolution.

# 7 The Non-Arab Third World and Antisemitism
## Barry Rubin

The emergence of the Third World, as a set of independent states and interests if not as the united bloc of its self-image, is one of the most important developments of our era. This new phenomenon has also had a serious, though easily over-stated, effect on the well-being and international status of the Jewish people and of Israel. (For the purposes of this article, the term 'Third World' is used throughout in reference to areas outside the Middle East.)

In reality, the Third World is defined more by differences than homogeneity. Even the most basic observations about it must be qualified. For example, the Third World cannot be called an area of non-Western culture since – most obviously in Latin America but also throughout Africa and Asia – Western ideas, institutions and social patterns have exerted a great effect there. While these states can generally be seen as economically developing, the degree of modernisation and industrialisation varies greatly. Some nations are newly, even arbitrarily, created; others have long histories of independence.

But one common factor for the Third World (when the Arab world and Iran are excluded) is its relative marginality for Jewish history. Few Jews, and hardly any indigenous ones, live in Africa or Asia today. While sizeable numbers of Jews live in some areas of Latin America, principally in Argentina and Brazil, their numbers and visibility are still proportionately far below what they have been or are today in Europe, North America and the Middle East. Nor do these states have a direct role in the Arab–Israeli conflict.

This relative marginality of Jews and Israel (or such events as the Holocaust and the long history of Jewish–Christian interaction in Europe) for their history and social order makes the attitudes of these Third World governments and peoples largely dependent on some intriguing and complex indirect factors. Given continuing Soviet and Arab propaganda, which often carries with it antisemitic themes, and the growing (though still small) power of the Third World, an analysis of these factors is of much interest. As shown by the votes in support of the UN resolution equating Zionism with racism, there are some immediate reasons for concern and action.

Among the forces shaping Third World attitudes toward Jews and antisemitism, the Islamic factor should not be overlooked. While not

85

implicitly antisemitic, there are trends in political and theological Islam that have pointed in this direction in recent decades. The existence of a conflict between Islamic states and Israel, propaganda from the Arab states, and a general anti-Western fundamentalism have all contributed to this orientation. Both Western and Marxist modernisation theory had predicted that new technology and social development would undermine the role of religion in society. This has not happened in a number of countries because of a growing association between religion and national self-definition. Technology has actually strengthened this bond. In Indonesia and Malaysia, and most obviously in Iran, the urban clergy was able to use better means of communication, transportation and organisation to regain a national intellectual dominance and to recapture the wavering provinces. As people were forced to confront the idea of their own nationhood, Muslims saw their religion as a central element in this process. Pakistan's whole reason for existence is as a Muslim state apart from the Hindu majority in India.

Since many Muslims today see themselves in conflict with Israel and the Jewish people, these tendencies have often produced antisemitic manifestations. Indeed, one can argue that isolation from the Arab–Israeli conflict lends these Islamic theories a degree of abstraction more conducive to an overall perception of Jews as a threat and as an evil force in the world. More antisemitic writings and statements have come from Pakistani theologians and publications than from virtually any other state. In Malaysia – where Islam has become a tool of the indigenous Malays against economically powerful and well-educated Chinese and Indian communities – the government sought to ban a visiting American orchestra from playing works by Jewish composers. This atmosphere is intensified by involvement of governments and Muslim notables in international meetings where anti-Israel and anti-Jewish themes are presented. The importance of Saudi, Libyan and Iranian financing for local mosques or other Islamic institutions also spreads such attitudes, particularly in the Asian Muslim countries. Similar trends are also present, albeit in much weaker forms, among Muslims in sub-Saharan Africa.

Christianity has also played an important role in shaping attitudes towards Jews with marked differences between Latin America, on the one hand, and Asia or Sub-Saharan Africa, on the other. Latin American Catholicism contains some strongly antisemitic elements. These may be due to the strong presence of medieval aspects in the Spanish Christianity of the Latin American continent, to the historical influence of the Inquisition there, and the continued hegemony of a highly traditionalist Church. This situation can be easily exaggerated, for only in Argentina is there a strong, consistent antisemitism. But it would not be inaccurate to say that inasmuch as Latin American Catholics perceive Jews through the prism of their religion, these are not favourable images. The advent of Liberation

Theology has had little or no effect here and, as always, threads of antisemitism from highly conflicting intellectual traditions merge with remarkable ease. Thus, the Nicaraguan Sandinistas have criticised Jews from a leftist standpoint (as supporters of imperialism, reactionary Zionism, and so on) and from a conservative theological stance (as persecutors of Jesus).

In Asia and sub-Saharan Africa, however, and particularly in the latter area, both Catholic and Protestant Christianity have generally taken on a different form, being both more flexible and more fundamental. A more recent and modernist theology avoids the medieval negative stereotypes of the Jews; a stress on the 'Old' Testament even creates a certain feeling of identity between the believer and the Israelites of those texts. Colonialist discrimination and persecution have reinforced this positive attitude toward those who suffered so much in the Bible yet still retained their attachment to Zion and hopes for a better future. Such views can easily carry over into producing favourable conceptions of Jews and Judaism. The important role often played by Christian clergy, mission schools and religiosity in these countries further magnify this influence, which has been noticed in Nigeria, Kenya, Zimbabwe and South Africa among other places.

'Third Worldism' in the sense of a loose ideology of self-identification and a set of political relationships stressing a sense of belonging to the Third World has undoubtedly been a much more dangerous factor encouraging anti-Jewish ideas. This trend was not inevitable but historically it has taken such a form. As a set of radical ideas rejecting Western influence (though usually not Western material goods) it is hostile to a West which, in spite of everything, remains relatively philosemitic. Thus 'Third Worldism' stands outside the liberal tradition with which Jews have been so often identified.

Antagonism to Israel has been defined, with much effort by the Arab states and pro-Soviet forces like Cuba, as a precondition for membership in the club. Again, one should not be too deterministic here – there is often a sharp variance between rhetoric and actual behaviour – but this formulation is essentially correct. The lack of experience of most African and Asian (and even many Latin American) societies with Jews and the lack of knowledge about Jewish religion and history prevailing there allows the most amazing atrocity stories and conspiracy theories to be circulated.

On the political level, either sympathy for the Arabs and Palestinians or a desire to obtain their economic or international support provides ample motive for a refusal to have relations with Israel and for public denunciations of the Jewish state. In part, this tendency has been a result of Arab oil power and money. Yet anti-Israel positions are also part of the glue that holds together the fragile Third World and nonaligned structures. Antagonism to Israel is the Arabs' principal issue just as rejection of South Africa is the African states' special concern. Allies endorse each other's preoccupations as a sign of mutual support and at almost no cost to themselves.

While the absence of Jewish citizens in these Third World states makes such sentiments a rather abstract matter, strong hatred of Israel inevitably becomes linked with antisemitism. When governments cynically make purely political gestures out of a sense of material interest, anti-Israel posturing may be of little importance and more easily reversible. Many African states, for example, maintain unofficial links with Israel. However, sincere belief is far more problematic and harder to affect than pragmatic adaptations which change with the times and external advantages. The presence of extreme left and Marxist influences plays an important role here. Social-democratic attitudes, which are still influential throughout the Third World, incline toward tolerance and pluralism and interact with important areas of Jewish involvement in social justice movements. Indeed, these sectors (for example the Socialist party in India and the veteran Socialist International cadre in Africa and Latin America) may be the most conscious of the Holocaust, the nature of Israel and the positive contributions of Jews to human society. More extreme ideologies, often influenced by the Soviet bloc and radical Arab nationalism, are much less sympathetic. They identify with the forces of revolutionary liberationism, of which the PLO is seen as a prime example, and reject Western definitions of terrorism. They are susceptible to the traditional mythology of some forces on the left which depict Jews as organic allies of capitalism. Regimes which espouse such ideologies are quite willing to vote in the United Nations in support of the 'Zionism equals racism' equation or to instruct delegations to international women's conferences to support similar resolutions.

Equally, the extreme right in Latin America often accepts the counterpart mythology of Jews as the purveyors of communism. The kind of military officers who make coups in South America are likely to see Jews in a way that combines a variety of views: the negative Catholic stereotype, the idea of Jews as simultaneously plutocrats and Marxists, and the ultra-nationalist suspicion of Jews as having dual loyalties. Bolivia, Paraguay, Argentina and Chile gave refuge to Nazi war criminals after the Second World War; Jews were singled out for arrest, torture and murder by the Argentine military *junta*. Once more, though, it is necessary to point out that the outcome of this kind of thinking, particularly outside of Argentina, has been limited. The existence of such attitudes has also helped to maintain a favourable image of Jews on the part of moderates in the politics of those countries.

It should be stressed that the question of Jews and antisemitism (and even of Israel) is a very secondary issue within the Third World political context. This very fact, however, also makes it easier to take extreme positions influenced by considerations (Arab money, Soviet propaganda, political log-rolling) that would not be allowed to affect more central and vital concerns. The lack of contact between many of these countries and organised Jewish communities and their lack of knowledge about Judaism and Jewish history generally means that there is little to counter these other pressures and promises. In Latin America, active local groups do have an effect, particularly on moderate, democratic governments where they exist. Ironically, another positive factor can be the very belief by some African and Asian leaders in the reality of international Jewish influence. Overestimating Jewish power may encourage them to seek better relations with it rather than to adopt antisemitic stereotypes. In some cases, as in the decisions of Zaire and Liberia to reestablish relations with Israel, there figured a rather practical estimate of the benefits of having American Jewish support when the US government determined foreign aid levels.

Western cues do play an important role in the Third World regimes' attitudes toward Jews. On the Zionism equals racism resolution there is a surprising correlation between the votes of African states and the identity of the former colonial (and still influential) European power. Ex-British colonies voted overwhelmingly against the resolution while ex-French counterparts overwhelmingly supported it. It seems logical to assume a correlation between France's more critical stance toward Israel in the Gaullist era and Britain's friendlier position in shaping the attitudes of their Third World political and cultural associates. Similarly, the clear North American stance against antisemitism probably plays a real part in discouraging Latin American governments from actively or rhetorically attacking the Jews.

Surprisingly, Western Jewish liberal efforts on behalf of the Third World have had much less effect, outside of some felicitous personal contacts with specific leaders. The reason for this is that the sympathetic positions taken by Jews acting within a national framework, particularly in the United States, are not clearly identified to the people and politicians of Third World countries. Lacking knowledge about how such systems function, and even more so about the activities of Jewish institutions, there is little appreciation of the positive role played by Jews in supporting independence struggles, foreign aid and other measures of benefit to those countries. More influential has been the concept of 'Jewish power', picked up second and third hand from a variety of sources, including antisemitic ones. While not necessarily hostile, these attitudes seem to correspond to those so common in the West fifty to a hundred years ago.

An important but rarely appreciated ingredient in Third World attitudes toward Jews is the use of local analogy. The identification of local ethnic groups or political standpoints with Jews can have a major impact on intellectual and political thinking. For example, in Nigeria the Ibo tribe, given its entrepreneurial skill and willingness to migrate into parts of the country where it was a minority, led it to identify itself with an interpretation of Jewish experience. The bloody pogrom against Ibos that led to the

Nigerian civil war intensified this sentiment, which was mirrored by the Muslims of northern Nigeria who often had negative feelings toward the Ibo. To this very day, the Ibo have a special relationship with Israel, which a number of their leaders have visited.

From a very different standpoint, the Ethiopian monarchy, which claimed descent from the Queen of Sheba (Emperor Haile Selassie's most prized title was the Lion of Judah) had similar positive views. This did not prevent constant pressure and periodic persecution against the Falashas, Ethiopia's Jews, stimulated by Christian antagonism, but the relationship was a complex one.

The historical experience and psychological self-definition of Jews, whether through their presence in a given country or only in theory, represent a disturbing notion for many Third World nationalisms. These governments are, after all, seeking to create a unitarian nation, overcoming ethnic, regional and communal divisions. The idea of a group that has both national and a transnational identity and loyalties is very difficult to comprehend and can seem quite threatening. This very point has been a central feature in the antisemitism of the Latin American right. Its most extreme manifestation, which periodically re-emerges, is the claim of the Argentinian Right that the Jews are conspiring to establish a separate state in the southern part of the country.

The Holocaust experience can also be a stumbling block for the Third World, particularly as new generations replace those who still remember the Second World War. These events seem extremely remote to many in the Third World. To cite an extreme case, when former Ugandan dictator Idi Amin praised Hitler it is not clear that this statement had the horrific significance for his listeners in Africa that it did in the West. Furthermore, the idea of the Holocaust's uniqueness may seem alien to those for whom, rightly or wrongly, the claim that they suffered centuries of persecution and genocide is so important for their own newly emerging self-image.

Much of the Third World today, then, is a *tabula rasa* for attitudes toward Jews and antisemitism. Consequently, what is taking place now is a battle of definitions in which the ideas and positions reached may hold intellectual, cultural, and political hegemony for centuries to come. The current conflict in South Africa provides an interesting, if undoubtedly special, example of this situation. On the one hand, there are the progressive attitudes of South African Jews who form a very large portion of those whites who are seeking major reforms and black civil rights. In addition, there are the positive religious attitudes, even identification, on the part of black Christians toward Jews. Some black leaders, like the Zulu Chief, Gatsha Buthelezi, cite their personal experience with Jewish friends and supporters in forming their attitudes.

In contrast to these factors stand some negative, even antisemitic trends. The Third Worldist liberationist ideology, augmented by PLO help for the

African National Congress and Libyan assistance to even more extreme groups, does not bode well for the future of the South African Jewish communities. Black anger over Israel's co–operation with South Africa, often greatly exaggerated by the media and by Soviet and Arab propaganda, is also a worrisome sign. The view of Jews which may one day be taken by a future black regime in South Africa is yet to be determined.

Perceptions of Israeli policy and actions also plays a major role in the broader attitudes toward Jews. On the positive side, Israel's historical policy of aid to the Third World, including the provision of innovative technology and specially tailored training programmes, created a great deal of goodwill. Yet these efforts did not prevent virtually all black African states from breaking relations with Israel in 1973 as expected Arab economic aid and Third Worldist ideology proved more powerful attractions. The membership and leading role of Arab states in the Organisation of African Unity also gave them some special advantages and leverage.

It is generally not understood, however, that Israel was always critical of South Africa and constrained in the bilateral relationship as long as the black African states gave Jerusalem an incentive to act in this manner. Once they broke off relations with Israel the attitude towards South Africa was not surprisingly modified. Only when these links are reestablished will Israel have a reason and alternative for changing its policy. Also generally unnoticed is the fact that Israel has been able to maintain good behind-the-scenes relations with several key African countries despite the formal isolation. Even more ignored have been the important ties (particularly in supplying oil) between Arab states and South Africa. Since black African states have been so disappointed in the small or non-existent aid actually supplied by Arab oil-producing states (financial assistance often made necessary in the first place because of the high cost of petroleum imports) disillusion may be creating a new area of opportunity for Israel in those areas. Egypt's peace with Israel and Libya's bullying arrogance and broken promises tend to push in this same direction.

Economic considerations remain an important, if somewhat wavering factor in the policies of Third World states. While the appeal of Arab oil money may have already passed its peak in Africa, it remains important for the newly industrialising states of East Asia, the needy nations of South Asia and for Latin American countries seeking new markets. There is a price, or at least one perceived by the non-Arab partners, in regard to relations with Israel that might also carry over into attitudes toward Jews.

Despite all these concerns, the overall picture is not so gloomy. There are no signs of a wave of antisemitism in the Third World but there is ample evidence of a lack of understanding and knowledge about Jews and Judaism. There is a great deal of confusion about the origins and roots of Israel and the relationship between Zionism and Judaism. Obviously, there are forces that would like to portray those questions in a manner most harmful to Jews but there is plenty of room for alternative interpretations and for the activities of Jewish groups to encourage more positive definitions and more beneficial attitudes.

The views taken towards Jews are also largely shaped by Third World attitudes towards dictatorship and democracy, pluralism and intolerance, local factors and conditions, beliefs and goals. The absence of Jews in almost all of these countries not only implies the lack of a practical outlet for antisemitism but also the unlikelihood that it will develop at all to a point of any importance. Nevertheless, it is important to point out that while Jewish life and status in the world has hitherto depended almost exclusively on conditions and attitudes in Europe, the Middle East and North America, whole new areas of the world are currently formulating their views and actions on these matters. These Third World states and societies are doing so from a basis of little experience and contact, albeit sometimes coupled with great curiosity, about these matters.

# 8 Anti-Zionism and Antisemitism in Latin America
## Natan Lerner

Any intelligent discussion of the connection between anti-Zionism and antisemitism in Latin America must be preceded by a clarification of the notion of anti-Zionism. I take the view that anti-Zionism is not precisely the same as antisemitism although their manifestations may be closely linked and may often appear simultaneously. Obviously, one may lead to the other. However, ideological and political adversaries of Zionism need not have the characteristics of typical antisemites. Opposition to particular policies of the Israeli government are not *per se* expressions of antisemitism. But there are certainly discrepancies concerning the *degree* to which the denial of the legitimacy of the existence of a Jewish state – the essence of Zionism – can be considered as antisemitism. Some will maintain that denying to Jews that which is accepted for any other nation – that is the right to self-determination – is a form of antisemitism; others will not identify such a denial with antisemitism as defined by the *Encyclopaedia Judaica*: 'a term denoting all forms of hostility manifested towards the Jews throughout history'. A Palestinian Arab opposed to Zionism may not be an antisemite in the indicated sense. Much of anti-Zionism – and sometimes anti-Israelism – doubtless carries with it ingredients deserving to be identified as antisemitism. But this is not *always* the case and a theoretical distinction can be made.

One criterion linking anti-Zionism with antisemitism may be the presence of elements contravening the law in those cases and countries where antisemitism is considered an offence. This means that whenever the voicing of 'anti-Zionist' views or slogans has the purpose or *effect* of engendering antisemitic sentiments or behaviour then we are confronting a manifestation of antisemitism against which legal measures may be invoked. This perhaps overly legalistic criterion might help to distinguish legitimate opposition to Zionism from the variety that merely masks traditional anti-Jewish prejudice. When acts, deeds, arguments or slogans have the purpose or effect of engendering hatred, hostility, discrimination, humiliation or persecution towards Jews then those acts are antisemitic even if their perpetrators claim to be only anti-Zionists. In recent years some countries have made judicial decisions which throw light on the notion of antisemitism and the possibility of applying anti-racist legislation to antisemitic activities or incitement. If the indicated method were adopted, politically motivated anti-Zionism would not fall under the category of antisemitism.

In the following analysis I argue that in Latin America there is very little anti-Zionism, properly speaking. Instead one finds a dangerous, old-fashioned and primitive antisemitism. But as Martin Luther King said in one of his last speeches (Harvard University, 1968): 'When people criticize Zionism, they mean Jews. You are talking antisemitism.' However the question arises as to whether one can discuss Latin America intelligently on a continental basis – the Caribbean is not included here – with regard to Jewish problems? While for some, Latin America is a single, dislocated country, for others no serious comment on its society is possible without clearly differentiating between the various sub-regions and countries. In referring to Latin America from a Jewish perspective we are not dealing with the entire area south of the Rio Grande nor with a representative cross-section of Latin American society. The Caribbean is of little importance and Central America, though an explosive region in world politics, is also secondary in Jewish terms; the smaller communities are declining through emigration and Jewish life is mainly concentrated in the two countries of Panama and Costa Rica.

The Latin American governments of Cuba and Nicaragua openly describe themselves as anti-Zionist, particularly in the United Nations. Both countries have a negligible, barely existent Jewish population and both are aligned with Communist bloc. Some commentators categorise both governments as antisemitic and it is well known that there are countries without Jews where antisemitic agitation occurs. Is this the case with Nicaragua? A 'Statement on Nicaragua' published in 1985 by the National Jewish Coalition (whose honorary chairman is the well-known Jewish leader Max Fisher) spoke of 'formal and systematic' persecution of Nicaraguan Jews. It also referred to troubled prospects 'for the 10,000 Jews still living in Central America'. Some Jewish publications have also quoted Sandinistan anti-Jewish statements. The 1979 seizure of the Managua synagogue was presented as a clear antisemitic step. (Later press reports announced that Managua offered to restore the synagogue to Jewish administration.) However, there is another viewpoint which regards the charges of antisemitism against Nicaragua as being politically inspired by the needs of United States foreign policy.

The case of Cuba seems more clear-cut. The Castro government has systematically taken an anti-Israel stand at the United Nations and has been outspokenly anti-Zionist. However no antisemitic measures have been announced or adopted. There seems to be a parallel with the situation in some East European countries. The anti-Israeli, anti-Zionist stand of both Nicaragua and Cuba is apparent: the question is whether there is also plain antisemitism. One might also ask whether the voting in the United

Nations in favour of the 'Zionism is racism' resolution has not had the effect of creating antisemitism. This is particularly relevant in the Latin American context. Two important Latin American countries – Brazil and Mexico – both with a substantial Jewish population, voted in favour of the resolution though they later tried to justify their action. Here we are on unsafe ground. Equating Zionism with racism can be perceived as a wholesale, indiscriminate assault against World Jewry, carrying with it implications of group libel. Beyond doubt this attitude *may* result in antisemitism. The legalistic criterion does not help in this case. We shall return later to the Brazilian and Mexican vote.

From a practical viewpoint the connection between anti-Zionism and antisemitism in Latin America needs to be discussed in relation to the major concentrations of Jews in Argentina, Brazil, Chile, Uruguay and Mexico. In all these countries anti-Zionism is not really an independent ideological category. Rather it is the outcome of an anti-pluralistic, monolithic conception of the nation which cannot accept cultural identity as a legitimate right of all components of society. In some cases it is accompanied by primitive, childish, but dangerous expressions of vulgar and officially illegal antisemitism. A brief overview of the Latin American attitude to the Zionist movement and Israel may help to understand the wider picture. But again, we should be warned that these generalisations are not necessarily valid for all of Latin America.

The role of Latin America as a whole in the political and diplomatic process which led to the establishment of the State of Israel and its acceptance in the United Nations is well known. On 29 November 1947 Latin America's vote on the partition question was decisive: 13 in favour, 6 abstentions, 1 against. In 1949 the Latin Americans helped to ensure Israel's admission to the UN. In 1968 10 out of a total of 15 foreign embassies in Jerusalem were Latin American.

There are many reasons for Latin America's support of Israel. After the Second World War the countries' governments extended their support to the Jewish people and to the young Jewish state born out of the Holocaust. Public expressions of support were also extended. The pro-Jewish trend was particularly strong among the middle classes, the democratic parties, labour unions and intellectual circles. After the mid-1940s pro-Zionist committees headed by prestigious leaders were established in almost every Latin American country. Subsequently institutions for cultural co-operation between Israel and the various countries were established and these engaged in pro-Zionist activities. Spokesmen for the democratic, progressive and liberal sectors of society generally gave their support to Israel and the Zionist movement.

On the government level, bilateral relations were generally good although Latin America's voting record in the United Nations and in other international forums was uneven, eventually deteriorating by degrees. The

Latin American vote on the Jerusalem problem reflected the stand of the Catholic hierarchy.

The liberal and progressive parties, including the democratic left, voiced unequivocal opposition to manifestations likely to carry antisemitic implications. Their attitude on matters of pluralism, assimilation, integration and cultural identity has been less clear. At the other end of the political spectrum, antisemitism has been part and parcel of an anti-pluralistic, chauvinistic, xenophobic, extreme Catholic-oriented trend. This includes authoritarian groups that had always opposed liberalism in Latin America and had been influenced by the French radical right, fascism, Falangism and Nazism. It is among these extreme right-wing circles that one can find the more extreme expressions of hostility towards Jews, often combined with 'anti-Zionist' expressions. It may thus be proper to examine in some detail their origins and sources of inspiration.

The distinguished Argentine historian, Jose Luis Romero, has summarised, in a concise volume on the Latin American right, the evolution of the 'dual society' which developed on the South American continent. Here the colonial aristocracy came to maintain an absolutist system on a religious, racial and class basis. An initial conviction of the superiority of the civilised, Christian Europeans over the barbarian pagan Indians and negroes, developed into what Romero describes as 'the social and political conception of the manorial groups'. Eventually this belief crystallised into a political force of the right once the new and different social sectors, created by immigration, challenged their central role in society. The result was the consolidation of an extremist, intolerant, anti-liberal, traditionalist and xenophobic front. It included some of the first Latin American tyrants (prominent among them the powerful Rosas in Argentina) as well as distinguished writers who denounced the rapidly growing democracy fed by immigration, and finally a radical and violent school of nationalism which has contaminated public life since the 1930s. It is this last group which has consistently produced antisemitic publications of a markedly primitive nature as well as engaging in anti-Jewish incitement and violence.

It is difficult to discern a single, clear cut philosophy common to the different and sometimes conflicting antisemitic groups. This is particularly true of Latin America where right-wing antisemitism has expressed itself more in 'activism' than in ideology. Nevertheless there are various recurring motifs which characterise the loosely defined worldview of the anti-liberal groupings in Latin America. These include an emphasis on power and military strength; the return to a Catholic, traditional way of life; opposition to liberalism, parliamentarianism, democracy and secularism; hatred of foreigners, freemasons, socialists, communists and of course Jews. In some cases there is also an accentuation of *indigenismo* (the native Latin American's way of life) and of Latin American unity. In these circles emphasis on *Hispanidad* as a central value is common.

Violence first became an important ingredient in these circles during the 1930s when the Nazi model was beginning to supplant integral nationalism (*à la* Maurras), Spanish Falangist and Italian fascist influences. By the 1950s and 1960s in Argentina, for example, antisemitic gangs such as Tacuara and Guardia Restauradora Nacionalista identified themselves with Nazi symbols and attitudes. Hitler's picture presided over meetings and blood-centred Nazi ceremonies were frequent. In other countries such as Chile, Uruguay, Brazil and Mexico, similar groups were active. On occasions, they even gained influence over some Latin American governments.

Despite their hostile attitude towards the Jews, most of the right-wing groups and organisations initially ignored Zionism. But anti-Zionist slogans with unmistakeably anti-Jewish ingredients began to appear in the 1950s, gradually becoming more insistent in the following decades. Populist nationalism, of which the best-known example in Latin America is the Peronist movement in Argentina, also played an important role in the proliferation of anti-Jewish sentiments. Influenced by extreme right-wing nationalism it, too, came out against forms of co-existence based on liberal, pluralistic philosophies.

As to the extreme left, it became strongly opposed to Israel and Zionism, but as a rule, tried to avoid antisemitic pronouncements. However, there have been instances when the leftist press – communist or otherwise – indulged in writings that may be considered plain antisemitism. Moreover there is evidence of co-operation between these sectors and anti-Israel Arab organisations. It should be pointed out that both the anti-Zionist and anti-Jewish groups have been active under all kinds of regimes, including the democratic governments that came into existence in the 1980s, as we shall point out later on.

The language and modes of operation of Latin American anti-Zionism change from place to place, but some common elements are undoubtedly present. In most cases, there is clear evidence of support extended to the anti-Zionist agitation by external factors, particularly local Arab and PLO representatives. On occasion there has been a remarkable convergence between Arab, right-wing and extreme left utterances against Zionism; sometimes it has been domestic political purposes which have been in the forefront. In other instances the attack on Zionism has been inspired by the needs of foreign policy as in the Mexican vote on the 'Zionism equals racism' resolution in 1975.

By the 1950s, confused anti-Zionist utterances were being made more frequently in Latin America, particularly in Perónist Argentina. Perón himself denounced the *Sinarquia*, a bizarre coalition of conspirators against the nations, including Zionism. In the early 1960s, during the relatively democratic interregnum, a wave of wild physical attacks against Jews was followed by what could be described as anti-Zionist agitation with antisemitic components. At the time, the then President of the Delegación de Asociaciones Israelitas Argentinas (DAIA), the representative body of Argentine Jewry, stated that the neo–Nazis suddenly 'became *anti-Zionists* and advanced the claim that the DAIA and the Jewish community were communists and Zionists at the same time. They utilised the well-worn argument of *dual loyalty*, attempting to exacerbate the nationalistic sentiment of the peoples of the Continent, and used the accusation of *communism*, with a view to isolating us from American solidarity.'

In 1964 Argentine Jews were distressed by the attempt of a right-wing Perónist Congressman to initiate legislation to investigate Zionist activities through a special Interparliamentary Commission on Anti-Argentine Activities. Zionism was described as a 'dangerous conspiracy which threatens the essence of our nationality', 'a menace . . . to the permanent values that are the basis of *argentinidad*, such as our faith, our culture, our traditions and our social order . . .' The Perónist Congressman spoke of the dangers of Argentine becoming dominated by the 'Israelite minority, with its economic power and its domination of the educational and cultural media, and the schools and Zionist paramilitary camps'. The Congressman wrote a book that year in which he denounced Zionism, claiming that it intended to take over the whole of Hispano-America.

During the 1960s the anti-Zionist offensive in Argentina – strongly supported by the then representative of the Arab League – coincided with similar waves in other Latin American countries. A decade later Argentina was again the scene of anti-Jewish violence and also of attempts to delegitimise normal Jewish community life. In the early 1970s Jews had to defend themselves against the absurd, but widespread charges that they were behind the so-called 'Andinia' plot to take over the southern part of the country. This accusation is still repeated today in the antisemitic literature of Argentina and elsewhere.

During the neo-Perónist regime and the subsequent military dictatorship events reached the point where *Newsweek* quoted a Jew as saying 'What antisemites are calling for is an ethnically pure Catholic and monolithic Argentina. The line is – the Jew has to assimilate or get the hell out – or die'. The right of Jews to a distinct presence within the general society was now clearly challenged. In June 1977 *Carta Política*, a widely read and intellectually respectable monthly, ran a leading article on the 'unsolved' Jewish problem in Argentina. It differentiated Argentine Jewry as a 'genetic community' from the North American model with its 'high degree of religious, cultural and social dispersion'.

The issue of the anti-Jewish excesses suffered during the military dictatorship has not always received the careful consideration that it deserves. Whilst this essay is not the place to cover these events in detail, what is relevant is the extent to which one can distinguish an *anti-Zionist* from a 'normal' antisemitic intention behind anti-Jewish acts. Two authoritative reports on human rights violations in Argentina under the military regime refer specifically to antisemitism. Both describe the interrogation of detained and tortured persons from whom information was elicited on Zionism, Zionist 'conspiracies' and Israeli matters. The *Report of the Situation of Human Rights in Argentina*, issued in 1980 by the Inter-America Commission on Human Rights of the Organisation of American States, quotes a victim from whom information was demanded on the 'Zionist conspiracy that was trying to take over Argentina'. *Nunca Mas*, the 1984 report of the National Commission on the Disappearance of Persons, established by the new Argentine democratic government, mentions instances of interrogation under torture which related to Israel, Zionism, the Jewish Agency, kibbutz organisations, the 'Andinia' plot and similar subjects. The recurrent feature is generally an openly pro-Nazi attitude amongst the torturers together with the reiteration of traditional anti-Jewish stereotypes. Again there seems to be no significant pattern pointing to an anti-Zionist attitude opposed to, or different from, classical antisemitism.

Argentina is of course a special case because of its extraordinary recent history and the fact that it became a focus of world attention. However, now that democracy has been restored and recent tragic events can be investigated it seems possible to locate the Jewish problem within the general picture of the society – without attempting any far-reaching conclusions. While the picture is painful from a Jewish as well as a general perspective there is no specific or significant anti-Zionist pattern that can be separated from the persistent and traditional varieties of antisemitism.

At present the situation is ambiguous. Since the restoration of Argentina's democratic regime Jews have played a striking role in political as well as intellectual life, to the extent that antisemites currently complain of 'Sinagoga radical' (i.e. domination of Alfonsin's Radical Party by the Jews). On the other hand, the Jewish community recently felt sufficiently motivated to organise a huge demonstration – more than 20 000 participants – against anti-Jewish incidents. Some of these incidents had spectacular implications and echoes in the world's press. At the same time neo-Nazi symbols and literature re-appeared on the streets. The recent election victory of Perónist presidential candidate Carlos Saul Menem, a Catholic of Syrian Moslem ancestry with close ties to Syria, is a further cause for Jewish anxiety, especially at a time of economic chaos and renewed fears of a military takeover.

The trends described in Argentina can be found in other Latin American countries. From time to time the Zionist theme is invoked. Thus the Brazilian Foreign Minister, in his attempt to justify his country's vote at the UN argued that it was 'a vote of love towards the Brazilian Jews'. 'What we want', he said, 'is that the Jews born in Brazil be Brazilians'. However, following the restoration of democracy in Brazil, the late Tancredo Neves stated unequivocally that he dissociated himself from the anti-Zionist vote and promised to revise it. As for Mexico – the other country which had voted in favour of UN Resolution 3379 – its government were at pains to convey to Israel and Jewish organisations that it did not really identify Zionism with racism and considered Zionism to be 'honourable'. However, in international affairs Mexico's behaviour in this respect continued to be equivocal. Internal developments in Mexico, particularly in the economy, had some influence on the feelings of security of the members of the Jewish community.

In Uruguay, another country that has returned to democracy, an unusual statement of support for Zionist ideology was made in June 1986 by the President, Julio Maria Sanguinetti. He urged his Jewish countrymen to avoid assimilation and to support Zionism. However, in general, Latin America's stand on the 'Zionism equals racism' issue – at the UN General Assembly, the Geneva conferences on racism and in other international forums – was not as favourable to Israel and Zionism as one might have hoped in view of the persistently good bilateral relations. Indeed it fell below West European, not to mention North American levels of sympathy and support.


POSTSCRIPT

At the time of writing new threats in Latin American countries are beginning partially to obscure the important political changes that took place earlier in the 1980s. The caretaker Alfonsin regime has been forced to declare a state of siege in the face of a staggering national debt, rampant inflation, a failing currency and food riots. It seems unlikely that the victorious Perónist Party will be able to do much about this massive economic crisis. In these uncertain circumstances, a large surge of emigration by Argentine Jews (some of whom may well go to Israel) is distinctly possible. Equally, antisemitic agitation of a violent kind, sometimes masked as anti-Zionism, could well serve again as an instrument of the right to destabilise the reborn Argentinian democracy. In Brazil and Uruguay, where democracy has also been restored, economic prospects are equally gloomy and in both countries traditional anti-Jewish forces continue to be active. In Chile pressure for democratic change is increasing. The question is how long the military dictatorship will be able to resist internal and external clamour for political change. In the meantime repressive policies continue to be the norm. Thus whilst democracy has made progress throughout most of the continent, the almost ubiquitous economic crisis and social unrest have created a climate of opinion that may rebound against the Jewish population.

The unpredictable is a permanent feature of Latin American life. It would thus be irresponsible at this stage to propose any unequivocal prognosis for the future. However, when looking at the general picture it seems that anti-Zionism as an ideology is only a marginal phenomenon in Latin America. While it is capable of making the Jewish situation unpleasant it is unlikely to carry dangerous consequences unless the continent is thrown into complete chaos by new upheavals, or active antisemitism translates itself into a major political factor. Nevertheless, antisemitism continues to be an ingredient – its strength related to particular places, periods and circumstances – in the authoritarian and xenophobic ideologies propounded throughout Latin America. Although this sometimes takes the form of anti-Zionism it is not hard to see that what is really involved is a grotesque and brutal antisemitism, far removed from any pretensions of being a serious confrontation with Zionist ideology. The 'anti-Zionists' in Latin America are motivated less by animosity to the idea of a Jewish state or the right to self-determination of the Jewish people in Palestine, than by traditional antisemitism which opposes any form of Jewish self-identification in their own societies.

# 9 Anti-Jewish Attitudes in the Arabic Media, 1975–1981
## Raphael Israeli

Arabs in general use the words 'Jews', 'Zionist' and 'Israelis' inter-changeably, imputing what they conceive as the evil of the one to the nature of the other. Their usually negative stance towards these terms and what they symbolise stems from three sources.

First, the traditional anti-Jewish attitudes that were cultivated by the Holy Qur'an and other Islamic writings; second, an incremental layer of Christian antisemitic stereotypes which seeped into the Arab world either via Christian Arabs who are part of the Arab Nationalist Movement, or through the intermediary of outright importation of such European writings as the *Protocols of the Elders of Zion*; third, as a result of the Arab–Israeli conflict and the consequent need of the Arabs to dehumanise Jews in order to justify their annihilation, specific Arab-made derogatory stereotypes of Jews were elaborated to serve this purpose.

## THE ISLAMIC ELEMENT

Much has been said and written about the anti-Jewish stereotypes in Islamic tradition. However, Islamic sources are not free from ambivalence in this respect. Indeed, while some verses of the Qur'an come close to praising the Jews and their heritage, others are overwhelmingly poised against them.

The residue of bitterness, not to say disgust and suspicion, that the Muslims harbour towards the Jews stem from the Prophet Muhammad's experience and confrontation with them, in the City of Medina, where he launched his career as a political leader of his community. As the Muslims see it, the Prophet had regarded the Medinian Jewish community as one of his potential allies. However, the Jews, far from accepting the Prophet on his own terms, ridiculed him and bluntly refused to either acknowledge him spiritually and religiously or to co-operate with him politically and militarily. The result was that he felt obliged to remove the challenge that the Jews posed to his authority as the ruler of Medina, and he persecuted and eventually evicted them from the city and the entire Arabian Peninsula.

After the death of the Prophet, the rapid expansion of Islamic rule eastwards and westwards came to incorporate, within a rather short period of time, a wide array of countries and peoples into the realm of Islam. Thus two differentiations were elaborated in Islamic political theory to respond to the new expediences: one, the conquered territories were categorised as the Abode of Islam (*dar-al-Islam*) as contrasted with the remaining part of the universe – the Territory of War (*dar-al-Harb*); second, a cleavage within the peoples of the world was determined between Muslims, the *dhimmis* (the protected 'People of the Book') who were to be tolerated and defended by Islam as long as they submitted to the superior Islamic sovereignty, and the pagans or 'unbelievers' who were to be fought into submission to Islam.

The ingathering of the Jews into modern Israel constitutes from this traditional Muslim viewpoint, which is still upheld by Muslim scholars of the Holy Law and probably by many of their Muslim constituencies, an unbearable challenge to the authority of the Muslim faith.

## EUROPEAN ANTISEMITISM

Arab borrowings from Western antisemitic literature are apparent in the repeated 'Shylock' depictions of Jews and Israelis and in such publications as the *Protocols of the Elders of Zion* which are still widely reproduced by state-owned printing houses and circulated *en masse* in Islamic lands. Even blood libels against the Jews have been recurring in literature and on the stage in some Arab countries, if not in actual life.

In Arab political publications as well as in their state-controlled media, many themes are copied from European Christian antisemitic arsenals:

1. The 'international conspiracy' of the Jews and 'World Zionism' aimed at undermining the world socio-economic and cultural systems with the ultimate purpose of bringing them under their domination.
2. Zionism and world Jewry are often likened to a horrendous octopus which ventures its tentacles whenever possible in a relentless and long-term drive to advance its ambitions of enslaving humanity.
3. In order to achieve its objectives, world Jewry allies itself to aggressive forces akin to it, such as imperialism and colonialism.
4. The Jews in general, and American Jews in particular, dominate and control the banking system, the media and the political arena. They plot behind the scene, concoct intrigues and support shadowy figures in order to advance their cause.
5. At times, Jews and Zionism are envied by their Arab slanderers for their determination and *savoir-faire* and for the meticulousness of their planning, devilish as it may be.

## THE IDEOLOGICAL RATIONALISATION OF THE CONFLICT

While the previous two categories have marked their indelible, and thus unchanging, imprint on the Arab perception of Jews and Israelis, the present one has been characterised by rapid change which runs parallel with the political fortunes of the Arab–Israeli conflict. So, while the basic stereotypes of Jews are more or less a constant of Arab political thought, a process of development is discernible in the way their anti-Israel attitudes are articulated in accordance with current political expediencies. Thus, extensive campaigns of vilification and vituperative accusations against Israel on specific matters may follow particular events where Israel was involved. In fact, Israel is not regarded in a uniform way, but as a kinetic entity which exposes various faces under different circumstances:

1. Israel lacks the prerequisite elements of a state, but it also has the power to assert itself and make the impact of a strong nation.
2. Israel could not survive without the aid of imperialism and colonialism, but Israel also manipulates world powers for its own ends.
3. Israel is found to evince 'Nazi arrogance' but it is also a frightened ephemeral entity.

Such rationalisations also serve another specific purpose: while it would be humiliating to recognise inferior Israel's superior power and military prowess, it is a much more respectable and acceptable proposition to be at the mercy of a great power such as the United States. Since the US puts her entire weight behind Israel, and the two have become inexorably intertwined in Arab perception, a protracted struggle is imperative in order to rid the Arabs of the dominion of this double evil.

The question remains, of course, as to whether the mass media which we propose to analyse are an authoritative, true and accurate reflection of Arab thinking at the grassroots level. The answer is certainly a resounding 'no', because the media in virtually all Arab countries are controlled by the same ruling elites who may make peace or wage war, and therefore they do not necessarily articulate the *vox populi* even where there is one. Moreover, unlike the media in the Western liberal democracies the media in the Arab world are more in the nature of a tool to shape and guide public opinion rather than reflect it.

Conversely, opposition to the regime directs its own propaganda (*Da'wa*) to the public it desires to win over to its cause, and does not purport to represent, necessarily, any particular segment of the population. In other words, both the ruling regime and the opposition to it are totalistic in their aims and totalitarian in their means.

In contemporary Egypt, the mouthpiece of the Muslim Brothers is called *Da'wa*, the very same term of political propaganda that the Abbasids adopted during their struggle against the Umayyads in the medieval Islamic world. In both cases, the *Da'wa* was devised to prepare the public for the coming overturn of the ruling house and the institution of a new ruler who would inaugurate an era of redemption and plenty. In both cases, the opposition stated its desire to restore a replica of the Muslim state as it is perceived to have existed in the times of the Prophet Muhammad. Therefore, even though most attention below is given to state-controlled media, the organs of opposition should not be ignored. In Egypt, this is all the more so because it is the late President Sadat's policy of accommodation with Israel which is considered an aberration of history while the 'Brothers' in Egypt follow the Islamic traditional norms of total rejection of Israel.

## The 'racist and imperialist' nature of Israel and Zionism

'Israel is bound to expand as a condition for her continued existence'. This is the message of most Arab media. Zionism, in concert with world imperialism, provides the ideological rationale for Israeli expansion 'from the Nile to the Euphrates'. Moreover, Israel aims to impose its domain on all peoples of the Middle East and Africa and eventually over the whole world. Zionism is a godless creed whose insatiability will not be satisfied until the universe is enslaved by the Jews. To further its ends Zionism will not flinch from any crime or horror, however great – the Entebbe operation in 1976 was a case in point. Zionism is to be likened to the classical models of colonialism.

Concurrent with a policy of external imperialist aggression, Israel conducts a campaign of domestic racist aggression directed towards its Arab and oriental Jewish citizens. For Zionism is in essence a racist ideology which maintains the Jews as the master race in Palestine. These racist attitudes are anchored in Jewish sources such as the Talmud; thus Israel believes it has the right to expropriate lands, deny the Arabs their rights and discriminate against its own oriental Jews. Such behaviour amounts to a Western onslaught against the people of the East. As a racist entity Israel is the natural ally of racist regimes, notably South Africa, with whom it connives in acts of aggression against Middle East and African nations.

So when the General Assembly of the UN adopted its 1975 resolution to condemn Zionism as a 'form of racism' the Arab media rushed to provide both a rationale and a 'historical background' for the resolution. The following excerpt is from an Egyptian magazine with a mass readership:

> Zionism is racist because this is the religion of the Jews only. Judaism is a family religion which is transmitted by tradition. No missionary activity is practiced in Judaism and it is extremely difficult to become Jewish or to acquire Israeli nationality . . . The Jewish engineers, doctors and

rabbis who had migrated into Palestine, were constrained to 'import' inferior dark-skinned Jews in order to perform the menial labour in Israel. In this fashion they carried out the 'Magic Carpet' operation whereby they brought in Yemenite Jews to sweep the streets and cultivate the land . . . Zionism is interested in white Jews, but discrimination obtains even against white Jews from Western origin who are considered inferior as compared with white Jews from the East: the Poles and the Russians . . . But all these bands of Jews are regarded as superior to the Arabs dwelling in Israel.[1]

The author singles out the Jewish people as evil and he accuses the Jews of being racist. It goes without saying, then, that such a demonic entity as Israel could only have been planted in the Middle East by the satanic world force of imperialism. America is described as the life artery of Israel and both are bent on depriving the Arabs of their rights in order to dominate them. Hence the duty of all Arabs is to struggle against Israel and its supporters, not merely in order to check Israel's imperialist ambitions but also to bring about the physical disappearance of the Zionist entity.

The Arabs were even more disillusioned and angry when Israel's government changed in 1977 and the Likud Party, led by Menachem Begin, came to power. From their point of view, this merely exacerbated an already difficult situation. 'All talk about a prospective peace has fallen silent,' wrote *Al Thawra* of Syria. 'Begin's rise to power has broken all branches of peace and consumed them in the flames.' A favoured method of the Arab media to give salience and credibility to their conception of Israel and Zionism is to quote 'scientific' research, 'investigative' reporting or international proclamations condemning the 'racist and imperialistic designs' of the Jewish polity; the rationale, of course, being that a world consensus and 'objective' findings cannot easily be refuted by Israel nor disputed by anyone who respects a majority opinion. After all it is inconceivable that most people are wrong all the time or that Israel could mislead all the people most of the time. A 'study' of this sort was published by the Jordanian daily *Al-Dustour*[2] in three instalments.

Of all the international gatherings, the annual Islamic Conferences and the triennual non-aligned conferences provide the most congenial surroundings for the Arabs to voice their anti-Zionist concerns. At the Colombo Conference of August 1976 a reference was made to Israel's imperialistic and racist schemes, and a neat comparison was made between these schemes and the South African government's designs in Africa.

In July 1976 there was another flurry of anti-Zionist sentiment in the Arab media surrounding the International Conference on Zionism in Tripoli, Libya. There was a similar response a few months later when a conference on 'Zionism as a racist movement' was held in November in Baghdad. These conferences boasted the participation of 'thinkers, writers, researchers and journalists from all over the globe'[3] but the level of virulence against Israel and Zionism did not abate. The Arab media exuberantly reported: 'Qadaffi will in person open the International Symposium on Zionism and Racism . . . All 30 participants from all over the world are among those who play a positive part in exposing the Zionist Monster and the dangers it poses to the world.'[4]

The Baghdad Conference was equally ungenerous towards Zionism. Some of the participants avowed that 'the stream of history flows against Zionism and the Arabs are ultimately bound to emerge victorious'; others reiterated the 'danger inherent in Zionism, not only to the Middle East, but to the entire world'.[5]

President Sadat of Egypt used the occasion of the Conference of Solidarity with the people of South Africa, convened in Addis Ababa in November 1976 to divulge his views on Zionism to the press: 'Egypt has been pursuing its struggle to liberate its land from the racist Zionist conquerers . . . Egypt is urging the intensification of efforts and actions until this burdensome yoke of reprehensible racism is removed from the conscience of humanity.'[6]

Sadat's call for the eradication of Zionism was echoed at the time throughout the Arab world. A Jordanian newspaper predicted that 'a common fate is awaiting all racist regimes and Zionism will follow in the footsteps of Rhodesia and South Africa'.[7] The visit of South Africa's Prime Minister, Mr Vorster, to Israel in 1976 was seen as a sign of the growing complicity between Zionism and apartheid and was treated accordingly. The commentator on Radio Cairo found 'striking similarities' between the South African government's treatment of blacks in South Africa and Namibia and Israel's behaviour towards the Palestinians in the occupied territories.

The publication of the Koenig Report[8] in Israel in the autumn of 1976 provided yet another opportunity for an outburst of anti-Zionist rage in the Arab media:

The Koenig report ought to be circulated among all members of the UN and discussed at the Civil Rights Committee . . . Even though the formal Zionist majority in Palestine may persist it will always remain an enclave within the Arab Motherland. Zionism ought to realize that it can never attain the strength of Nazi Germany, neither will the Arabs in Israel ever assume the status of the Jews in Hitler's Germany.[9]

Finally, a non-political event that reflects, on the one hand, the Arab media's concern with life in Israel and its scrutiny of all Israeli publications, and on the other hand reveals its sensitivity to any perceived act of humiliation by Israel. (The fact that the Arabs have been heaping humiliations on Israel in the process is beside the point.) In August 1976 a case of incest between a brother and sister was widely reported in Israel since it led to the baby born of the illicit relationship being killed by the mother of the siblings. The attorney's defence was quoted verbatim in an Arab newspaper and interpreted as typical of Israeli policy:

> The Defence Attorney described the family in question as one which had immigrated to Israel from Iraq whence it had imported Arab customs and mentality . . . The defendant claimed that the boy saw no wrong in sexual intercourse with his sister, because this would be acceptable in an Arab milieu . . . Our hands tremble from anger and rage as we write down the words of the defendant, who repeated racist words without compunction. This is the basest manifestation of the overt Zionist stance against the Arabs, and of the degree to which Israeli racists have descended.[10]

**Zionism and Israel undermine the world order**

'The racist and imperialistic propensities of Zionism' do not explain everything. The Arab media mystifies Zionism to the point where it becomes a mammoth Satan bringing misery and calamity to all humanity. One of the most emotionally-charged accusations levelled at Israel and Zionism is a supposed commitment to fighting world Islam. There are routine Arab accusations that Israel has been 'Judaizing Arab lands and destroying the holy places of Islam'.[11] The most forceful illustration of Arab media fervour at Israel's perceived demonic intentions towards Islam is the annual remembrance of the Aqsa Mosque arson of 1969.[12]

> It has been eight years since the Zionist occupying forces set fire to Al-Aqsa Mosque in the framework of a well-educated scheme to . . . annihilate the Islamic heritage and place all holy places under Zionist control. This act of provocation, which encroached upon the sentiments of the Islamic world and constituted a blow to international law, was designed to alter the status of Jerusalem. The occupying authorities are also pursuing their digs around the Aqsa Mosque, thus posing a threat to its foundations . . . Since it took over Jerusalem in 1967 Israel has controlled one of the gates of this city, set up a military check-post there and allowed Israelis to enter the Aqsa and some of the Rock Mosques. The Israelis, who thus entered through this gate, performed dancing parties while in a state of drunkenness, and at the same time other groups attacked Muslims who were praying, in an attempt to hold their parties within the Mosques . . . Because of the resistance of the Arabs in the face of these Israeli attempts, the Israeli authorities were forced to expose their criminal face as they set fire to the Mosque on 21 August 1969 . . .

Israel committed the same sort of crime against the Nativity Church on 29 March 1971, when an Israeli entered the chruch, chased the visitors and began wreaking havoc and destruction to the Holy Tomb . . . he attacked the priests who tried to restrain him but they delivered him to the police. Israel has ever since tried to cover up this story . . .[13]

Israel and Zionism are not only cultivating their hatred of Islam but are also conspiring in shadowy designs to undermine the Arab world in order to dominate it. Today's Zionists are comparable to yesterday's Nazis; their barbaric deeds against the Muslims and Arabs even surpass Nazi crimes.[15] Israel knows no respect for international laws and has ignored the Geneva agreement regarding civil rights in occupied territories. Israel has thus become an outlaw, like South Africa and Rhodesia.[16] Israel's attempt to cause chaos begins, of course, in the Middle East. All wars which break out in the Middle East are Israel's fault and the Arabs are innocent victims. Israel is the major terrorist of the Middle East,[17] an international pirate,[18] an unscrupulous oppressor who has no regard for Arab culture and tradition. The list of accusations against Zionist Israel is long:

1. Israel has confiscated Palestinian lands under the pretext of self-defence and declared them 'closed zones'.
2. More land was expropriated under the excuse of dispersion of the population and concern for social and environmental development.
3. Israel has established garrison settlements along its 1967 borders, under the cover of Kibbutzim, thus usurping more land; its ultimate goal is to turn the Palestinian peasants into industrial workers.
4. Israel has been harming Arab culture and perpetuating illiteracy among its Arabs.
5. Israel grants higher salaries to the Palestinian Arabs in industry than in agriculture, with a view to encourage Arab migration from their land and the establishment of new settlements.
6. Israel's policy towards the Arabs exposes the cancer-like expansionist trends of Zionism and its philosophy of imperialism, capitalism and colonialism.[19]
7. Israel is pursuing a genocide war against the Palestinians.
8. Israel does not implement UN Resolutions regarding the return of the refugees to their homes.
9. Israel has taken over natural resources in the occupied territories, confiscated Palestinian real estate and bank accounts.
10. Israel has been destroying Arab houses and villages in the occupied territories.[20]

The most convincing proof of the illegality of Israel's deeds is, of course, the plethora of condemnations of Israel at the UN General Assembly, in the Security Council and other UN agencies. The result of all this is that the Arabs' right to defend themselves against Israel's excesses is well established, therefore the Arab boycott of Israel cannot be considered other than a legitimate step of self-defence.[21]

Islam and Arabs apart, while Israel's schemes to undo stability and to foment disorder are world-wide they focus more particularly on the Third World. Proof of this can be found not only in the proverbial co-operation between Israel and the racist government of South Africa[22] but also in Israel's intervention in the affairs of other countries and its 'plans' to take over the oil wells of the Arabs.[23] The tension between Ethiopia and Sudan at the beginning of 1977 was thus interpreted by a Syrian newspaper:

> The Ethiopian regime has been playing an imperialistic role as a proxy of imperialism and Zionism, which are historically linked together. The problems with Sudan emanate from the fact that she is bound in a military treaty with Egypt; in other words, the occupying Zionist forces are using to their advantage this situation at a time when the world is looking forward to a peaceful solution in the Middle East . . . Israel is always ready to push the Ethiopian regime to confrontation with African Arabs, as a link in the Zionist-imperialist conspiracy.[24]

Along the same lines, Israel's commando operation in Entebbe, Uganda in July 1976 was viewed as a flagrant encroachment by Israel on the sovereignty of Uganda and also as a threat to the whole of Africa.

Israel's political, military and economic conspiracy to corrode the world order is matched by an equally perverted plot in the moral sphere. Israel has been extorting money, indulging in moral excesses, engaging in organised crime and international espionage. Such illicit acts are indicative as much of Israel's decadent nature as of its meddlings in the international area.

**Zionism and Jews**

Although in most cases no differentiation is made between Jews and Zionism with the latter often virulently attacked in antisemitic terms, at times Jews receive slightly preferential treatment. The grounds for such generosity lie in the argument that the Jews have fallen victim to Zionism and imperialism. Zionism is claimed to have been contaminated by the Jewish myth of superiority, namely that it is the national movement of the 'chosen people' who have ingathered back in the 'chosen land'. Zionism has used these symbols to mislead the Jews with an illusory promise of security. But this promise has proved vain and Jews have begun to emigrate from Israel, not to mention the majority who never wanted to go there in the first place. On the operative level the Arabs ought to struggle against Israel by encouraging the Jews of Israel, particularly those who had migrated from Arab countries, to return to their lands of origin; the Arab states should make practical arrangements to absorb them.

By dominating the Jews, Zionism has, in turn, made them the enemies of mankind. Thus, instead of curing their condition, it has, on the contrary, contributed to reinforcing the negative stereotypes attached to them. Instead of traditional Judaism, Zionism has forged an 'Israeli' culture which is actually unauthentic, uprooted and inhuman. It is a corrupt and infamous culture which feeds upon conquest and military aggression.

The UN Resolution condemning Zionism as a form of racism was an opportunity, as one Arab magazine put it, to 're-open the Zionist file'. The fact that the Western countries voted against this resolution is ascribed to their 'guilt complex'[25] in having failed to prevent Nazi persecution of the Jews and to Israeli and Zionist success in exploiting this complex for their own ends. The Arabs then have no recourse but to 'launch an extensive information campaign in order to awaken world consciousness to the dangers posed by Zionism to many human and cultural values and to the democratic principles and their political, educational, social and economic ramifications'.[26]

The Jews who have been 'infected' by Zionism can be cured. The Palestine Liberation Organisation is the 'mending and liberating factor' for the Jews who have either been, or are likely to be, incorporated into Zionist ranks. To achieve these sublime humanitarian goals, it is imperative that (a) Israel's attempt to monopolise the contacts, dialogues and representation of world Jewry be contained; (b) Israel's efforts to create total identity between Judaism and Zionism be thwarted, so as to prevent the subjection of the Jews to Israel's political aims.[27] This analysis implicitly admits elsewhere that some Arab countries exercise a measure of discrimination (against the Jews?) in their domestic policies, but while this is a mismanagement which calls for redress and condemnation, the discrimination practised in Zionist Israel is a matter of creed because it lies at the very foundation of Zionist existence. Unlike Arab nationalism, which makes for Arab partaking of human values, Zionism denies the Jews such a process, thus allowing discrimination to become a value and an ultimate goal unto itself.[28]

The Arabs are so worried by the apparent success of Zionism and at the same time so fascinated by it, that they devote to it much attention and 'scientific' research. Symposia, 'scientific publications' and 'academic conferences' are given considerable publicity in the media throughout the Arab world.

**The Jews**

Apart from Zionism, which has 'poisoned' the Jewish spirit, the Jews as such are treated in a derogatory fashion by the Arab press. Indeed when the 'Jewish character' is analysed, straight antisemitic stereotypes are invoked. Political and religious leaders of Islam are called upon to reinforce these stereotypes:

> Jews have no right or title in Palestine because they are not the offspring of Abraham, Isaac and Jacob. Jacob is not Israel, and the latter is a different person who had nothing to do with the Patriarchs or the prophets; he was the forefather of the Jews . . . It is a pure act of arrogance on the part of the Jews, the killers of Prophets, to advance the claim that they are the Prophets' descendants . . . Jews are ambushing Muslims and plotting against them the best they can . . . They bask in the illusion that they can exploit the division in the Arab world to their advantage . . . During the war that took place in Ramadan (1973), Arabs/Muslims waged war while believing in Allah, and Allah made them victorious as he had promised us . . . Oh Muslims in the East and the West! We must shatter again the arrogance of the Jews, and this can be accomplished only when we unite in the cause of recovering Jerusalem! Jerusalem is Arab and Islamic, and the Messenger of God will not be satisfied until Jerusalem reverts to being Arab and Islamic again.[29]

However, rather than appearing to condemn the Jews as such, allusion is sometimes made to the corrupting nature of Zionism on them, and so the vicious circle is complete; Jews were debased and humiliated in the first place; Zionism is marked by the derogatory traits that are characteristic of Jews; and in turn Zionism and Israel further debase the Jews by their inherent inhuman attitudes. Israeli politics, society and culture are all imbued with the evils that Jews have transmitted from one generation to another. Exactly as the Jews are thieves, so is Israel who follows the laws of the jungle: whoever can, steals and robs others.[30] Even the proverbial 'Jewish mother' is charged with perversion in the Arab media, inasmuch as she 'uses murder, terror and torture against Palestinian Arabs'.[31]

The logical conclusion is that there is no point in talking to the Jewish polity in terms of the norms of international law, morality and values, because an entity that is founded on piracy and terror, racism and communalism and despises religious values, does not deserve to be talked to with logic. The only recourse is the escalation of the armed struggle which would intimidate the Jewish forces of colonialism and imperialism in Palestine.[32]

## The international power of Jews

Despite their innate defective traits Jews have succeeded in attaining key positions of influence in world politics and the world economy. Such Jews are in a position to harm the Arabs and to put themselves at the service of Zionist propaganda. Israel is merely an extension of this world-wide endeavour of the Jews, and its success in spreading its values and in penetrating world markets is only one manifestation of international Jewish activity. Jewish propaganda is particularly directed to youth and to Arab youth specifically, because this population is the most malleable to outside influences.

The most striking characteristic of Jews is their penchant for organis-ation on a world scale. They are presented as a huge confraternity, a network of lodges where decisions are taken secretly and whence orders flow to the outside world. Since most activities of world Jewry are illicit the organisation is reminiscent of a mafia-type set up which can manipulate funds, push its members to occupy posts and even decide the fate of people.

## FOLLOWING SADAT'S PEACE INITIATIVE

After President Sadat's visit to Jerusalem in November 1977, the image of Israel in the Arab media hardly improved. On the contrary, in some respects the anti-Israeli/Jewish/Zionist malice gathered momentum, as the Arabs felt 'vindicated' in their acceptance of certain stereotypes. The only change was that President Sadat and his entourage were cast by non-Egyptian Arab media in the same mould as the Jews/Zionists.

However, the Egyptian press slightly veered toward a more realistic evaluation of Israel and its chances of survival. At the beginning of the peace process, the press was continuously optimistic about the prospect of detaching Israel from its Zionist-imperialistic nexus, and hope was even expressed that an Israel alienated from Zionism might very well facilitate its assimilation into the Middle East. Thus, even though Zionism con-tinued to be regarded as an extension of imperialism, the cure of Israel from that disease seemed attainable by peaceful means.

Other indications of a more positive approach also began to emerge. For example, at times Israel's birth was attributed only to world Jewry and Zionism and not to imperialism. One reason for this slight mitigation might be the rapprochement which occurred at the same time between Egypt and the United States. Another reason might have been Israel's commitment to withdraw from the Sinai, thus blunting the Arab accusation of Zionist expansionism. A further change in Egyptian attitudes was a less wholesale rejection of Zionism. The most probable explanation for this is that it was no longer credible to claim that Israel was seeking to undermine the security of the world while negotiating peace at a considerable cost to her own security. Moreover, had Israel's démarche been seen as 'subversion', the Egyptian press would have played into the hands of the Arab rejec-tionists who hurled precisely the same indictment at both Sadat and Israel. And since peace was concocted in conjunction with the US, (the paradigm of imperialism) Zionism, was now more conveniently compared with communism and atheism, the twin evils which had allied themselves in their commitment to eradicate Islam and introduce anarchy.

Before the peace initiative Israeli Jews were generally identified with Zionism and therefore all of them were perceived as aggressors and warmongers. But after 1978 a distinction was made between Israeli Zionists and non-Zionists and the slogan has often been repeated: 'we accept Jews among us, not Zionists'. This was, no doubt, an elegant way for the Egyptian leaders to justify their peace negotiations with Israel. They had made peace with Jews who want shelter, peace and stability, not with Zionism which has never given up its inherent evils. At the same time, however, the point is made that peace with the Jews does not necessarily mean a love story with them, but only a pragmatic arrangement.

Embarrassment in the media was evident, immediately following Sadat's visit to Jerusalem, at how to present and justify the fact that Arabs had made peace with the Jews – how to advocate the merits of a deal with Satan. Hence the seemingly contradictory statements made with regard to the Jews: *they* are welcome, not Zionism – their national movement; *they* are as bad as they have always been, but pragmatic considerations have dictated the peace process. Consolation was sought by the Arab media in that Judaism has actually borrowed its principles from other religions; that the Israeli–Zionist identity had been on the decline following the Yom Kippur war and that the spiritual vitality and original creativity of Israel had been waning as their nihilistic literature demonstrated. Consolation is also sought in the hope that since it was Jewish fanaticism that created Zionism, Jewish moderation under the aegis of peace might very well bring about its disappearance and the return of the Jews to normalcy.

Whilst Jews have been moderately treated by the Egyptian media of the post-initiative era in the context of their Zionist–Israeli identity, there seems to be no let-up in the virulence against them when they are treated separately as an ethnic religious group. Worse, an aggravation of previous stereotypes is discernible in some cases.

Moreover the peace process sheds a new light on the international power of the Jews, especially their economic power. Indeed fears have often been expressed in the Egyptian press of Israeli penetration into Egypt's economy. To allay some of these fears, other Egyptian writers advanced the argument that Israeli economic penetration poses no more of a menace to Egypt than any other foreign country which markets its goods there. The difference, however, lies in the limitless resources and resourcefulness of the Jews when they spread their propaganda and by implication their commercial advertising round the world. The Jews, it is argued, control international organisations such as Rotary, which in turn helps them to take over positions of power all around the globe.

Many illustrations of both generalised and 'personal' stories of 'evil' Jews can be found in the Egyptian press. Personal attacks on Prime

Minister Begin, beginning in 1977, also reached an unparalleled level. There was a further flurry of anti-Israeli and antisemitic writings in the Egyptian press in connection with the Camp David conference of September 1978. While before the conference the Egyptian media were sceptical about its results, blaming Israel and Begin in advance for any eventual failure, the success announced at the end of the Conference was attributed mostly to the innate grandeur of Sadat. Before the Conference, commentaries were written to the effect that:

1. Israel's stated positions are but a repetition of old ideas. They want to continue to occupy the lands, to oppose the Palestinians. If Israel wants to be part of the Middle East she has to behave like a state, not to confuse security with peace and to desist from acts that may fan the conflict in the future.[33]
2. Egypt stands to lose nothing if Begin's stratagems and plots to undermine Camp David are successful. Begin has a chance to be recorded in history if he follows Sadat's example.[34]
3. Begin desires to keep Arab lands. His political outlook is based on his religious creed. He believes that religion is not a matter for negotiation or debate and therefore uses religion to preclude negotiations.[35]
4. The staunchest supporters of Israel have begun to revise their positions. Austrian Chancellor Kreisky, appalled by Begin's obstinacy accused Israel of being a police state led by generals from Central Europe who know nothing of politics, although they have proven their worth in war and aggression.
5. Israel has made considerable progress in the domain of urbanisation, but her psychological state leaves much to be desired. The Israelis are divided and have no confidence in the future of their country; they are always preoccupied with an imminent emotional crisis. Can Camp David change the Zionist character of Israel?[36]

As long as the Camp David Conference proceeded it seemed that the Egyptian media were restraining themselves in expectation of the final results. But, paradoxically, when the Conference was completed and the agreement was announced, the Egyptian media released the steam that had bottled up:

Begin's book [*The Revolt*] is important because its author is at the apex of the Israeli government that we are facing and which has entered a cultural struggle against us in order to earn gains for itself . . .
There is a big similarity between *The Revolt* and Hitler's *Mein Kampf*; the books are comparable in style and wording. Both books are replete with racist incitement, with hatred for others and with the sacrifice of everything else in order to attain self-interest.[37]

Other articles accused the Zionist movement of founding its ideology on the 'racial purity' of Jews, and for that purpose it had allegedly encouraged Jews to migrate into antisemitic countries and to emigrate from liberal nations where they were likely to be assimilated. Jews were blamed for falsifying the past, collecting some documents and forging others in order to condemn people they did not like. They took revenge on the living and the dead alike, tarnishing the stature of persons they disliked such as the composer Richard Wagner and the writer Nietzsche.[38] Egyptian journalist Anis Mansur resorted to depicting the Jews as 'so fearful of losing their land that you can hear a peace hysteria in Israel'. Other journalists charged that racial discrimination in Israel remains as evident as ever and Oriental Jews continue to suffer at the hands of Western Jews. If Israel failed so dismally to normalise her domestic inter-communal relations over thirty years, how can she hope to normalise contacts with her enemies of hundreds of years? Israel will create chaos in the Middle East and will remain as it is with America standing behind it. The Israelis are afraid of peace because their existence is founded on *no peace with non-Jews*.[39]

So while it was conceded that peace was likely to modify Israel, Israel's procrastination and the obstacles she erects on the road to peace remained very tangible in Egyptian eyes. In this respect Jews have been accused of reverting to their greed, out of fear that peace might turn Israel into a normal society, preventing her from being able to collect money across the world.

The Egyptian media also promised that Egypt would rush to help other Arabs in case of war with Israel, and that Egypt was not striving for a separate peace but for a complete Israeli withdrawal and the recognition of Palestinian rights. Egypt, it was emphasised, remained as committed as ever to the needs and aspirations of the Arab nation.[40] Exactly as there cannot be war without Egypt there can be no peace without Palestine.[41] Other Egyptian writers urged mistrust of Israel on the grounds that she did not want Camp David.

## CONCLUSIONS

1. No basic change occurred in the substance of the conception of Jews, Israelis and Zionism in the period which followed Sadat's visit to Jerusalem, compared to the previous level of the pre-peace initiative period.
2. While the fortunes of the process of negotiations were reflected in the fluctuations of anti-Israel virulence in the Egyptian media, one cannot escape the feeling that the controlled press of Egypt played a game of nerves with Israel in order to influence the process.
3. Mixed feelings were expressed as to the future of Israel after the peace treaty. Some writers remained optimistic about a basic modification of the

Israeli 'evil', but for the most part the fundamental beliefs, stereotypes and prejudices against Israel remain firmly intact.

4. Even when Jews are described more leniently and there is some readiness expressed to accept them and assimilate them into the region, the same negative spirit against Zionism is preserved throughout. Moreover, at times the peace treaty is depicted as a means to liquidate Zionism.

5. Despite repeated Arab and Egyptian confirmations to the contrary, antisemitic onslaughts have been the norm rather than the exception in the media whenever there is need to attack Israel and Zionism.

6. While some fluctuations in anti-Israel utterances marked the Egyptian press during the peace process, other Arabs maintained, or even increased their accusations, because peace constituted for them a new threat concocted by the Jews and Zionism. The only difference was that this time Sadat, not the Egyptian people, was cited as a 'collaborator' of Zionism and vilified accordingly.

It is fair to observe, however, that in the early 1980s, while public opinion as reflected in the Arab media in general remained rather persistent in its violent hatred of the Jews and Israel, the Egyptian press showed rather less consistency and relentlessness than the rest. This is admittedly a positive change but when references to Israel and/or the Jews were made in the Egyptian press, in a political context, such as the Lebanese war or the Taba crisis,[42] the old anti-Jewish and anti-Israel stereotypes were invoked with exactly the same intensity and viciousness as before.

What is particularly alarming in the Egyptian press is the fact that while the mainstream followed the ups and downs of the normalisation process in the aftermath of the peace treaty, the organs of the opposition in Egypt, both on the Socialist left and the Muslim right, persisted throughout in their antisemitic agitation. Regardless of whether the regime has been unable or unwilling to control that propaganda, which expressly runs counter to its stated policy towards Israel, this remains indicative of the predisposition of the Egyptian masses to absorb it. When one peruses the books containing antisemitic motives (based on the *Protocols*) which apparently still enjoy wide circulation, this alarm is not likely to be allayed. Two cases in point are popular books, 'The War of Survival Between the Qur'an and the Talmud' and 'The Jews, Objects of the Wrath of God' which were in demand by the Egyptian public during the Cairo Book Fair of February 1981.[43]

Anis Mansur, current editor of *October*, has recently and unashamedly reaffirmed his antisemitic leanings and his books seem in great demand. In his book *The Wailing Wall and the Tears* (1979) he ridicules, slanders, condemns and calumnates the Jews as no other antisemite in recent years has dared to do: Jews are enjoined by their faith to 'ravish all women of other religions'; the 'Secret Constitution of the Jews' – the *Protocols* –

encourages Jews to pursue the profession of obstetricians in order 'to specialize in abortion and so reduce the number of non-Jews'; children in the Kibbutzim are raised to 'hate anybody who is not Jewish'; the Talmud advises Jews to kill any non-Jew; and 'their souls are full of hostility to all people without exception' – these are only a few pearls from Mansur's repertoire.

The apogee of antisemitism, the blood libel, also made its re-appearance in Cairo in 1981 under the 'respectable' guise of a 'scholarly' book by a Dr Kamil Sa'fan – *Jews, History and Doctrine*. It recounts in gory detail as a historical fact, the Damascus blood libel of February 1840 and affirms that 'similar cases went unnoticed by the chronicles or were so manipulated by the Jews that the friends of the victims were unaware of this'. These accounts, which were given full 'confirmation' by Anis Mansur in his aforementioned books and are supported by a host of similar antisemitic publications, place a long, dark tunnel at the end of the light which the peace treaty kindled in the hearts of most Jews and Israelis.

In more recent years there has been no end to the virulence and anti-Israeli and anti-Jewish statements. Here, for example, is *Al-Watan* (Kuwait) of 2 September 1988:

> The Zionist gangs constitute the trash of the nations of Eastern Europe . . . This riff-raff claims that they are the descendants of Abraham's own father, and they link themselves to him with an imprudence that generates disgust . . . The documents of the 'Masonite' Zionist Protocols are the greatest world conspiracy against humanity . . . We see complete correspondence between the content of the Protocols and their plans and the content of the Jews' Torah & Talmud.

At a UN Seminar in Geneva (5 December 1984) on the encouragement of understanding, tolerance, and respect in matters relating to freedom of religion or belief, the Saudi representative, Ma'uf Dawalili said, *inter alia*:

> Why did Nebuchadnessar expel and scatter them [the Jews] throughout the world? Why did Hitler want to exterminate them? . . It is because they call themselves the chosen people and allege that they were chosen by God from among all the peoples . . . What has brought oppression of the Jewish world from these ancient times to this very day is their belief.

Some Arab antisemitic statements blatantly justify the Nazi number of 6 million Jews, others deny altogether that the Holocaust ever took place and claim that it is a complete fabrication by the Jews and the Zionists. The stories about the torture and murder of Jews in camps, about the gas chambers, etc., are all dubbed 'Zionist propaganda'. Israeli society and

Jews are slandered in the harshest language. Thus *Roz el Yussuf* on 6 August 1987:

Israeli society is a racist society, hostile to other religions . . . The Jews claim that . . . other peoples are merely creatures who may be killed and slaughtered whose blood may be shed and used for baking matzoth for the holidays of the Jews.

According to *Al-Akhbar* (26 December 1987):

Zionism has a written constitution and its name is the Talmud . . . It contains a call upon Jews to corrupt the world with sex, drugs, and infiltration, the mixing of races while maintaining the cleanliness of the Jewish race, the imposing of an iron hand on the economy of the world and the media in order to force them into the service of Zionism, which is simply total control of the world.

Antisemitic trends against the Jewish people and by extension against Zionism and the State of Israel, are not isolated exceptions in the Arab world. What is saddening is that these unmitigated expressions of hatred and bigotry are not condemned by governments (including Egypt's) or by the artistic and intellectual communities of the Middle East. Undoubtedly, utterances that should have been long relegated to the dustbin of history will not serve peace. This can only be achieved through a profound mental and cultural metamorphosis in the Arab world.

This essay was first published in *IJA Research Reports* (London: Institute of Jewish Affairs), no. 15, September 1983. The author subsequently added a brief postscript to cover more recent developments.

**Notes**

1. *Akher Sa'a* by Chief Editor Anis Mansur, 3 December 1975, pp. 5-8.
2. *Al-Dustour* (Jordan), 9, 12 and 17 January 1977.
3. *Al-Jihad* (Libya), 20 July 1976.
4. Ibid.
5. INA, 13 November 1976.
6. MENA, Cairo, 3 November 1976.
7. *Al-Dustour*, 7 November 1976.
8. Israel Koenig is the northern district commissioner in the Israeli Ministry of Interior. He reported to the government of his concern about the rapid growth of the Arab population of the Galilee which in the long run, if unchecked, might give rise to an Arab majority in that area and to demands of secession from Israel on grounds of 'self-determination'. The report was publicly debated but never adopted as government policy.
9. *Al-Ba'th* (Syria), 29 March 1977.

10. *Al-Ra'i* (Jordan), 22 August 1976.
11. See for example MENA, Cairo, 7 March 1977.
12. On 21 August 1969 a young Australian tourist, Michael Rohan, set fire to the Asqa Mosque in Jerusalem. Despite Israeli condemnation of the act, the conviction of the culprit and the rush to extinguish the fire as soon as it erupted, Israel was widely accused in the Arab world of arson. Incidentally, the incident brought about the first Islamic Summit Conference which met in Rabat in 1969 and thereafter instituted the annual meeting of the Foreign Ministers of the Islamic countries.
13. MENA, Cairo, 21 August 1977.
14. *Al-Thawra* (Yemen), 21 August 1977.
15. *Sawt-al-Arab* (Cairo), 7 November 1976.
16. Radio Cairo, political commentary, 8 November 1976.
17. *Al-Sabah* (Tunisia), 7 July 1976.
18. MENA, Cairo, citing Algerian and Moroccan press, 5 and 6 July 1976.
19. *Al Ba'th* (Syria), 29 March 1977, 15.
20. *Al-Anwar* (Lebanon), 26 July 1977.
21. Ibid.
22. Radio Cairo, quoting President Sadat, 7 March 1977.
23. *Akher Sa'a* (Egypt), 21 July 1976.
24. *Al-Ba'th* (Syria), 4 January 1977.
25. *Shuun Filastiniyya*, December 1975, p. 6.
26. Ibid., pp. 9-10.
27. Ibid., pp. 10-11.
28. Ibid., p. 11.
29. *Al-Idha'a Wal-Telefizion* (Egypt), 6 August 1977; *Al-Akhbar* (Egypt), 15 August 1977.
30. *Al-Ra'i* (Jordan), 16 August 1977; *Al-Musawwar* (Egypt), 22 April 1977.
31. *Al-Dustour* (Jordan), 6 November 1976.
32. *Al-Madina* (Saudi Arabia), 17 August 1977.
33. *Al-Akhbar*, 4 September 1978.
34. *Roos-al-Yusuf*, 4 September 1978.
35. *Al-Gumhuriyah*, 4 September 1978.
36. *October*, 3 September 1978, p. 50.
37. *Jaridat Misr* (Egypt), 19 September 1978, p. 12.
38. *Al-Ahram*, 27 November 1978, p. 18.
39. *Akhbar Al-Yawm*, 2 December 1978, p. 8.
40. *Akhbar Al-Yawm*, 16 December 1978, p. 8.
41. *Al-Gumhuriyah*, 17 December 1978, p. 12.
42. Taba is the tiny stretch of land on the Eilat–Aqaba Gulf coastline which until very recently remained contested between Egypt and Israel, following the latter's otherwise complete withdrawal from the Sinai in April 1982.
43. *Al-Idha'a Wal-Telefizion* (Cairo), 7 February 1981. For this and the following references I am indebted to my colleague, Mrs Rivka Yadlin, who drew my attention to recent publications and shared with me some of her reflections on them and on unpublished writings.

# 10 Fictive Anti-Zionism: Third World, Arab and Muslim Variations
## Antony Lerman

There are two main problems in any discussion or analysis of anti-Zionism: first, defining what it means, what it refers to; second, deciding what *kind* of phenomenon it is.

Applied too loosely, the term ceases to serve any useful purpose. For example, it cannot be appropriate to describe as anti-Zionism both opposition to the policies of the Israeli government and the denial of the right of Jews to a state. Similarly, it would make no .sense to equate all Arab anti-Zionism with the anti-Zionism of such groups as the British National Front. In popular usage, however, all these applications of the term are often used indiscriminately. What seems to be the case, increasingly, is that any negative or critical attitude to anything remotely relating to the State of Israel is labelled anti-Zionism.

Confusion as to the *nature* of anti-Zionism is also apparent. It is regarded variously as an ideology, a threat to Western civilisation, a form of prejudice and a synonym for antisemitism, among other things. It is often discussed in terms of its delegitimising or dehumanising effect on Israel and Jews. Sometimes it is seen principally as serving the ends of Soviet propaganda. Alternatively, Arab states or the UN system are regarded as the propagators and initiators of anti-Zionism.

Many writers on and observers of anti-Zionism make three fundamental assumptions: that those who espouse it are opposed to a single, identifiable phenomenon called Zionism; that what they are opposed to actually does exist in the real world; that the anti-Zionism espoused is a unitary phenomenon which can be understood without a differentiated analysis. However, the fact that confusion exists as to the definition of anti-Zionism, and about what kind of phenomenon it is, suggests that such an assumption is unworkable. If this thing called 'Zionism' which arouses so much animosity were single and identifiable the confusion would surely not exist.

This confusion can be mediated by distinguishing between two types of anti-Zionism: the first is a political ideology practically directed at opposing the state of Israel as a state born out of and expressing the aspirations of the Jewish movement for national self-determination; the second bears no relationship to anything that exists in the real world but is rather a fictive construct intended to serve the particular internal and external political purposes of those who espouse it.

The first type of anti-Zionism is principally advocated and practiced by the Palestinian national movement in its various forms, by certain Arab groups, and by others, non-Jews and Jews, who maintain a consistent ideological position against the Jewish state. These might be Marxists of various types, revolutionary communists and so on. The second type of anti-Zionism is found among Third World states, the Arab and Islamic worlds in general and the states of the non-aligned movement and also of the Communist bloc. It refers to the Zionism debated and discussed at the United Nations, at international Third World conferences, and mentioned in the international relations discourse between Arab and other states. However, this anti-Zionism, which we might call *fictive anti-Zionism*, is also found amongst some of those who adhere to the political ideology of anti-Zionism. This is a fundamental distinction which is not often made but without it it is very difficult to understand the nature of contemporary anti-Zionism.

This paper is devoted exclusively to the phenomenon of fictive anti-Zionism (though not the variety emanating from the Communist bloc). By isolating fictive anti-Zionism I do not intend to suggest that the problem of anti-Zionism is purely semantic although somewhere along the line of distortion of Zionism the question of meaning does become important. This aspect has been touched on by a number of observers. For example, Walter Laqueur writes about 'psittacism', the habit of using words without thought.[1] The distortion of Zionism in international affairs can be seen generally as part of a tendency towards imprecision in foreign policy discourse. On the other hand, what has happened to Zionism can also be seen as a deliberate misuse of language. Ehud Sprinzak refers to this as a 'corruption of language'[2] and the 'deliberate destruction of language and rational discourse'.[3] Daniel Patrick Moynihan sees it as 'the totalitarian manipulation of words and symbols' designed to undermine the liberal societies of the West.[4] And Yohanan Manor, in an attempt to discuss the similarities between anti-Zionism and antisemitism, believes that the 'creeping' phenomenon of criticism of the politics and actions of Israel taking 'the form of a mass condemnation of Israel itself . . . often starts through a language bias'.[5]

One problem with the semantic approach is that it can encourage belief in the idea that the situation could be improved by a concerted effort to return to the correct meaning of the term 'Zionism'. If what we face is to a great degree sloppy thinking, the notion of a global clarification of terms has some superficial attraction. But as this paper will show, such hopeful solutions are beside the point. The distortion of Zionism, and of anti-Zionism, is deliberate and calculated.

The use of fictive anti-Zionism in foreign policy and political discourse is, of course, not a recent development. Whilst it is virtually impossible to quantify the phenomenon and make reliable comparisons with previous decades, this abuse of Zionism has accelerated as an ever increasing number of states have expressed public sympathy and support for the Palestinians, and have given some form of diplomatic recognition to the Palestine Liberation Organisation.[6] The principal clearing house for these developments has been the United Nations, which has acted as an important means of communication between those states, national liberation movements and non-governmental organisations wishing to express their support for the PLO by opposing the ideology of the state which they see as denying the rights of the Palestinians to self-determination. The main impetus in recent years has come from UN General Assembly Resolution 3379, passed on 10 November 1975, which declared that 'Zionism is a form of racism and racial discrimination'.[7] This linked Zionism with what has come to be the main social evil of the last twenty to thirty years – a social evil whose unique status owes so much to the effects of the Nazi regime – and therefore gave anti-Zionism a form of international legitimacy and status which it had hitherto lacked.[8]

If it were possible to identify a period in which the language of anti-Zionism was used in a limited and consistent way, that period has long since passed. The absurdity of the current situation was nicely captured by the Irish journalist and author Conor Cruise O'Brien:

Radio Outer Mongolia habitually calls the Chinese 'Zionists', Communist shop stewards in Paris call Arab immigrant workers 'Zionists'. Just as the Christian church was (and perhaps is) 'the true Israel', *verus Israel*, so in contemporary rhetoric true Jews are said to be the Palestinian Arabs (as victims) while those who claim to be the Jews, out there, are in truth Nazis (as masters), as well as being Chinese, and even Arabs . . .
Further, since the Arabs of Paris are *Zionists* – just like the Chinese – they are responsible for what the Jews, that is the Nazis, did in Palestine to the real Arabs, who are really the Jews.[9]

A similar point is made by Daniel Patrick Moynihan, although without the irony: 'In the lexicon of modern international politics, Zionism has first been used as a euphemism for "traitor". Then it had been determined to be a form of racism. Finally, according to the Cuban-led non-aligned movement, Zionism became "a crime against humanity". And one didn't have to be a Zionist, or even Jewish, to become a victim of this campaign.'[10] Michael Curtis has made a similar point: 'The equation of Zionism with illegitimacy has now turned to farce, with the Soviet Union in Outer Mongolia denouncing the Chinese as Zionists and Haitian exiles attacking the Zionism of the ruler Papa Doc Duvalier.'[11] What these quotations indicate is the extent to which Zionism has ceased to possess any objectively consistent meaning when used in these contexts, and has taken on a deliberately fictive character, becoming a general term of abuse designed, for example, along with other key words, as a simple way to identify an enemy.

### Classifications

There are two main ways in which examples of fictive anti–Zionism can be classified. First, according to the agent or group of agents using the anti–Zionist discourse; for example: individual entities like the PLO, Libya, Syria; organisations and groupings like the Islamic Conference Organisation (ICO), the non-aligned movement, the Organisation of African Unity (OAU), the United Nations; states in some form of conflict relationship like Iran and Iraq, Libya and Egypt. Second, according to the context in which Zionism is said to operate, or according to the object of Zionist 'machinations' – for example: the media, individual states, the Third World, the economic arena, international organisations and so on.

It is probably more interesting and revealing to classify the phenomena according to the second method because this provides a means of surveying the vast arena in which Zionism is said to operate and the amazing and far-reaching power which Zionism is said to possess. Moreover, I attempted the classification of abuses of anti-Zionism according to the first method in an earlier paper.[12]

### The Media

'Zionist' control of the media is often presented as a worldwide phenomenon, not even confined to those states in which professed Zionists actually live. Yasir Arafat, addressing the General Federation of Palestinian Writers and Journalists in May 1985, said that 'Zionist information' dominated the Arab people through its 'penetration of the Arab media, a penetration made possible by agents of US imperialism in the region'. No explanation is given of how this actually operates. More important is the effect which this domination has supposedly had. Arafat claimed that Arab information has made no attempt to fight back – giving the siege of Beirut as an example. This longest of Arab–Israeli wars, lasting 88 days, had allegedly been ignored by the Arab media because of propaganda penetration in favour of the 'Zionist devilish machine'.[13]

Such use of the notion of 'Zionist' control of Arab media is quite common where the accuser feels that his viewpoint is being ignored or when a version of events inimicable to him is being presented. Thus, the Iranians blame misrepresentation of their case on the media more generally. Denying reported links with Israel in May 1985, Iranian President Ali Khamane'i said:

> Rumours about our purchase of weapons from Israel and on the dispatch of a number of Iranian Jews to Israel constitute a new scheme by world arrogance aimed at accusing us of having relations which we deem both religiously unclean and forbidden and at preventing the exposure of the political collusion between certain Arab and Muslim leaders and world arrogance. . . . It is essential to remind you that every year, on the eve of the ceremonies marking world Jerusalem Day, observed throughout the world at the suggestion of the Islamic republic, such rumours are disseminated by the imperialist and Zionist mass media.[14]

In fact Tehran claimed in June that negative reports by 'Western countries and the countries of the region on 'Jerusalem Day' marches and demonstrations [unparalleled since the Islamic revolution] . . . have been mere fabrication and bereft of truth' because they were sent by 'their agents and correspondents affiliated to Zionism and imperialism'.[15] Indeed, 'This issue [that the Iranian nation does not have the enthusiasm which marked the early days of the revolution] has consistently been flaunted conspicuously and widely by the Zionist media.'

The 'Zionist–American information services' were also blamed by Abu Abbas, at the time of the highjacking of the cruise liner *Achille Lauro* in 1985, for 'inventing' the idea that anyone had been killed by the 'Palestinian youths'.[16] This was done to 'justify America's piratical and terrorist action against the Egyptian airliner which was carrying the Palestinian youths after the peaceful resolution of the problem of the Italian ship'.

The BBC is often a target for attack and two appointments at the corporation, in 1983 and 1985, provided an opportunity. First, the appointment of Stuart Young as Chairman of the BBC's Board of Governors was widely seen in the Middle East as serving the interests of Zionism. Mr. Young, who died in 1986, had close connections with many Jewish and Zionist causes. Even the Egyptians, more restrained than most, managed to exaggerate reaction to the appointment: 'Arab quarters in London have expressed dismay and concern over the appointment of the new Chairman of the BBC, due to his strong links with Israel and the Zionist movement. His appointment has caused a political row and anger in opposition parties in Britain.'[17] Tehran radio was more outspoken: 'In order to justify [Zionist aggression] from the propaganda standpoint, [Zionism] will now enjoy more effective support and backing from Britain's government radio and television.'[18] Other Islamic media also reported critically.[19]

The second appointment was of Benny Amar, an English Jew of Egyptian origin, as assistant head of the BBC's Arabic section. Syrian radio claimed that a 'clamour erupted inside the BBC and among the Arab diplomatic circles as a result of this decision for fear of its effects on the Arab media coverage in the programme'.[20] The Syrians said that he was a spy for the 'British, the Americans and the Zionists' in Cyprus after he left Egypt following the Suez crisis. 'Now he has a new role to play.'

More recently, the Prime Minister of Malaysia, Mr Mahathir Mohamed, invoked Zionism as a cause of his country's problems. On 26 September 1986 he expelled two *Wall Street Journal* correspondents and banned the paper for three months in exasperation at the critical articles appearing in the Asian edition about his country. 'The Prime Minister regards reporting of [corruption, inefficiency and the existence of a fuzzy line between politics and business] as a 'Zionist' conspiracy against Malaysia by the foreign press'.[21] Mr Mahathir also accused the Malaysian press of being under Zionist influence. When a negative report appeared in a Chinese-language newspaper Mr Mahathir alleged that 'well-known media organizations were controlled by Jews, either as owners or as holders of key posts, such as editors and journalists'.[22]

In an interesting commentary on the Malaysian Prime Minister's habit of blaming Zionists and Jews for his troubles Dr Michael Liefer, an expert on the politics of South-East Asia, says that Mr Mahathir's 'anti–Zionism has a source in his fervent support for Palestinian nationalism. In the case of Malaysia, where Islam is the official religion, support for Palestinian nationalism tends to be understood also as support for fellow Muslims. Such support serves a domestic function.'[23] Dr Liefer quotes some vitriolic anti–Jewish and anti–Zionist statements by Mr Mahathir, including the statement that the Jews 'have been apt pupils of Dr Goebbels'. But he puts even this down to essentially domestic considerations and says: 'It suggests a pathological view of Malaysia's alleged detractors and enemies that goes beyond support for the Palestinian cause and the need to counter Islamic fundamentalism at home.'

### The 'Alliance of Zionism with Imperialism, Racism, Neocolonialism' and other Evils

The formula of linking Zionism with imperialism, racism, neocolonialism and so on has become a staple element of resolutions at the United Nations, at gatherings of Third World countries and also at Arab and Islamic forums. Whilst the Palestinian issue does not play such a prominent part in these arenas as it did before 1982, final communiqués, statements and speeches by participants never fail to repeat the formula. Heads of state and other national leaders at the seventh non-aligned summit meeting in New Delhi in 1983 included the ritual condemnation of Zionism in their remarks. Libya's Major Jallud referred to 'imperialism, Zionism, racialism, fascism and reaction'.[24] President Samora Machel of Mozambique said 'Non-alignment is by definition anti-colonialist, anti-apartheid, anti-Zionist, anti-fascist and anti-imperialist'.[25] He expanded on the link between fascism and Zionism: 'In order to deny [the right of the Palestinian people to self-determination] Israel is using the most brutal forms of genocide typical of Nazi-fascism, as happened at Sabra and Shatila in Lebanon.' The South Yemen President, Ali Nasir Muhammad, said: 'It is important to point out that the Israeli provocations against Syria represent a link in the imperialist-Zionist plot to degrade the Arab peoples . . .'[26] Even in Central America it is important to make the right noises. Thus, President Daniel Ortega Saavedra of Nicaragua: 'Today we say to the enemies of our movement that, instead of being neutralized, we are now more active, that is, that every day we are more anti-imperialist, more anti-racist, more anti-Zionist, more anti-apartheid, more anti-colonialist, more anti-neocolonialist . . .'[27] And President Souphanouvong of Laos added his voice: 'he said non-alignment represented a clear solemn task against colonialism, neocolonialism, imperialism, Zionism, apartheid and racism and for the cause of national liberation and social progress of the movement'.[28]

Examples of the use of this formula are practically endless. But the very fact that it is a formula makes it difficult to assume the expression of opposition to Zionism can be classified in any sense as an ideology. It rather serves the purpose of establishing the speaker's credentials as part of a broad Third Worldist ideological tendency. In order to be recognised as a member of the club, you have to repeat the litany on every occasion that the club meets together in formal session. It is neither necessary to have any understanding of what Zionism is, nor is it necessary to take any practical action against Zionism. It is enough simply to repeat the catechism for absolution to be granted.

**The Worldwide Zionist Plot**

In a sense most examples of fictive anti–Zionism can be classified under this heading but some are more expressly couched in terms of plots and conspiracies. These plots are designed to undermine individual states or the Third World or Arab world as a whole; they aim to curtail freedom, to enslave the unsuspecting, to create instability.

Such plots do not have to be traced back to the 'Zionist regime' in Israel. President Assad, for example, addressing a meeting of Syrian doctors living in the USA, gave this warning:

Our people admire and respect the American people. On several occasions, I told US officials, with whom we disagreed, that we are struggling to preserve our freedom in the face of the Israeli usurpation that is planned by world Zionism.

As for you in the USA, you must struggle to regain your freedom which was usurped by Zionism, by millions of organized Jews in the USA.[29]

Those participating in the 'Zionist conspiracy to rule the world' are not only Jews. A court in Candia, Crete, ruled in 1984 that the Jehovah's Witnesses sect bears a close resemblance to Judaism and is part of 'the Zionist conspiracy to rule the world from Jerusalem'.[30] The court cited the purported beliefs of the Jehovah's Witnesses, drawn from the Old Testament prophet Ezekiel, to claim that the sect seeks a 'theocratic Zionist state' in which 'some of them will be appointed as governors of the most important areas of the world and that the ruler of Jerusalem will be issuing directions concerning world affairs'. The court further stated that the Jehovah's Witnesses are 'against Christianity and the nation' and have the 'political-economic character of an organization close to Judaism. . . .'

Colonel Qaddafi uses the plot theme with great regularity. On Israel's co-operation with Black African states he commented in 1984: 'The hidden objective is to prepare militarists within the African armies in order actually to stage coups in the future and set up governments formed by the military who have been prepared by the Israelis so as to place their countries in the service of Zionism.'[31] But Qaddafi gave this exposition an economic twist which has also become a staple means of abusing Zionism:

Next, they [the Israelis] want to infiltrate economically. The Jewish organization cannot live except in banks and on economic activities, some of which are covert. They want to infiltrate African activities, African markets, African concerns and African companies. They offer experts not to serve the interests of the African countries but to serve Zionism.

Similar attacks on Zionism as a means of Third World economic exploitation can be found expressed in other forums. At the 12th session of the Economic Commission for Western Asia in Baghdad in April 1985, Iraq's First Deputy Prime Minister, Taha Yasin Ramadan, remarked that 'South Africa, the Zionist entity and Iran . . . were linked by a common objective – to confuse and obstruct the development process, shake political stability and paralyse economic and regional co-operation among the developing countries with the aim of keeping them economically backward'.[32]

Perhaps the basic text for citing the economic power of Zionism can be found in the Economic Declarations of the non-aligned movement. These declarations proclaim the benefits of the 'New International Economic Order' which the movement believes should replace the existing order. The barriers to implementation were spelled out clearly at the last non-aligned summit in Harare, Zimbabwe, in September 1986:

The Heads of State or Government reiterated that colonialism, imperialism, neo-colonialism, interference in internal affairs, apartheid, zionism, racism and all forms of racial discrimination, foreign aggression, occupation, domination, hegemony, expansionism, exploitation and destabilization constitute fundamental obstacles to the economic liberation of developing countries and reaffirmed their commitment to individually and collectively take effective measures to put an end to these practices.[33]

The Iranians are especially exercised by plots and conspiracies against them and against the Islamic world in general, and they see the hand of Zionism operating everywhere. After the release of an Amnesty report critical of the regime's human rights record, Prime Minister Mir Husayn Musavi said: 'We discussed the conspiracies hatched against our country to undermine the influence of the Islamic revolution by painting an ugly picture of the Islamic Republic. Among these are the activities of the human rights committee and Amnesty International, which are usually backed by the global Zionists.'[34] Musavi went on:

My focus of attention is the billion strong Islamic society. We must make it understand how a political Zionist sect which in the 100–150 years since its establishment has carried out conspiracies and espionage work for foreign countries, particularly Britain and later Israel, receives support and [make it understand] what is the nature of its belief, and whether its approach in our country has a religious or political nature. I believe that it has a political nature.

In August 1986 President Ali Khamane'i dwelt in detail on the nature of the link between Zionism and the plots against Iran and Islam:

The plot consists of Islamic communities being made increasingly subservient – from the political, economic and military standpoints – to world arrogance, and particularly in our region to Israel. The plot of establishing relations with Israel, recognizing Israel, accepting Israel as a reality, the plot firstly of covert relations and then overt relations between the Zionists and certain Islamic governments: all these are components of that huge plot, that deep-rooted and extremely dangerous plot against the Islamic world. . . .
The issue does not concern Jews as such, for it is the issue of Zionism. There may be many Jews hostile to the Zionists. There may have been many Jews who have made revelations about the Zionists. Zionism is an extremely short-sighted racist Judaism. . . .
We do not say that all the Jews should be thrown into the sea. We say

that the Zionist government should be eliminated root and branch and that all the Palestinians, be they Muslims, Christians and Jews, should live together as brothers. [Shouts of God is Great and slogans] The struggle against the Zionist regime is a religious obligation, a duty.[35]

The range and scope of the 'Zionist plot/worldwide conspiracy' is truly extraordinary, though the examples given here are by no means fully comprehensive. In many instances Zionism is referred to without connecting it to Israel or to any specific country. It certainly makes the conspiracy theory more sinister and, in a strange sense, more plausible, if Zionism is seen to be *global* and *multinational*, equally at home in New York, London or Tel Aviv. But there is a whole area of fictive anti-Zionism which consists of states and individuals being specifically singled out as Zionists.

**The 'Other' is a Zionist**

Since Zionism has become a code word for identifying the enemy, it is not at all surprising that it is one of the charges hurled back and forth in various inter-state conflicts throughout the world. Conor Cruise O'Brien drew attention to this in the quotation given above. Nowhere was it more freely used than in the war between Iran and Iraq. Back in September 1980 the Iraqi President, Saddam Husayn, in a long speech justifying Iraq's view of the conflict, saw it as a Zionist-imperialist conspiracy to which the Iranians had succumbed: 'We will confront the machinations of the suspect agents in Iran – who have rancorous and backward mentalities and racist motives, . . . hostile colonialist, Zionist and racist machinations.'[36] The Iranians responded in kind. A former foreign minister, Sadeq Qotbzadeh, declared: 'The criminal government of Iraq has . . . been entirely in the hands of international Zionism and has acted against the interests of the Arabs and the Muslims and for the Zionists.'[37]

This theme was pursued relentlessly throughout the war. When Israel bombed Iraq's nuclear reactor, that country's First Deputy Prime Minister Taha Yasin Ramadan asserted that this 'Zionist aggression . . . confirmed the strong link between the Zionist entity and the Iranian rulers'.[38] In March 1986 Teheran radio, broadcasting in Turkish and proclaiming 'victories scored by the Islamic righters', claimed that: 'The Muslims in the northern districts of Iraq and the people of Sulaymaniyah have described their reaction [rejoicing greatly over the recent news] as stemming from the Zionist Iraq Ba'thist regime's oppression of the people of the region and from its pressure and massacres . . .'[39] For the Iranians, it is not only the Iraqis who are Zionists or are in alliance with 'world Zionism', those states which help Iraq are also implicated. In July 1984 Ayatollah Montazeri said: 'Today, Islam and Muslims are dealing with government leaders who are either ignorant and uninformed about Islam or [are] agents and mercenaries of the enemies of Islam and international Zionism . . . He accused the Riyad government of corruption and subservience to Zionism.'[40]

Just as the Iranians provide theoretical justification for their abuse of Zionism, through their militant Islamic fundamentalism, so too do the Iraqis, though using different methods. An article in an Iraqi journal, entitled 'Similarity and conformity of Iranian and Zionist propaganda',[41] argued, using the scholarly apparatus of footnotes and quotation, that Iran's 'attack on Iraq [*sic*]' was 'in conformity with the contents of Zionist propaganda'. The war serves the interests of Zionism and imperialism.[42] The Iranian attitude of wanting to export 'so-called "Islamic revolution" . . . reminds us of the aggressive expansionist, racist Zionist phenomenon, a phenomenon which employs religion, utilising various types of propaganda to cast doubt and to defame Arab-Islamic civilization'.[43] The similarity between Iranian and Zionist propaganda is based on 'a wider, ideological conformity wrapped in a religious wrapping'. The ideological parallel does not lie in the concepts and ideas but in objectives and goals and in the justifications used to support these objectives.[44] The article sums up the similarities as (1) their stand on Arab nationalism; (2) expansionism and hostility towards Arabs; (3) 'arrogance and haughtiness' as a consequence of racism and racist thought.

But on the whole, calling your enemy 'Zionist' requires little justification. In the past it was a feature of Syrian–Jordanian relations. In early 1981, when already strained relations between the two countries worsened, troops were ostentatiously moved to their common border. Moves on the ground were accompanied by propaganda activity: 'Arab Syria . . . would always support the fraternal people [of Jordan] in its national and pan-Arab struggle against the imperialist-Zionist plot in which King Husayn's regime was taking part.'[45] But according to King Husayn it was Syria who was secretly serving Zionist interests: 'Syria wants to divide the whole region so that some of it is subservient to the West and some of it to the East, Syria wants to internationalize the Arab-Zionist conflict. With that goal it agrees with Zionism.'[46]

Syria has other targets for its anti-Zionist rhetoric. Following Britain's breaking of diplomatic relations with Syria in October 1986, the full force of this rhetoric was turned on Mrs Thatcher's government. In an article in *Tishrin* entitled 'Britain from colonialism to Zionisation', the British step against Syria was said to come 'within the framework of an old colonialist-imperialist-Israeli scheme in which Britain plays a planned role'.[47] Held directly responsible for an act of terrorism, the Syrians indulged in convoluted explanations of terrorism and of its ultimate link with Zionism:

Zionist-imperialist circles have sought to confuse terrorism with legitimate national struggle to liberate the land and regain the rights in order to exonerate the Zionist enemy, who is guilty of organized terrorism

against civilian aircraft, violates the sovereignty of UN member states, occupies, destroys and carries out the ugliest crimes which in their barbarity have surpassed the crimes of the Hitlerite Nazis. . . .
Terrorism is originally a form of imperialism, just like racism, Nazism, fascism and Zionism which has carried out serious and great crimes against our Arab nation, particularly in Palestine, whose people it expelled and made homeless.[48]

Other states came to Syria's support using similar links between Zionism and the United Kingdom.[49]

**Variations on Themes**

The spread of fictive anti–Zionism should already be evident from the examples quoted above. However, variations on these themes show the malleability of the discourse which abuses Zionism. For example, the Iranian Islamic Republic's leaders' intense dislike and distrust of the Baha'i faith has been apparent since the revolution, and an unknown number of Baha'i adherents have been murdered on the pretext that they were Zionists. One such execution was announced in March 1985: 'A man called Ruhollah Bahram Shani, son of Geshtasb, was charged with committing espionage for the Zionist regime, getting direct orders from Israel and smuggling hard currency out of the country to Israel through the national Baha'i network.'[50] In South Africa it was reported that the township of Soweto was 'being flooded with pamphlets calling for a boycott of nine major South African companies – among them the giant Anglo–American corporation – on the grounds that they are 'Zionist organizations which send 80 per cent of their profits to Israel which buys arms to murder our Arab brothers'.[51] The PLO representative in Nicaragua, questioned on the radio as to what Zionism's interest is in Argentina, replied: 'It seems they have the same intentions they have in Palestine, that of forming their second state. They have called on the 500 000 Jews in Argentina to form their second state in the area of Patagonia.'[52]

As the one group actively involved in physically opposing Zionism and Israel, as opposed to indulging only in rhetoric, the PLO has been mostly left out of these examples. They tend to be more ideologically consistent in their anti–Zionism. Nevertheless, they too regularly indulge in the abuse of Zionism even whilst making strenuous efforts to show that they are not antisemitic. An example of this type of approach can be seen in the PLO's response to a radio station calling itself 'The Voice of Vengeance, the Voice of Holy Hatred', which began transmission to the Arab Maghrib region early in 1985, broadcasting 'violent statements replete with racism, and calling publicly for violence, terrorism and murder against Arab

Jewish citizens in the Arab Maghrib countries'.[53] The PLO radio went on:

> We in the PLO are anxious to make clear that the method of black propaganda which this radio uses is the same as that used by the Zionist radios which were directed, during the second world war, at the German Jews and, during 1947–51, in our Arab region, and exactly the same as the Zionist intelligence organs are employing now to incite the Jews of Lebanon, Yemen and India . . .
> The PLO condemns this suspect radio, and the parties responsible for it – though all the indications are that it is an Israeli radio which is used by the Zionist broadcasting services in their well-known propaganda campaigns to incite the Arab Jewish citizens and spread panic and terror among them with the aim of inciting them and forcing them to emigrate from their homelands to occupied Palestine to feed the Zionist war and aggression machine with manpower.

One need hardly point out that the number of Jews in Lebanon, Yemen and India amounts to no more than a few thousand.

**Conclusions**

Zionism, an ideology of national self-determination, applicable in one tiny part of the globe, has become a universally applied epithet, a fundamental 'evil' made responsible for most of the world's problems. As the examples quoted above show, the range of the abusive references to Zionism which make up the discourse of fictive anti-Zionism is enormously wide.

It is tempting to draw parallels between this fictive anti-Zionism and antisemitism especially because of certain features common to both. First, the attribution of mutually exclusive characteristics: antisemitism sees Jews as both controlling communism and capitalism, as possessed of both great prowess and yet racially inferior; fictive anti-Zionism sees as Zionists opposing sides in the same war, controlling West and East and so on. Second, both have conspiracy theories at their centres. Third, both show a tendency to rabid utterances, so extreme as to constitute verbal violence. Fourth, both Jews and Zionism are seen as demonic.

However, to draw a parallel in this way does not prove that anti-Zionism and antisemitism are one and the same. It is one thing to show that they have similar characteristics; it is quite another to claim an equivalence. Moreover, it fails to take into account the fact that many of the countries which use fictive anti-Zionism could easily abandon it if there was a change of government or policy. We need to look at why this phenomenon of fictive anti-Zionism has become so widespread in the cultural and ideological patterns which are dominant in the states which use it.

## An Excuse for Failure

One important tendency in the Arab world is the inability to face the real implications of defeat, the need to explain failure by reference to external factors. This is indicative of a certain fatalism and a wish to escape the consequences of taking responsibility for one's mistakes. An explanation of how this expresses itself in relation to political events is given by Fouad Ajami in an account of Arab political thought and practice since 1967.[54] A Lebanese professor of philosophy, Kamal Yusif al-Hajj, had written that the Arabs were wrong to blame the West for their misfortunes because the West was merely deceived by Zionism. The Arabs must save the West from the hold of the Zionists: 'The formidable powers of the West would then be under our influence instead of the influence of the Zionists.'[55] Here, a theory of conspiracy and demonic powers is taken absolutely seriously. 'This explains why the Protocols of the Elders of Zion were taken seriously by some Arab writers . . . If the Protocols are believed, then the Arab defeat would make sense: The Arabs would be another deceived, dominated people, and what overwhelmed them would not be a small state but a vast conspiracy', writes Ajami.

A large part of the rhetoric of fictive anti-Zionism is couched in the revolutionary ideological language of Third World radicalism. As Menahem Milson has noted, traditional Islamic concepts have been transformed into the revolutionary language of twentieth-century political ideologies: 'This radiant vision inspires millenial tendencies in which religious fervour is transformed into political zeal, fanaticism is virtue, and compromise is tantamount to treason.'[56] As Earl Raab suggests, anti-Zionism must be related to the 'ideology of extremism' which has four features: political moralism (all opponents are evil, not just wrong); a conspiracy theory; anti-democracy; bigotry.[57] Zionism therefore has become a point of common interest to the exteme left and to regimes which brutally suppress human rights and abhor Marxism.

The language of revolutionary rhetoric, however, is more than just an ill-fitting uniform worn only when it is necessary to identify with a certain view for the sake of political expediency. Fictive anti-Zionism shows all the signs of being part of the expression of a specific and identifiable world-view. Peter Berger has written of a 'series of propositions' which form 'the common core of the Third World ideology' and 'constitute an intellectual and moral whole'.[58]

they are based on a set of presuppositions about the nature of the world and they also put this view of the world into a moral context, a view of what the world *ought* to be. Moreover, this ideology, culled from a variety of sources (most of them, incidentally, of pro-Western provenance), is not an abstract intellectual enterprise. Rather it is a political instrument used to legitimate specific objectives. Thus the broad acceptance of this ideology by Third World governments has gone hand in hand with various political initiatives, almost all of them within the United Nations system.

This ideology has its theorists, like Professor Ali A. Mazrui,[59] Anouar Abdel-Malek[60] and others, who provide it with an academic quasi-academic or pseudo-academic underpinning.[61] Mazrui has recently written about the linkages between Zionism, Nazism and apartheid and considers Israel 'as the most arrogant sovereign state in the world since Nazism'. While Mazrui concerns himself specifically with Zionism, Abdel-Malek provides the grand theory which justifies Third World revolutionary rhetoric as a whole. He argues that 'the roots of violence, the roots of global war, the road toward armament, lie in the historical structuration of the international order, i.e. in the historical formation of Western hegemony, rooted in historical surplus value, beginning in the fifteenth century'. 'The Zionist operation', Abdel-Malek writes elsewhere, '[is] the most intense form of imperialism the Middle East has ever known'.[62] This language bears all too much resemblance to the theorising of the Iraqi writer, quoted above, who drew an equivalence between Iranian and Zionist propaganda as a means of showing their identity of aims. And there are many other examples, especially in the proceedings of the United Nations Seminars on the Question of the Palestinian People organised within the UN framework and in the gatherings organised by Colonel Qaddhafi and others.[63]

This fictive anti-Zionism has perhaps reached its peak in the non-aligned movement where repeating the litany of condemnation of Zionism is a ritual basic to the nature of the movement. It must be understood that the hyperbole and the great outpourings of words in long speeches and in gargantuan declarations are the only weapons at the disposal of the non-aligned. The movement's impotence in its chosen areas of concern makes the word-glut a form of therapeutic massage. As Peter Willets writes, the non-aligned movement operates as an 'institution for the aggregation of demands'.[64] These demands reflect three levels of powerlessness: international (they have no way of influencing East–West relations, the functioning of the world economic system etc.), continental (specifically in Asia and Africa), and national (domestic policies have mostly failed to produce the kind of social and economic advances implied in the ideology they espouse). Fictive anti-Zionism is one element in the response to this powerlessness. The use of anti-Zionist rhetoric indicates obeisance to an ideological position which legitimates the regime domestically (principally with the political party or movement which forms the basis of the regime's power and support) and within the Afro-Asian political context.

This conclusion follows from the rhetorical forms of anti-Zionism quoted in this paper, but it can be demonstrated in another way. A significant number of states which espouse this anti-Zionism operate in an entirely different manner on the practical political level. As Ehud Sprinzak wrote, in a paper prepared specially for the World Zionist Organisation; 'Anti-Zionist sentiment in these countries is mainly a political stand taken by the government for political reasons. It is likely to change to pro-Israelism a day after the government has changed its official position.'[65] Broadly speaking it is this kind of mechanism which operates in Africa. The OAU called for a total diplomatic boycott of Israel in 1973. Three refused; four have since restored relations; Egypt signed a peace treaty; and another three or four are close to resuming ties with Israel. Moreover, if Israel were to distance itself from Pretoria, other African governments would probably be ready to restore diplomatic relations.[66] Meanwhile, these states continue to repeat anti-Zionist rhetoric.

To conclude that fictive anti-Zionism constitutes such a large part of the anti-Zionism expressed worldwide (and this analysis touches on only a small part), and is directed towards fulfilling the particular political needs of the regimes and organisations which use it, should not be interpreted as a message of reassurance. But any critical approach to anti-Zionism must seek to understand the phenomenon and the basis of understanding is differentiation. Only by separating out its different forms is it possible to assess the danger that anti-Zionism really represents.

## Notes

1. Walter Laqueur discusses psittacism in international affairs in Foreign policy and the English language', *Washington Quarterly*, Winter 1981, pp. 3–12. See also, by the same author, 'Is Khomeini a neoconservative?', *New Republic*, 8 December 1979, pp. 9–11.
2. Ehud Sprinzak, 'Anti-Zionism: from delegitimation to dehumanisation', *Forum* (Jerusalem), no. 53, Autumn/Winter 1984.
3. Ehud Sprinzak, 'The damage of anti-Zionism. A preliminary analysis', *The Threat of Anti-Zionism* (series) (Jerusalem: World Zionist Organisation, 1984), p. 3.
4. Daniel Patrick Moynihan, 'On the "Fascist, Zionist, Reactionary Alliance"', an address to the Friends of Hebrew University of Jerusalem, London, 19 January 1982, p. 3.
5. Yohanan Manor, 'The new anti-Zionism', *Jerusalem Quarterly*, no. 35, Spring 1985, p. 133.
6. See for example 'The international status of the PLO', *IJA Research Reports*, no. 16, 1981.
7. See Thomas Mayer, 'The UN resolution equating Zionism with racism: genesis and repercussions', *IJA Research Reports*, no. 1, April 1985.
8. Seymour M. Finger and Ziva Flamhaft, 'The issue of "Zionism and racism" in

the United Nations', *Middle East Review*, vol. 18, no. 3, spring 1986, pp. 55–8.
9. *Observer* (London), 11 December 1983.
10. Moynihan, p. 11.
11. Michael Curtis, 'Introduction: antisemitism – the baffling obsession', in Michael Curtis (ed.) *Antisemitism in the Contemporary World* (Boulder and London, 1986), p. 8.
12. Tony Lerman, 'The abuse of Zionism', *IJA Research Reports*, no. 20, December 1981. Some material from that paper has been incorporated here.
13. Voice of Palestine (Algiers), 14 May 1985. (All quotations from radio broadcasts and news services are as monitored and translated by the BBC and published in *Summary of World Broadcasts for the Middle East and Africa*.)
14. Tehran home service, 17 May 1985.
15. Tehran home service, 15 June 1985.
16. Kuwait News Agency (KUNA), 13 October 1985.
17. Middle East News Agency (MENA) (Cairo) in English, 25 March 1983.
18. Tehran in Persian for abroad, 5 August 1983.
19. World Jewish Congress press release (London), 29 August 1983.
20. Damascus home service, 10 November 1985.
21. *Economist*, 4 October 1986.
22. Michael Liefer, 'Mahathir's anti-Zionist rhetoric', *International Herald Tribune* (Paris), 9 October 1986.
23. Ibid.
24. Tripoli home service, 9 March 1983.
25. Maputo home service in Portuguese, 8 March 1983.
26. Aden home service, 10 March 1983.
27. Radio Sandino ((Managua) in Spanish, 9 March 1983.
28. Vientiane home service, 12 March 1983.
29. Damascus home service, 15 August 1985.
30. *Jewish Telegraphic Agency* (New York), 28 December 1984.
31. Voice of the Greater Arab Homeland (Tripoli), 2 August 1984.
32. Iraqi News Agency, 24 April 1985.
33. Economic Declaration, Eighth Conference of Heads of State or Government of Non-Aligned Countries, Harare, 1–6 September 1986, published in *Review of International Affairs* (Belgrade), 20 September 1986, vol. 37, p. 66.
34. Tehran home service, 4 December 1985.
35. Tehran home service, 16 August 1986.
36. Baghdad home service, 17 September 1980.
37. Tehran in Persian for home and abroad, 5 April 1980.
38. Iraqi News Agency, 24 April 1985.
39. Tehran in Turkish for abroad, 4 March 1986.
40. Tehran home service, 31 July 1984.
41. Nawaf Adwan, 'Similarity and conformity of Iranian and Zionist propaganda', *Al-Khalij al-'Arabi* (The Arab Gulf) (Basrah), vol. 15, no. 24, 1983.
42. Ibid., 26.
43. Ibid., 27.
44. Ibid., 28.
45. Damascus home service, 2 February 1981.
46. Amman home service, 21 March 1981.
47. Damascus home service, 27 October 1986.
48. Damascus home service, 26 October 1986.
49. For example, Tehran home service, 26 October 1986; Algiers home service, 26 October 1986.

50. *Jomhuri-ye Islam* (Tehran), 5 March 1985.
51. Jewish Chronicle News Service (Johannesburg), 15 November 1985.
52. Radio Sandino (Managua) in Spanish, 31 March 1981.
53. Voice of Palestine (San'a), 15 April 1985; *Aufbau* (New York), 24 May 1985.
54. *The Arab Predicament, Arab Political Thought and Practice since 1967* (Cambridge and New York, 1981).
55. Ibid., pp. 33–4. Ajami here paraphrases the argument of Sadeq al-Azm, an American-educated Syrian intellectual, whose book, *Al Naqd al Dhati Ba'd al Hazima* (Self-Criticism After the Defeat) (Beirut 1968), he describes as 'one of the most impressive and controversial pieces of Arabic political writing in recent times' (30). The quotation from al-Hajj is from al-Azm's book.
56. 'How to make peace with the Palestinians', *Commentary* (New York), May 1981, p. 31.
57. Earl Raab, 'The two anti–Zionisms', *Midstream* (New York), vol. 22, no. 3, March 1976, p. 52.
58. 'Speaking to the Third World', *Commentary*, October 1981, p. 31.
59. See for example two articles by him in *Alternatives: A Journal of World Policy* in 1983 and 1986.
60. See for example his piece in *Review* in 1979.
61. For example, the writers in *Judaism or Zionism? What Difference for the Middle East?*, edited by EAFORD (International Organisation for the Elimination of All Forms of Racial Discrimination) and Ajaz (American Jewish Alternatives to Zionism), (Bath, Avon: EAFORD and Zed Books, 1986).
62. 'Introduction' in Anouar Abdel-Malek (ed.) *Contemporary Arab Political Thought* (London, Zed Books, 1983), p. 23.
63. See for example, 'The Baghdad Ideological Conference on Zionism', *IJA Research Reports*, December 1976.
64. Peter Willets, *The Non-Aligned in Havana, Documents of the Sixth Summit Conference and an Analysis of their Significance for the Global Political System* (London, 1981), p. 4.
65. Sprinzak, 'The damage of anti–Zionism', p. 7.
66. Colin Legum, 'Israel reviews its policy on South Africa', *Colin Legum's Third World Reports* (London), 13 November 1986. See also Colin Legum's article, 'The Third World, Israel, and the Jews' in William Frankel (ed.) *Survey of Jewish Affairs 1982* (Rutherford and London, 1984), pp. 227–35.

# Part III
# Western Anti-Zionism

# 11 The Christian Churches on Israel and the Jews

## Norman Solomon

A recent survey lists over 20 000 different sects of Christianity in the world today. If they cannot agree on Christian doctrine or Church structure it is hardly likely they will share one consistent view on Jews and Israel. Group tendencies can be discerned and described, but one must always be wary of thinking of Christians, any more than Jews, as a monolithic entity. Nor should one overestimate the significance of 'Christian' views in contemporary Western society, where professing Christians are probably a minority.

How then do we start assessing the attitude of 20 000 different Churches to (a) Jews and (b) Judaism? We shall boldly prune and sort. Four categories will suffice. We will first consider the Evangelical 'fundamentalist' Churches, for they provide a simple model of naive Christian response. We then move on to the World Council of Churches (roughly 400 Churches belong to the WCC) and the mainstream Protestant Churches, most of which belong to it. We shall then consider the Roman Catholic Church, which boasts the largest number of adherents (perhaps 600 million), though it can by no means speak for all Christians. The Eastern Orthodox Churches, particularly the Middle Eastern ones, must also not be overlooked, though there is no room here to deal with them other than to refute the common assertion that they are intransigently set against all improvement in Christian–Jewish relations; they are however, through the World Council of Churches and their contacts with other Churches, an important factor in the Churches' reluctance to espouse wholeheartedly the cause of Israel.

## WHAT IS THE CHURCHES' PROBLEM?

It took some four centuries after the death of its founder for Christianity to produce its scriptures, its patristic writings and the conciliar definitions of doctrine which shaped the Christian traditions we now know. During most of this period it fought a running battle with Judaism, whose scriptures it appropriated as its own and sought to use as justification for its claims. But if the events involving Jesus were really the 'fulfilment' of the Hebrew scriptures, why did the Jews themselves not become Christians? Either Christian claims were in fact wrong and the Jews right, which the Church fathers were certainly not prepared to concede; or else there had to be something very seriously amiss with the Jews themselves, some wickedness or wilful blindness which had concealed the truth from them. The Jews were therefore seen as 'rejected' by God. But they could not be *totally* rejected; even Paul[1] had warned Gentile Christians not to vaunt themselves, 'the wild olive branch', over 'the native branches' (the Jewish people). Nor does the New Testament lack assurance that the Jews will eventually come to the 'true faith'. Translated into social terms, and backed up with discriminatory anti-Jewish legislation from Constantine onwards, these considerations nurtured the 'teaching of contempt' which characterised medieval Christian attitudes to Jews and found its culmination in the Holocaust. It was only too easy to point to the Destruction of the Temple, the Exile and the generally low status of the Jews as demonstrating that God had rejected them, though in His mercy He would remove the veil from their eyes and welcome them back at the end of time.

It was hard enough for Christians with this sort of background to welcome Jews as equals when the Emancipation finally, though with painful slowness, granted them equal civil rights. Indeed, many Christians had favoured removing discriminatory laws because they felt that once Jews were better educated and 'civilised' they would embrace Christianity. When Jews not only retained their identity but actually rose to positions of prominence and influence and, in many instances, led the way in the arts and sciences and other activities, the traditional European concept of their inferiority was challenged. This provoked the antisemitism that climaxed in the Holocaust. Once the West had finally learned to accept Jews as *individuals*, as *minorities* within a broader culture, the new challenge of a Jewish state came into being. The West, generally, welcomed the new state – otherwise it would not have been set up at all – but those Christians who were still encumbered by medieval theological concepts found it difficult to come to terms with the reality of Israel. Was not the actual *empowerment* of the Jewish people before the Second Coming (without conversion, and in a position of authority over a Christian minority in the Holy Land itself) contrary to all traditional Church teaching?

The late Canon Peter Schneider[2] tells the possibly apocryphal story of a Western Christian theologian 'thoroughly enjoying his new found camaraderie with rabbis, visits to the synagogue and even exchange of pulpits' but declaring, in the wake of the Six Day War: 'We have just got over the shock of having to treat Judaism as a real religion. Indeed, theologically we can now cope with that and then almost immediately, you Jews go and spoil it all by insisting in this day and age in tying up your religion with a piece of real estate.'

Basically, Western Christian theologians have found three ways to handle their dilemma. None of them actually *want* to be antisemitic or anti-Jewish, and there must be very few who *want* to be anti-Israel or anti-Zionist; but conventional Christian patterns of thought set up great tensions, and these have to be resolved. One method, prevalent among the 'fundamentalist' sects is to see Israel as a harbinger of the Second Coming. This sometimes results in an embarassingly pro-Israel stance where the Christian Zionist appears well to the right of Menachem Begin and Yitzhak Shamir. Another option is epitomised by those who are prepared to make a radical revision of Christian teaching on Jews and Judaism. Rosemary Ruether, for instance,[3] has forcefully argued that anti-Judaism is integral to the original self-definition of Christianity, from its scriptures onwards. Hence, an unequivocal rejection of this element within Christianity is called for. Others maintain that anti-Judaism is not essential within Christianity, but can be 'explained away' as part of the polemical situation in earlier times. Whichever of these views one takes, a radical review of actual teaching is called for, and when accomplished this can pave the way for a more positive relationship with Jews and Judaism, and a less tense attitude to Israel. Finally, without abandoning any part of Church dogma or the triumphalist claim to being the 'true faith', some Christians emphasise the command to love all people, including the Jews, because this is what Jesus wanted. This somewhat patronising attitude does at least lead to the sincere condemnation of antisemitism; however, it makes for ambivalence on the question of Israel, since it neither provides a theological justification for the existence of a Jewish state nor a path to 'normal' relations with it.

Arthur Hertzberg, a Vice-President of the World Jewish Congress who has himself taken a leading role in the dialogue process, has observed: 'Christianity at its deepest level continues to grapple with the problem of the rejection of the New Dispensation by Jews when it first appeared among them.'[4] All of the documents addressed by Christians to Christians on the subject of Jewish–Christian relations demonstrate the truth of this observation, particularly in their soul-searching on the relationship between their twin commitments of dialogue and mission. A distinction is made, as we shall see later, between 'proselytism' or 'improper and unfair ways of persuasion and coercion', rejected by most mainstream contemporary Western Churches, and 'witness' or 'mission', considered to be of the essence of Christianity. Many Jews take exception to the whole idea of Christian 'mission' and are frightened by the term 'missionary'. I believe this is an inept reaction for two reasons. First, there is no real dialogue unless one is prepared to hear the 'other' talk about what he feels most deeply; 'mission' in some sense is at least as central to Christian concerns as Israel is to Judaism. Second, as an orthodox Jew (and I am sure Reform and other religious Jews will share this with me) I am also a 'missionary'; the Torah is not an 'exclusive club' but, in its main aspects, a message for me to proclaim to the world. I also 'witness', in my humble way, the truth of that which is entrusted to me. Should I expect the Christian to do less? What I *can* object to, and in this I am joined by mainstream Christians, are 'improper and unfair ways of persuasion and coercion', as above.

## CHRISTIAN FUNDAMENTALISTS, JEWS AND ISRAEL

Few people like to be called 'fundamentalists'. The term lacks precision and tends to be used pejoratively. It applies to a type of 'mind-set' rather than a particular Christian, Jewish or other sect. I shall nevertheless first say something about characteristic attitudes of some of the Christian groups commonly known as 'fundamentalist evangelicals', because these attitudes form a sort of raw material, theologically simplistic, which arises from a rather literal reading of Christian scriptures. It thereby provides a springboard for us to move on to consideration of the more sophisticated attitudes of the major Churches.

Teddy Kollek, who for as long as anyone can remember has been Mayor of Jerusalem, writes in his foreword to a recent book by Michael J. Pragai,[5] 'It is the story of heartwarming testimony and a stirring expression of brotherhood that joins Jews and Christians in perhaps the most significant event of this century, the rebirth of Israel. It is a story of faith . . .' Pragai's book is a serious study of individuals and movements amongst Christians (virtually all of them what we would now call 'fundamentalists') from the seventeenth century onwards who espoused the idea of the return of Israel to its land. He singles out Thomas Brightman (1562–1607) as 'father' of the British concept of the Restoration of the Jews. Brightman prophesied the overthrow of the Antichrist (identified with the Papacy) to be followed by the dissolution of the Turkish Empire and the 'Calling of the Jews' who would be 'Kings of the Orient'. Wild as such ideas may seem today (one still hears remarkably similar talk from fundamentalist evangelicals) theological support for a Jewish return to the Holy Land has, if in modified form, remained a dominant influence and there is an unmistakable line from Brightman through Finch, Toland and others to Lloyd George and the Balfour Declaration. From the Jewish point of view, it has not always been easy to balance the advantage of such support against the disadvantage of its linkage with a programme or at least a hope for conversion.

Dr Pragai also reminds us of those Christians who have themselves 'returned', many of whom have played a distinguished part in building up the land. Dr Pragai is not numbered amongst those Jews who see a proselytising missionary within every Christian; he dramatically presents the 'International Christian Embassy' as the response of friendly Christians to the withdrawal of several Western embassies from Jerusalem in 1980, and as 'a dynamic witness of a friendly and supportive Christian presence and. . . . a most welcome part of Jerusalem's heartbeat'. He concludes with a survey of the tributes found in Israel to its Christian supporters – kibbutzim and forests named after them and special monuments.

There is, then, a positive stream to be discerned in fundamentalist Christian thinking about Israel. At a 'National Prayer Breakfast in Honor of Israel' in Washington DC in February 1986, the American fundamentalists Jerry Falwell, Jimmy Swaggart, Oral Roberts and Pat Robertson 'praised Israel and the Jewish people in speech and song', and were warmly applauded by Jewish leaders.[6] Pat Robertson had indeed told the Anti-Defamation League of B'nai Brith (ADL) in 1980: 'It is my considered judgment that there is a firm biblical mandate in both the Old and the New Testament for the establishment of the nation of Israel in the Holy Land.' But Robertson also wrote, not much later: 'TV is a national pastime in Israel . . . News of the Messiah is going to reach families in . . . Jerusalem [and in] Tel Aviv . . . Miracles are to abound. God's chosen ones are about to see more and more of the direct revelation of Jesus Christ! And when they see Him, they're going to believe.' Falwell, like many other fundamentalists, still maintains that Jews are collectively guilty for shedding the blood of Christ – though Falwell *is* nice to Jews and *does* speak up for Israel. Probably most Jews, including the ADL leadership, will take the cynical view: 'These guys are nuts, but we want all the votes we can get for Israel, and we can't afford to worry about the theological niceties.'

Gershon Greenberg[7] has sounded a note of caution. 'American Jews discredit themselves,' he writes, 'by ignoring the Judaic *telos* to Zionism. They deceive fundamentalists thereby as well. Fundamentalists delude themselves by ignoring Christian teleology – which with bitter irony promotes affection for Jews as a prelude to apocalypse. The leaders deceive their followers, who read in the Bible of Jewish guilt for deicide while their leaders appear like philosemites. Groups that have been deceived are known to turn around and attack their leaders and their collaborators-in-deception, with malice.' As the Jews are quite certainly not about to 'accept Christ' one wonders whether and how the next generation of Falwells will justify support of Israel? The profound ambiguity in the attitude of fundamentalist Christianity subsists, despite the proclamation of friendship for Jews and support for Israelis which is rooted in a certain way of reading Scripture.

I have argued at length elsewhere[8] that it is wrong and dangerous to base contemporary political decisions on the literal reading of Scripture, and that it is presently a cause of much of the misery in the world. The trouble is, if theology is *not* consciously and critically developed, a simple-minded, fundamentalist theology is unconsciously assumed and is not challenged because people do not know how to do so and even feel threatened when questions are asked.

THE WORLD COUNCIL OF CHURCHES AND SOME
PROTESTANT CHURCHES

It was the National Conference of Christians and Jews in the United States
which first mooted the question of holding an International Conference
after the Second World War to redefine attitudes to Jews and Judaism in
the light of the terrible events which had taken place. The Conference was
held at Oxford in August 1946, and marks the initiation of that serious
Christian reappraisal which has resulted in growth of Jewish–Christian
Dialogue in the post-Holocaust period.[9] It promulgated a statement on
'The Fundamental Postulates of Christianity and Judaism in Relation to
Human Order' and put forward two practical proposals. The first of these
was that a smaller conference should be held the following year at which
the problem of antisemitism should be addressed. The second was to set up
an International Council of Christians and Jews.

The newly created World Council of Churches held its very first Assembly in Amsterdam in 1948. 'We cannot forget that we meet in a land
from which 110 000 Jews were taken to be murdered. Nor can we forget
that we meet only five years after the extermination of 6 million Jews', runs
the report *The Christian Approach to the Jews*, which the Assembly
received and commended to the churches for serious consideration and
action.[10] There is nothing ambivalent about the forthright condemnation of
antisemitism articulated in this document, nor about the acknowledgment
of the failure of the churches to 'manifest Christian love towards our
Jewish neighbours' and the way this contributed to antisemitism. The
emergence of the State of Israel is acknowledged, though the attitude
expressed towards it is ambivalent: 'On the Political aspects of the Palestine problem . . . we do not undertake to express a judgment.' The real
sting in the tail is a theological one. It appears that the way that
Christians should atone for their past animosity to Jews is by *redoubling
evangelistic efforts towards them* – after all, how better to show your
Christian love for anyone than by bringing them to Christ? No doubt the
Jews of the time (I have not searched the archives for confirmation),
fresh from Hitler's gas chambers, thanked these loving Christian
churchmen for their pious sympathies and their condemnation of antisemitism. Inwardly they must have groaned 'Hitler took our bodies
from us; have we survived that for our souls and those of our children
to be snared by the missionaries?'

In the years since Amsterdam the World Council of Churches has
learned much. Antisemitism is consistently condemned (New Delhi, 1961,
produced perhaps the strongest condemnation ever). Israel is still a hot
potato, especially as the World Council of Churches is anxious to give
voice to Eastern Christians. But Jews are not targeted for mission, though
there is a difference of opinion as to whether they should be excluded from
it. The World Council of Churches, unlike the Vatican, is a federal rather

than a hierarchical structure. Its proclamations represent consensus rather than decision – in some ways, of course, this is a strength rather than a weakness. But its numerous component units and Committees are not and cannot be straight-jacketed into mutual consistency. The 'Programme Unit on Faith and Witness' has a sub-Unit for Dialogue with People of Living Faiths and Ideologies (names of Units change every now and then) and a section of this handles Jewish/Christian relations. Its achievements are many and valuable and its individual members are leading international figures in the dialogue, largely sympathetic to Israel as well as to Jews and Judaism. But this cannot prevent the World Council of Churches – through whichever of its units – coming out from time to time with statements perceived as hostile towards Israel. It is not helpful either when Jewish delegates 'punish' – for instance by boycotting conferences – the unit for dialogue because of some World Council of Churches statement which the unit's members deplore as much as anyone.

In July 1982 the Executive Committee of the World Council of Churches 'received and commended to the Churches for study and action' a statement entitled *Ecumenical Considerations on Jewish–Christian Dialogue*.[11] This document had been drafted over several years by the Dialogue Working Group of the Consultation on the Church and the Jewish People (does the World Council of Churches have more committees than it has constituent churches?), and there had been much consultation with Jews, notably through the International Jewish Committee for Interfaith Consultations. One of the preparatory conferences took place in Jerusalem in June 1977 and the conference paper it adopted significantly commences with the words: 'Proselytism, as distinct from Mission or Witness, is rejected in the strongest terms by the World Council of Churches . . . This rejection of proselytism is the more urgent where Jews are concerned'.[12] Allan R. Brockway, Secretary of the Consultation on the Church and the Jewish People, frankly admits that the *Ecumenical Considerations* 'left unsaid or said far more minimally' than was done in the original paper many things, 'particularly concerning the Land and State of Israel'.[13] This, he alleges, was to comply with comments received from the Middle East churches. Brockway himself asks 'Can the dialogue assist the churches and the ecumenical movement actively to understand that concern for, and identity with, the Palestinian people is not necessarily incompatible with concern for, and identity with, the Jewish people who today are inseparable from the State of Israel, its well-being and continued existence?' He sums up: 'Dialogue between Jews and Christians has become sophisticated religiously and is having significant effect on Christian teaching about Jews as well as revision or elimination of anti-Judaic liturgies and preaching. At the same time the *relation* between the Churches and the Jewish people has deteriorated and tension between them continues to mount because of different interpretations of the State of Israel and the war between Israel and its Arab neighbours.'

This depth of misunderstanding is underlined by various reports on the Middle East produced in recent years by such bodies as the British Council of Churches and the Australian Council of Churches. The reports, which to me at least appear to be a mixture of political naivety and genuine compassion for the perceived 'underdog' (the Palestinians), have aroused strong resentment amongst Jewish and other supporters of Israel and this, when strong feelings are expressed on both sides, has tended to sour the Jewish–Christian relationship. But this merely serves to enhance the importance of continued dialogue, and the great need for it to address fearlessly not only theological and social problems but political ones.

The World Council of Churches' work on Jewish–Christian dialogue has both fed into and been fed by the work of its constituent Churches, many of whom have produced their own Guidelines of value and importance. In Britain the 1980s have seen the United Reformed Church engaging in regular discussions with Jews,[14] and the Church of Scotland produce its own excellent Guidelines both on antisemitism and on Jewish/Christian relations generally.[15] The Church of England held its first high-level Consultation with Jews in 1980 and the second at Shallowford House, Stafford, in April 1987.[16] On a broader scale the Lutheran World Federation has been especially active in this field,[17] and recently there has been a growth of interest behind the Iron Curtain, in Hungary, Poland and East Germany.[18] Third world countries are involved also, and in November 1986 a highly successful major Consultation was held in Nairobi with delegates of the non-Roman Catholic African Churches and the International Jewish Committee on Interreligious Consultations.[19]

## THE ROMAN CATHOLIC CHURCH

The Roman Catholic Church, with its long history of vilification and oppression of Jews, started on the wrong foot so far as modern Zionism is concerned when in 1904 Pope Pius X sent Theodor Herzl away with the words: 'The Jews have not recognised our Lord so we cannot recognise the Jewish people. If you come and settle your people there, we shall have churches and priests ready to baptise all of you.'[20] In the years preceding the Balfour Declaration the Vatican consistently opposed any priority being given to Jews in the Holy Land and meddled unsuccessfully to ensure that the mandate for Palestine would be given to a Catholic power.[21] Pius XII's infamous *concordat* with Hitler is the nadir of modern papal diplomacy, in no way redeemed by his sheltering a few Jews who happened to live beneath his walls. After the war, when other Western Churches were expressing their profound dismay at the Holocaust and beginning to think of constructing a new relationship with Jews and Judaism, the Roman Catholic Church remained aloof. It did not, and still will not, become a member of the World Council of Churches, continuing to regard itself as the only 'authentic' Church.

It is against this inauspicious background that we must assess the present position. Only in the mid-1960s, during the pontificate of John XXIII, did the Roman Catholic Church, through the medium of the Second Vatican Council, address itself realistically to the modern world. For the first time it recognised the value and importance of the ecumenical movement, and took stock of the fact that there were people of other faiths on the planet and that even non-Christians might have spiritual insights and integrity, though they might still not be 'saved' other than through Christ. At Vatican II the Roman Catholic Church did not relinquish (nor has it subsequently relinquished) its claim to the full truth in matters of 'salvation'; its recognition of others is polite, even friendly, but ultimately condescending. Though enlightened Catholic theologians have striven to overcome the triumphalism of the Roman Church, Vatican statements have softened rather than removed it. Jews should beware of the error of reading friendly Vatican overtures to Jews (or to any other non-Roman Catholic group) as recognition of full spiritual equality and legitimacy. Jews who want to understand what Vatican II offers them should not read only *Nostra Aetate n.4*, to which we shall return, but such sections of the Vatican II documents as that relating to 'The People of God' (Chapter IIa) in which it is made abundantly clear that the 'People of God after the flesh' (the Israelites) has been superseded by the people 'after the spirit', that is, the believers in Christ – even though this is not taken to mean that God has 'rejected' the Jews.[22]

Nevertheless, thanks to the strenuous efforts of exceptional Catholics such as Cardinals Bea and Willebrands, and with the encouragement and assistance of a galaxy of inspired Jews including the late Jules Isaac and Abraham Heschel, the Vatican published on 28 October 1965 a short document, *Nostra Aetate*, on relationships with non-Christians, and about one third of its length (section 4 of the 5) is about Jews and Judaism. We do not know for certain (since Vatican archives are not open even to *bona fide* scholars) what were the pressures and circumstances which led to the drafting and redrafting of the document. Unlike earlier drafts, however, the final text contained no explicit mention of the Holocaust, not even an implicit mention of the State of Israel. Yet it was hailed, even by Jews, as a momentous step forward. Why? It was admittedly strong in its condemnation of antisemitism and this was something new for Jews to hear spoken with the full authority of the Church. It also laid down that Jews collectively, even those of the time of Jesus, should not be held responsible for the crucifixion of Jesus.

This was indeed music in the ears of Jews who since childhood had suffered the mindless taunts of 'You killed Jesus', and perhaps they did not notice that *Nostra Aetate* nevertheless maintained that 'the Jewish auth-

orities and those who followed their lead pressed for the death of Christ'
(an opinion, curiously, shared by Maimonides). If they had noticed this
they would not be so surprised when the present Pope, around Easter time,
preaches on the New Testament passages on which this assertion is based
and makes no attempt to 'clear' the Jewish leaders of the time. *Nostra
Aetate* moreover stresses the positive bond (the 'common spiritual heritage') between Jews and Christians, and calls for special love of Jews by
Christians. For me, such sentiment is rendered somewhat otiose by the
realisation that I am to be loved not for myself as a Jew, but because I am
'the stock of Abraham' who prefigured the Church. *Nostra Aetate* is still
knee–deep in – arising out of rather than arisen from – the Middle Ages,
the Church Triumphant and Christian supersessionism. But let us not be
ungenerous. Measured against Pius X's flea in Herzl's ear, or Pius XII's
infamous *concordat*, it is revolutionary. No doubt it carries the seeds of
greater things to come.

The real test of *Nostra Aetate* was whether it would lie forgotten in the
Vatican's commodious archives or whether it would be taken up as a
turning point in Jewish–Christian relations. Already in March 1967 the US
National Conference of Catholic Bishops published a very practical set of
*Guidelines for Catholic–Jewish Relations*.[23] Then, on 22 October 1974,
Pope Paul VI rose to the challenge. He set up a Commission for Religious
Relations with the Jews and asked them to recommend ways of implementing *Nostra Aetate*. It was thus that in January 1975 the second
major Roman Catholic document on Christian Jewish Relations was
published, under the title *Guidelines and Suggestions for Implementing the
Conciliar Declaration 'Nostra Aetate (n.4)'*, by the Vatican Commission
for Religious Relations with the Jews.[24] This document states 'such relations as there have been between Jews and Christian have scarcely ever
risen above the level of monologue. From now on, real dialogue must be
established.' The document shows itself sensitive to Jewish suspicion of
Catholic motives and missionising. There is a call to exercise great care in
liturgy and homiletics so as to avoid portraying Jews and Judaism in a false
light, and recommendations on teaching and education 'at all levels of
Christian instruction' with a recognition that 'the history of Judaism did not
end with the destruction of Jerusalem, but rather went on to develop a
religious tradition'. Catholic–Jewish collaboration in joint social action is
urged. Once again, neither the Holocaust nor the State of Israel is mentioned. In the years since 1975 great efforts have been made in many
countries to implement these recommendations and even in Britain, which
has by no means led the field, the changes in Catholic teaching in schools
have been remarkable.

The third and most recent Vatican document on Christian–Jewish Relations appeared in November 1985 under the title. *The Common Bond:
Christians and Jews. Notes for Preaching and Teaching*,[25] and its pro-

duction and publication were instigated and encouraged by the present Pope, John-Paul II. It met with a mixed reception, including some howls of protest from leaders of the Jewish community, many of whom had evidently not troubled to read it. Most of those who did read it failed to understand that it was a document aiming to help Catholics teach other Catholics rather than a statement on Jews and Judaism addressed to the world at large. Once the dust had settled several important features became evident. It stressed that 'Jews and Judaism should not occupy an occasional and marginal place on catechesis; their purpose there is essential and should be organically integrated'. The Holocaust was mentioned; the State of Israel was mentioned – both for the first time and explicitly in an official Vatican document. Catholics, moreover, were to recognise and teach the profound spiritual significance of both these events to Jews. Jews will regard the treatment of the Holocaust in particular as somewhat cavalier; its spiritual significance surely touches Catholics as well as Jews and some element of acknowledgment of the Church's tacit complicity and 'preparing of the way' would have been opportune. The document is, nevertheless, replete with positive indications and with precise suggestions on such delicate subjects as how to handle Gospel reference to Jews or to Pharisees. Unfortunately it does not entirely escape supersessionism, and actually advocates a typological approach to the interpretation of Scripture – something which is shunned by many leading Catholic theologians today.

Many prominent Jews attacked *The Common Bond* because it counselled Catholics that 'The existence of the State of Israel and its options should be envisaged not in a perspective which is itself religious, but in their reference to the common principles of international law.' The attacks were ill-considered. As a Jew engaging in dialogue with Catholics I am, of course, anxious that they should understand the religious dimension of *my* attachment to the Land (though this religious commitment is by no means shared by all Jews and even religious Jews differ in their attitudes towards the *actual* State of Israel). *The Common Bond* accepts this: 'Christians are invited to understand this religious attachment which finds its roots in biblical tradition.' On the other hand, I have no reason to wish to persuade Catholics that they also should see my relationship with the Land, from the point of view of their own theology, in religious terms. In fact, to urge this would be to create problems and not to solve them. It would drive Catholics into the sort of position *vis-à-vis* Israel adopted by less sophisticated Christian theologians; typical approaches would be (a) the Jews, rejecting Jesus, forfeited their covenant right to the Land, and/or (b) the Jews are to return to the Land before the Second Coming, when they will recognise Christ as the Messiah. It seems evident to me that the *The Common Bond* disposes of this theological baggage at a stroke and leaves Catholics free to adopt realistic and 'normal' attitudes to Israel.

It is to be hoped that the Holy See will avail itself of this entrée into present realities and establish full diplomatic relations with the State of Israel, thus putting behind it a major irritant and one of the greatest obstacles to the real business of dialogue. The Church might reflect that at the present time there is still a readiness on the part of Israel to respond warmly. It is not clear what answer one would make to any Jews who felt that it was historically inappropriate to formalise a relationship of friendship with the Roman Catholic Church (the thought has, sadly, been expressed). Nor is it easy to reply to those who underline that the Roman Catholic Church is neither the only Christian Church nor even the original Church in the Holy Land. Nor does there appear to exist, in the modern system of international relations, a logical reason for the Roman Catholic Holy See, alone amongst religious organisations, to enjoy a unique status in international law. As Clifford Longley put it, 'it is difficult to imagine any other country in the world knowing or caring much whether the Vatican thought it existed or not'.[26] On the whole the Holy See stands to gain more from proceeding intelligently in this matter than Israel does.


CONCLUSION

There are well over a billion Christians in the world and perhaps 15 million Jews. The tensions between them in the past, arising in the period when Christianity and rabbinic Judaism first defined themselves, have been a paradigm of bad human relations, replete with stereotypes and 'false witness', not entirely one-sided. We now live in an age where it has come to be realised that the prime responsibility for all of us is to share the planet peacefully despite differences of belief or culture. Our traditions, naively understood, militate against this, and lead us to define ourselves against each other and to strive for domination or, if on the losing side, for survival. We are therefore called upon to develop the more eirenic elements which are also found in the traditions. This means listening to one another and sharing one another's concerns. The progress of this dialogue cannot be measured simply in terms of this or that pronouncement about Israel or 'mission'. It is a much deeper matter, involving mutual understanding and individual soul-searching. We all entertain hopes for 'short-term gains' from the dialogue process. Jews have hoped, for instance, that Christians would stop calling them 'Christ-killers'. This hope has been fulfilled, at least in the teaching of the mainstream Churches.

Jews still hope for a more positive attitude to Israel; this has been achieved only to a limited extent. Perhaps we have not explained our position with sufficient sensitivity for the deep concerns of the 'other side'. We shall certainly continue to try. And we note that it is not only the Christian side which has to do the listening. In a very important sense, the peace of the world depends on a successful outcome of this and similar dialogues. Religion still holds enough sway over people to propel them to Armageddon. Our task is to ensure that the life-enhancing power of religions overcomes their tendency to mutual destruction.

**Notes**

1. Romans 11:19-24 (NEB).
2. Peter Schneider, *The Christian Debate on Israel* (The Centre for the Study of Judaism and Jewish/Christian Relations, Selly Oak Colleges, Birmingham, England, 1987), p. 28.
3. Rosemary Ruether, *Faith and Fratricide* (New York, 1974). Professor Ruether's book stimulated a vigorous debate. For some of the reactions see, in particular, Alan T. Davies, (ed.) *Antisemitism and the Foundations of Christianity* (New York: Paulist Press 1979).
4. *Christian Jewish Relations*, vol. 18, no. 3, September 1985, p. 22.
5. Michael J. Pragai, *Faith and Fulfilment: Christians and the Return to the Promised Land* (London: Vallentine, Mitchell, 1985).
6. *Christian Jewish Relations*, vol. 19, no. 3, September 1986.
7. Ibid.
8. Norman Solomon, 'The Political Implications of a Belief in Revelation', in *Heythrop Journal*, vol. 35, no. 2, April 1984.
9. A moving, first-hand recollection of these events 'Forty years on' by W. W. Simpson appeared in *Ends & odds*, no. 30, October 1986, published for the Interfaith Dialogue Trust by the Centre for the Study of Judaism and Jewish/Christian Relations, Selly Oak Colleges, Birmingham, England.
10. This text as well as other major Church statements, both Catholic and Protestant, may be studied in *Stepping Stones to Further Jewish-Christian Relations* compiled by Helga Croner (New York: Paulist Press, 1977), pp. 69–72.
11. This is reproduced in the sequel to the previous volume, Helga Croner (ed.), *More Stepping Stones to Jewish-Christian Relations* (New York: Paulist Press, 1985) pp. 167–74.
12. Ibid., p. 165.
13. *Christian Jewish Relations*, vol. 18, no. 4, December 1985.
14. As a 'first fruit' of these Consultations, the United Reformed Church published (London, 1983) an admirable handbook *Christians and Jews in Britain* (London, 1983) A Christian (Iorwerth Thomas) and Jewish (Edie Friedman) account of the achievement of the Consultations to 1986 appeared in *Christian Jewish Relations*, vol. 19, no. 4, December 1986.
15. *Anti-Semitism in the World Today* and *Christians and Jews Today*, Scottish General Assembly, 1985.
16. Papers from the Amport House, Andover, Consultation, on the theme of 'Law and Religion in Contemporary Society', appeared in *Christian Jewish Relations*, vol. 14, no. 1, March 1981.
17. The Lutheran World Federation has published reports and texts such as *The Significance of Judaism for the Life and Mission of the Church* (Geneva, 1983) and *Luther, Lutheranism and the Jews* (Geneva 1984). It is impressive that the Lutheran Church has had the courage to repudiate totally the anti-Judaism of its reforming founder.
18. Several of these meetings have been documented in recent issues of *Christian*

*Jewish Relations*. A major Consultation, under the auspices of the International Council of Christians and Jews, took place in Buckow, East Germany, in September 1987, and plans are afoot for Consultations in Poland and elsewhere.

19. *Christian Jewish Relations*, vol. 20, no. 1, March 1987, is devoted to the Nairobi Conference.
20. This version of the conversation has been disputed by Catholics. However, until the relevant Vatican archives are made accessible to research there would appear to be no adequate reason to doubt Herzl's account.
21. See Sergio Itzchak Minerbi, *Ha-Vatikan v'Eretz ha-Kodesh veha-Tziyonut*, (Jerusalem: Yad Ben-Zvi Institute). There is a short review article in English by Geoffrey Wigoder in *Christian Jewish Relations*, vol. 19, no. 3, September 1986.
22. See Austin Flannery (ed.) *Vatican Council II: The Conciliar and Post Conciliar Documents*, (Dublin: Flannery, Costello Publishing Company, 1975).
23. *Stepping Stones to Further Jewish-Christian Relations* compiled by Helga Croner, (New York: Paulist Press, 1977), pp. 16–20.
24. *Loc. cit.* pp. 11–16.
25. Helga Croner, (ed.) *More Stepping Stones to Jewish-Christian Relations*, (New York: Paulist Press, 1985), pp. 220–32. *Christian Jewish Relations*, vol. 18, no. 3, which carries a Twentieth Anniversary Symposium on *Nostra Aetate*, reproduces *The Common Bond* as well as *Nostra Aetate* itself. There is also, on pp. 67–73, a critical commentary on *The Common Bond* by Norman Solomon.
26. *The Times* (London), 31 March 1986.

# 12 American Blacks and Israel
## Earl Raab

The 1967 war in the Middle East was a watershed for American black attitudes towards Israel, as it was for so many other contemporary developments affecting the Jews. However, as in the other cases, there were also prior factors. Before 1967 there was little publicly expressed interest in Israel; what there was tended to be favourable. Further back, before the establishment of the Jewish state the Zionist movement was regarded sympathetically by leading American blacks as a consequence of their own impulses towards self-determination. In 1919 W. E. B. DuBois wrote that 'the African movement means to us what the Zionist movement must mean to the Jews'.[1] And in 1941 he continued that Palestine was 'the only refuge that harassed Jewry has today'.[2] Menachem Begin recalled that, during Israel's War of Independence, Dr Ralph Bunche said to him 'I can understand you. I am also a member of a persecuted minority'.[3] With some reservations about the 'self-segregated' nature of Israel, as expressed by Walter White of the National Association for the Advancement of Colored People (NAACP), the relatively few comments from black leadership were generally favourable towards the establishment of the Jewish state. During the following fifteen years or so American blacks were understandably pre-occupied with their own struggle for freedom. For the most part the black press was mute about the 1956 war in the Middle East and there was very little coverage of Israel, critical or otherwise.

The first signs of change occurred when an explicit 'Third World' ideology began to emerge among American blacks during the so-called Black Revolution of the early 1960s. The decade of the 'civil rights revolution' was coming to a close. It had begun with the Supreme Court decision outlawing school segregation; with the establishment of anti-discrimination laws and agencies in most Northern and Western states; with the organised protests in the South. National civil rights legislation was about to come to fruition. But black consciousness was now on the boil. Historic resentment was fully out of the closet and at a high pitch. Centuries-old degradation no longer seemed bearable. The civil rights revolution scarcely looked like a revolution at all – at best the setting of the stage for a long evolutionary process of rehabilitation. There was no mood among blacks for such generational patience. The mood was for immediate reparations, immediate dignity and 'black pride' – at its most intense among young blacks who were beginning to attend college in numbers similar to their proportion of the population. It was during this period of radicalisation that the intellectual thread of Third World ideology emerged. At its core this ideology held that the racially oppressed people of the world – black, brown and red – had been colonised by white European and American imperialists. The black struggle in America was only part of that global Third World struggle; the remedy was to bring down the imperial powers, beginning with the United States.

This was, of course, an old line among ideological radicals. In the 1950s, one heard of the impending revolution of 'Asians and Africans in the New and Old Worlds' upon whom 'White Christian civilization' had hurled itself. But it was not until the Black Revolution of the early 1960s that Third World ideology became standard fare for black intellectuals. It was a rare young black leader on the university campus who did not read or know about Frantz Fanon's seminal book subtitled *The Handbook for the Black Revolution That is Changing the Shape of the World*.[4] He wrote that the 'Third World today faces Europe like a colossal mass . . .'[5] The Third World included American blacks; Europe included America. 'The poets of negritude will not stop at the limits of the continent,' wrote Fanon. 'From America, black voices will take up the hymn with fuller unison. The "black world" will see the light and Busia from Ghana, Birago Diop from Senegal, Hampate Ba from the Soudan, and Saint-Clair Drake from Chicago will not hesitate to assert the existence of common ties and a motive power that is identical.'[6]

Israel was not a notable target of Third World ideology in its earlier years. But the stage was set with the passing addition of the Arab nations to the Third World roster. Although he found some fault with local Arab nationalism, Fanon noted that 'the majority of Arab territories have been under colonial domination . . . Today in the political sphere the Arab League is giving palpable form to [the] will to take up again the heritage of the past and bring it to culmination'.[7]

In the shadow of the war against Nazism it was still not comfortable for the radicalised movements to attack Israel – or the Jews generally. However, the cracks in this reticence began to appear in the early 1960s, starting with some negative ideological linkage between American Jews and the plight of American blacks. The breakdown of this reticence paved the way for ideological anti-Israelism.

*The Reshaping of Black Antisemitism*
There was not much attention paid to any phenomenon of black antisemitism in the US before the 1950s. For one thing, the larger field of antisemitism was too overwhelming. In the 1930s, indeed, the vaunted 'Grand Political Coalition' was forged behind Franklin D. Roosevelt, and included at its most liberal edge the nationally organised elements of the labour movement, the blacks and the Jews. It was this liberal coalition

which stayed together during the 1950s to spearhead the 'civil rights revolution'. But as the blacks became more politicised, and as the black intellectuals became more radicalised, traditional patterns of everyday conflict between the Jews and the blacks were made more explicit.

James Baldwin, the well-known Black writer, who sharply criticised antisemitism nonetheless recalled: 'When we were growing up in Harlem, our demoralizing series of landlords were Jewish and we hated them. We hated them because they were terrible landlords that did not take care of the building . . . Our parents were lashed down to futureless jobs in order to pay the outrageous rent, and we knew that the landlord treated us this way because we were coloured and he knew that we could not move out. The grocer was a Jew and being in debt to him was very much like being in debt to the company store. The butcher was a Jew and, yes, we certainly paid more for bad cuts of meat than other New York citizens and we often carried insults home along with the meat. We bought our clothes from a Jew and sometimes our second-hand shoes and the pawnbroker was a Jew – perhaps we hated him most of all.'[8]

There was nothing new about this litany of complaints which referred to the well-publicised periods when Jews moved out of the urban ghetto areas just ahead of the blacks, retaining the ownership of most of the buildings and shops in those areas. Kenneth Clark, another black opponent of antisemitism, wrote in 1946: 'The antagonism towards the Jewish landlord is so common as to have become almost an integral aspect of the folk culture of the northern urban Negro . . . and all his obvious ills are attributed to the greed and avarice of the Jewish landlord.'[9] Those negative black attitudes towards Jews showed up on the various surveys and typically in the landmark survey done by the University of California Survey Research Center in 1964. This survey found that blacks were significantly more likely than whites to accept economic stereotypes about Jews. For example:[10]

|  | Whites | Blacks |
|---|---|---|
|  | (percentage accepting) | |
| Jews use shady practices to get ahead | 40 | 58 |
| Jews are shrewd and tricky in business | 34 | 46 |
| Jews are as honest as other businessmen | 27 | 35 |

Summarising the results, the authors found no significant difference in 'non-economic antisemitism' between whites and blacks, but found that 54 per cent of the blacks ranked 'high' on a scale of economic antisemitism, as against 32 per cent of the whites. While the level of antisemitism, as measured by this kind of economic stereotype, drops heavily for both groups as their educational level rises, nevertheless blacks continued to be higher on economic antisemitism than whites at the same educational level.[11] However, these measures of black antisemitism, based on daily ghetto experiences, became pertinent to black anti-Israelism only when they began to be integrated with the ideological attack which later characterised Third Worldism. Before that, they were rather taken for granted as the result of a conflict which would wither away once the phenomenon of Jewish ghetto landlords and their associations in black consciousness had faded.

But James Baldwin himself noted the *symbolic* ingredient in that earlier economic antisemitism, when he titled his 1967 article 'Negroes Are Anti-Semitic Because They Are Anti-White'. The use of the Jew as a stand-in for the white as the target of black anger became more common. It was in the course of *this* development that antisemitism came significantly out of the closet in the US after the Second World War.

It was probably not until the summer riots of 1964 that the issue of black antisemitism came to general attention. Cries of 'Let's get the Jews' were reported by the press. According to one report, 80 per cent of the furniture stores, 60 per cent of the food markets and 54 per cent of the liquor stores burned and looted in the Watts riots were owned by Jews.[12]

That was the old daily-life conflict, but in the hands of the new black ideological activists, antisemitism was again becoming something permissible in America. Moreover there was a new kind of economic conflict as the black middle class began to grow. In the bitter Brooklyn fight emerging black teachers and established Jewish teachers were at swordpoint and a nasty antisemitism developed. In 1969 a Jewish viewpoint was expressed about the dangers of this kind of emergent ideological antisemitism among blacks:

> This is not the anti-semitism which the black population shares with the white population. It is, rather, the abstract and symbolic antisemitism which Jews instinctively find more chilling. Negroes trying to reassure Jewish audiences repeatedly and unwittingly make the very point they are trying to refute. 'This is not anti-semitism' they say. 'The hostility is toward the whites. When they say Jew, they mean white.' But that is an exact and acute description of political anti-semitism. 'The enemy' becomes 'the Jew', 'the man' becomes 'the Jew' . . . But the ideology of political anti-semitism has precisely always been poetic excess, which has not prevented it from becoming murderous . . . Then, too, 'Third World' anti-semitism is becoming more of a staple, at least among the ideologues where it counts most.[13]

It was the fusion of this 'symbolic antisemitism' and Third World ideology (the restraints against expressive antisemitism having been loosened) which first presaged the strain of black anti-Israelism in America. It was in

1964 that Malcolm X, the black nationalist leader, formerly of the Black Muslim movement, said:

These [Jewish] people conduct their businesses in Harlem, but live in other parts of the city. They enjoy good housing. Their children attend good schools and go to colleges. This the Negroes know and resent. These businessmen are seen by the Negroes in Harlem as colonialists, just as the people of Africa and Asia viewed the British, the French and other businessmen before they achieved their independence.[14]

As a matter of fact, Malcolm X was one of the first to put all the Third World pieces together, including anti-Israelism. He expressed his anger at 'the Jews who with the help of Christians in America and Europe drove our Muslim brothers (i.e., the Arabs) out of their homeland where they had been settled for centuries, and took over the land for themselves'.[15] Malcolm X also pointed out that the aid sent to Israel to support its aggression against the Third World was taken from the pockets of American blacks.

*After the 1967 War: Full-Fledged Third World Ideology*
But it was the 1967 war which gave momentum to the full scope of Third World ideology. After all, it was only after 1967 that Israel could be plausibly cast in the role of 'colonialising' power. There had been some previous murmurs of approval for Nasser in Third World circles (as in Malcolm X) and some generalised sympathy for Arab attempts to decolonialise themselves, as in Frantz Fanon – but by and large these were circles that would have been uneasy with too vigorous support of some of the old feudal Arab regimes. However, the Palestinian Arabs were another matter. They and their cause were quickly gathered into the Third World conceptual fold. Furthermore, for the first time, in the wake of the Six Day War, Israel was clearly a major client of the US in the Middle East. The ideological mould was set.

Shortly after the end of that war in 1967, the Student Non-Violent Coordinating Committee (SNCC), one of the leading black activist organisations, issued a newsletter whose purpose was to discuss the problem of the Palestinians, who were described as 'Third World brothers' to the blacks. The following 'facts' were presented, among others:

The Zionists conquered the Arab homes and land through terror, force and massacres.

Israel was planted at the crossroads of Asia and Africa without the free approval of any Mid-Eastern, Asian or African country.

The US government has worked along with Zionist groups to support Israel so that America may have a toe-hold in that strategic Middle-East location, thereby helping white America to control and exploit the rich Arab nations.

The famous European Jews, the Rothschilds, who have long controlled the wealth of many European nations, were involved in the original conspiracy with the British to create the 'State of Israel' and are still among Israel's chief supporters [and] the Rothschilds also control much of Africa's mineral wealth.[16]

Among the radicalised black groups of the period who adopted some version of the full Third World syndrome were the Black Panthers, who came out in strong support of 'Arab guerrillas in the Middle East'. In 1970 that party's international co-ordinator, Connie Mathews, explained some of the connections:

The white-left in the U.S.A. is comprised of a large percentage of the Jewish population. Before the Black Panther party took its stand on the Palestinian People's struggle, there were problems, but the support of the white-left of the Black Panthers was concrete. However, since our stand, the white-left started floundering, and it has become undecided. That leaves us with no alternative then but to believe that a large portion of these people are Zionists and are therefore racists.[17]

*Third World Ideologues vs. Grass Roots*
It is necessary and important to make distinctions between these ideological developments among black intellectuals and the black population at large – without dismissing the importance of that ideology. First of all it must be noted that neither a coherent Third World ideology, nor a Third World ideological movement, has ever captured the black population at large. At the end of 1965, as the black revolution was reaching its highest pitch, and in the metropolitan non-South where the ideological black revolution thrived most, one out of ten blacks chose the pragmatic NAACP as that civil rights group which 'is doing the most at the present time to help Negroes'. One out of ten had designated the Congress of Racial Equality (CORE), known then for its militant activity on behalf of desegregation. The Muslims received only 3 per cent of the positive response.[18] In fact, among the half of all American blacks who ventured disapproval for any black leader, 97 per cent expressed disapproval of Malcolm X.[19] Moreover, when American blacks were asked whether the United States was 'worth fighting for', in case of another war, nine out of ten answered affirmatively – scarcely a response worthy of radical Third World ideology.[20]

With respect to these responses to radical ideology in general, two population characteristics of the American black population must be taken into account: education and religion. In 1960 about 8 per cent of all Americans and about 3 per cent of all blacks aged 25 or more had completed 4 years of college; about 40 per cent of all Americans and about 20 per cent of all black Americans over 25 had completed high school or more.[21] 'Militancy' itself, as the expression of conscious values, has generally been associated with educational level. In the 1964 study it was found that blacks with at least some college were three times more likely than grammar school graduates, and about half again more likely than those with some high school, to be 'militant'.[22] It was found that even among black college students, militancy was greatest among those of higher-status backgrounds.[23] To an even greater extent, direct participation in ideological movements has always been a function of education. Various studies indicated that the educational and middle-class status of activists in such groups as CORE and SNCC was dramatically high.[24]

Thus, the particularly sharp educational gap in those years between the black grassroots and the college-educated black ideologues provided one explanation for the failure of the new ideologies to sweep through the rank-and-file. The religious status of American blacks provided another clue. Church membership has been notably higher among blacks than whites for reasons which have been much discussed.[25] In the 1960s this pattern persisted.[26] Among blacks it was found that there was a relationship between frequency of attendance at worship services and 'militancy'. In the 1964 survey 18 per cent of those blacks who attended church more than once a week measured as 'militant', as compared with 34 per cent of those who attended less than once a month.[27] However, there may be a tendency to overstate the significance of the 'religious' factor in itself, because of the relationship of education to religiosity and to church attendance. In the 1964 survey when education was held constant, not only were church attendance patterns similar between whites and blacks, but the patterns of fundamentalist religious beliefs were also similar.[28]

Nevertheless, the *institutional* importance of the black church remains clearly disproportionate. The black population has twice as many churches per capita as the white population. The church, which became a prime social centre for American blacks after emancipation, has remained so. In the negro communities around the nation 'black leadership' has remained chiefly identified with religious leaders, never challenged for long by civil rights leaders and only recently threatened by emerging black political leaders. As one of Martin Luther King's lieutenants put it, the church is 'the most organized thing in the Negro's life. Whatever you want to do in the Negro community, whether it's selling Easter Seals or organizing a nonviolent campaign, you've got to do it through the Negro church, or it doesn't get done.'[29] That is one of the reasons why Martin Luther King was able to establish such a dramatic leadership in the black community. In 1962, asked 'which person [on a list of four] do you think has done most to help Negroes,' 88 per cent of the metropolitan non-South blacks identified Dr King. Roy Wilkins of the NAACP was identified by 6 per cent; James Farmer of CORE and Malcolm X were identified by 1 per cent each. The choice of Dr King was even higher in the South.[30] Martin Luther King was no Third World ideologue. The black Christian church in America, heavily fundamentalist in its formal lineaments, is not the most fertile ground for the growth of radical Third World ideology. Both education and religion have been factors in maintaining the gap between black ideologues and the grassroots.

*The Continuing Role of Third World Ideology*
Neither the radical Third World ideologues nor their organisations gained a significant foothold among the black population in general. SNCC and CORE, after they were captured by the ideologues, swiftly diminished in importance, as did the Black Panthers. (That was reminiscent of the typical collapse in America of both left-wing and right-wing groups, such as the Ku Klux Klan, when they have become politically extremist.) The radical Black Muslims remain a fringe in the black population. The mainstream black establishment, the leadership of the NAACP, the Urban League, the black churches and the Congressional caucus all publicly condemned a Third World ideology which included either antisemitism or ideological anti-Israelism. Nevertheless, the continuing effect of Third World ideology on black intellectuals cannot be discounted, as illustrated by the saga of the Southern Christian Leadership Conference (SCLC) and the dramatic episodes involving Andrew Young and Jesse Jackson.

Martin Luther King, who founded the SCLC in 1957, was close to the Jewish community and a strong supporter of Israel. In 1967, three months after the war, a National Conference for New Politics was held in Chicago: its black caucus included many activist blacks, including representatives of the SCLC. The Third World 'black militants' at the conference insisted on a resolution to condemn the 'imperialist Zionist war', which passed handily. This resolution marked the real beginning of the post-war momentum of black Third World ideology.

Martin Luther King responded to the protestations of the Jewish community by stating that the SCLC staff members who had attended the conference had been 'the most vigorous and articulate opponents of the simplistic resolution on the Middle East question'.[31] He then indicated that his support and that of the SCLC for Israel remained as firm as ever. However he was attacked by a black writer, John A. Williams, as 'a house Negro' who had been used by the bullying American Jewish community. Moreover, observers noted a schism within the SCLC. The SCLC never became a vehicle for Third World ideology and has never renounced its support of Israel, but after Dr King's assassination, it has, at the least, become more 'even-handed' with respect to the Middle East. It is the kind of even-handedness which makes the pro-Israel community feel some trepidation. Reverend Joseph C. Lowery, the president of the SCLC, while stating his commitment to a 'strong, secure Israel', refers pointedly to the 'pre-1967 borders', opposes the Camp David exclusion of the PLO from negotiations and calls for some reduction in American aid to Israel.

In 1979 the SCLC leadership went to the Middle East. They had requested but were denied an audience with Israel's Prime Minister. But they met with Yasir Arafat, and pictures were taken of Lowery embracing Arafat and of the SCLC delegation linking arms with him and singing *We Shall Overcome*. Reverend Walter Fauntroy, Chairman of the SCLC Board, said 'Mr Arafat appears reasonable and open to dialogue . . .'[32] Lowery, who opposed the 1975 UN 'Zionism equals racism' resolution, is admittedly no Third World ideologue. And it would obviously be a mistake to identify every anti-Israel pro-Palestinian Arab sentiment, or even every anti-Israel sentiment, as an exercise in Third World ideology. But the point is that the SCLC was moving in a different direction than mainstream America. The public opinion polls registered a rise in American opinion favourable towards Israel after 1967 which never receded significantly. Palestinian partisanship remained low among the American public. But the SCLC was moving in an opposite direction. It did so incrementally, and without becoming a vehicle for Third World ideology, but the movement reflected the effect of more radical forces in its midst and in the black intellectual world. For example, in its 1979 trip, the SCLC authorised only one black journalist, Samuel F. Yette, to make a public report, and that had an ideologically anti-Israel flavour. Among other things, Yette referred to the 'world Zionists' who 'decided to take all of Palestine for themselves . . .'[33]

It is important to distinguish between the SCLC becoming an ideological Third World agency – which it is not – and the SCLC as reflecting the effects of a pervasive Third World intellectual climate. It would be equally important to make that distinction in the matter of the 'Andrew Young affair'. Andrew Young, like Martin Luther King, had been close to the Jewish community and had been an explicit supporter of Israel. As UN Ambassador he met with Zhedi Labib Terzi, the PLO observer at the UN in 1979, although the US had pledged not to have any dealings with an unreconstructed PLO. The Israeli government protested and the American Jewish community rumbled.

It is possible that there was an over-reaction to the meeting, which Young said was inadvertent and without substance. But it is also possible that the meeting was neither quite that inadvertent nor insubstantial, since Young was reprimanded by the US administration for giving a false report on the meeting as well as for holding it. It is also probable that the meeting was given special significance because Young, a product of his particular intellectual environment, had previously given the impression of having some Third World tendencies. He gave that impression not because he hobnobbed with real Third World leaders, which was part of his job, but because of some of his public suggestions such as that Cuban soldiers were helping to bring order to Angola, or that there were hundreds or thousands of political prisoners in the United States.

Still, Young was scarcely a radical Black Panther and it was the reverberations from the Andrew Young affair, rather than the meeting with Terzi, which suggested the continuing viability of Third World ideology. Dorothy Pounds, a black columnist, questioned America's 'pro-Israel stance' following this affair and referred back to the Jewish landlords and grocers who 'oppressed' American blacks, coupling the attack on them with an attack on Israel's 'racism'.[34] The mainstream black press reminded its readers that the Palestinians were a 'darker-skinned people',[35] and James Baldwin accused Israel of having been set up to safeguard Western interests.[36]

The more recent episode with the Reverend Jesse Jackson, culminating in the 1984 Presidential election, was an even sharper example of the effects of Third World ideology. Jackson, a charismatic minister, had been part of the SCLC but had then established his own operation called PUSH, one of whose prime features was to motivate black youth towards excellence in school. This approach was quite agreeable to moderates, even conservatives; Jackson was not a political radical. Catalysed by the Andrew Young affair, Jackson made his own publicised trip to the Middle East. He was not received by Israeli government officials, who were unhappy with private party intervention, but he did visit Israel as well as the PLO. His remarks were generally addressed to the plight of the Palestinian Arabs and Israel's callousness towards them. He compared the condition of the Arabs in the West Bank and Gaza with the conditions of black slavery in America. He complained that the US government gave more money to Israel than to Palestinian refugees.

Jesse Jackson scandalised American Jews not so much by his private antisemitic reference to 'Hymies', for which he apologised, but for two episodes relating to Israel. In one case one of his supporters, Louis Farrakhan, the leader of a small Black Muslim organisation, declared that the creation of Israel and Israel's expulsion of Arabs was an 'outlaw act' and in the course of those remarks referred to Judaism as a 'gutter religion'.[37] While mainstream black leaders, such as the head of the NAACP, quickly condemned Farrakhan's remarks, Jackson was slow in doing so. Only after considerable pressure did he term Farrakhan's remarks 'reprehensible'. More definitively disturbing was the fact that Jesse Jackson asked James Zogby to be one of his official nominators on the floor of the Democratic Party convention. Zogby was head of the American Arab Anti-Discrimination Committee, the leading pro-PLO and anti-Israel organisation in America.

It is again important to note that a pro-Palestinian and an anti-Israel stance did not in themselves make Jackson a 'Third World ideologue'. But it is significant that like Young he was moving in a direction counter to that of mainstream American with respect to the Middle East; and that there were Third World ideological forces in his close entourage. Most significant of all, however, was the tenor of Jesse Jackson's general stance towards American foreign policy, of which his pro-Palestinian bias comprised only one piece.

It has become a matter of unconventional wisdom to perceive that American policy on Israel is a function of American foreign policy in general. According to this viewpoint, Israel's survival will depend more on the shape of American foreign policy in general than on any discrete American feelings or policy on Israel. America is not so likely to 'abandon' Israel in any forthright fashion; it is more likely to become less capable of critically supporting Israel because of some general withdrawal from advocacy on the world scene. This tendency has been generically called 'neo-isolationism'. It is a post-Vietnam phenomenon, which opposes American interventionism – the current focus has primarily been Central America – and military expenditures, calling instead for expenditures towards the relief of domestic problems.

This kind of 'neo-isolationism' is not Third World ideology, but is often compatible with that ideology and its anti-American perspective. Neo-isolationism is not explicitly anti-Israel in itself – indeed many policy-makers who are part of that tendency in general American foreign affairs are strong supporters of Israel. Symptomatic of their dilemma were Congressional votes on foreign aid in both 1984 and 1985. A number of traditional supporters of Israel voted against the aid to Israel because it was part of a package which included interventionist aid to Central America, which they opposed. Of course, they knew that Israel was going to get its aid somehow, but their dilemma was beginning to emerge. And of course it is possible to oppose a specific American policy in Central America without being 'neo-isolationist' in any of its various shadings – but a number of these Congressmen, it was perceived, were caught up in a larger tendency than that.

The Jesse Jackson presidential movement was seen as bringing together in one camp the activist neo-isolationist forces, Third World ideological tendencies, specific pro-Palestinian and anti-Israel attitudes *and* the American black community, which supported him strongly. While many pro-Israel Americans were mainly disturbed by Jackson's explicitly pro-Palestinian stances, others were more gravely concerned about the complex of forces he brought together, which they felt was objectively detrimental to continuing American support of Israel. It was the juxtaposition of the American black population which caused most concern. If the 'gap' were jumped between the ideological leanings of many black intellectuals, and the black grassroots in America, in conjunction with some general neo-isolationist forces, then a mass-based political movement could be created which would be inimical to Israel. The black population would obviously be the mass base for such an inimical movement.

It was for this reason that a higher percentage of Jews than of the general population expressed concern about Jackson in 1984 even though the Jews were disproportionately inclined towards Democratic Party candidates. In the national exit poll done for the *Los Angeles Times* on 6 November 1984, 58 per cent of the Jews expressed disapproval of Jackson, as compared with 42 per cent of the general population. It was for this reason that in the 1984 national Survey of American Jews, conducted for the American Jewish Committee, Jews considered blacks to be more antisemitic than any of the other 14 groups named, including big business, Catholics, fundamentalist Protestants and the State Department. About 17 per cent of the Jews thought that 'most' blacks, and 37 per cent thought that 'many' blacks were antisemitic (as distinct from 'some' or 'few').

*Assessment: American Blacks and Israel*
Nevertheless, the 'gap' between black intellectual Third World tendencies and the black grassroots was *not* jumped by the Jesse Jackson movement. His campaign was supported by all of the elements already indicated but, according to the evidence, they did not jell into a cohesive political movement. The black population supported Jackson's domestic agenda but were not drawn into his foreign policy agenda. The 'Measure E' campaign in Berkeley in June 1984 demonstrated the split in microcosm. Measure E was a referendum calling for the President to reduce aid to Israel by an amount equal to what Israel spends 'in the occupied territories of the West Bank, Gaza Strip and Golan Heights'. The referendum was introduced by James Zogby's American Arab Anti-Discrimination Committee in conjunction with the pro-Third World ideological forces in Berkeley.

Measure E was an echo of what Jesse Jackson had already called for. His tilt on the Middle East was well known in Berkeley. The supporters of the referendum who included Jackson's most prominent local supporter and one of Jackson's top lieutenants came to Berkeley to campaign for Measure E. In addition, the June 1984 election ballot carried both Jackson's candidacy in the presidential primary and Measure E. The blacks constituted 20 per cent of the Berkeley electorate. In that election Jesse Jackson overwhelmingly swept all of the eight black precincts – those that were 80 per cent or more black. In Berkeley as a whole Measure E was defeated by a 64 to 36 ratio. In the black precincts Measure E was defeated by a 58 to 42 ratio. If one were able to remove the Jewish votes – and the 'progressive' Jews of Berkeley *did* in fact rally against this measure – then there would have been no significant difference between the black and white votes. In effect, the blacks voted for Jackson's domestic policy and against his foreign policy.[38]

It has been noted that the social status and educational level of the grassroots black population is one factor which keeps it distant from ideological positions in general. Its preponderant domestic and everyday concerns generally keep it distant from foreign policy considerations. One additional factor that still keeps it from adopting anti-Israel or pro-Palestinian positions is the resistance of many of its leaders, especially on the political level. In Berkeley's Measure E episode, for example, only one black public official supported the measure; the others either opposed it or sat it out. The black press by and large (except under the stress of an 'Andrew Young affair') has supported Israel. For example, a survey of the black press after the 1973 war found that it was rarely hostile to Israel.[39] Furthermore, the America Israel Public Affairs Committee (AIPAC) has reported that 'sixteen of the twenty-one members of the Black Congressional Caucus (an even higher percentage than their white colleagues) have consistently voted for foreign aid to Israel and against major arms sales to those Arab nations still not at peace with Israel'.[40]

There is a blurred but effective split between the pragmatic and the ideological leadership in the black community. The pragmatic leadership is itself more a part of the mainstream American political process, which blunts its ideological edge; and it also finds American Jewry to be an important partner in most of its enterprises. For example, just as the Black Congressional Caucus is disproportionately disposed towards support of Israel, so are the Jewish members of Congress disproportionately disposed towards most black legislative causes. The signals which the grassroots black population receive from its pragmatic leadership do not urgently press that population towards ideological Third World or anti-Israel positions. In nine Gallup surveys between 1973 and 1983, American non-whites with opinions have indicated that their sympathies lie with Israel as against the Arabs by an average of two to one.

On the other hand, in the nine Gallup polls during those years, the total American public with opinions has indicated that its sympathies lie with Israel as against the Arabs by a 4:1 ratio. The difference between the blacks and the whites is not quite as great as it seems from those statistics. About 11 per cent of the general population, on average, indicated sympathy with the Arabs, as compared with about 15 per cent of the non-whites. The larger differential was in sympathy for Israel, an average of 45 per cent for the general population and 30 per cent for the non-whites.[41] It is in the relative absence of black opinion, or of positive black opinion with respect to Israel, that the concern lies. And that concern is buttressed by a statistical 'oddity' which the surveys have found: for the general population, favourable attitudes towards both the Jews and Israel have been correlated positively with level of education. But for blacks, this correlation has been less distinct.[42] There is a compelling suggestion that there is an ideological factor related to higher educational levels, not to mention contact with ideological movements on the college campuses.

At the time of the United Nations 'Zionism equals racism' resolution, both an expression and culmination of Third World ideology, the *Hilltop*, Howard University's student newspaper, typically applauded the resolution as condemning 'a political ideology used to justify continued displacement and subjugation of Arab Palestinians in their own land, Palestine'.[43] The apparent fact that educational level has a different impact on blacks than on whites with respect to both antisemitism and anti-Israelism, does not mean that there is an automatic relationship between these two antipathies. In their analysis of a comprehensive Louis Harris survey, Lipset and Schneider found no significant correlation, one way or another, between sympathy for Israel and conventional antisemitism in the general population. Nor was there a significant correlation between antisemitism and support for the PLO.[44]

However, in at least one current of the black intellectual climate, there does seem to be an ideological element which acts on *both* feelings towards Israel and feelings towards Jews. It is suggested that, as in the case with the general population, antisemitism is not the source of the anti-Israelism (non-economic antisemitism is not disproportionately high among blacks), but that anti-Israelism can be the source of antisemitism, given the prominent American Jewish role in support of Israel.

The American black grassroots population is neither prevalently anti-Israel or antisemitic, as American Jews are sometimes wont to see them because of the vocal Third World stream in the black intellectual climate. The American black population has not been harnessed to either a Third World ideology or an anti-Israel stance. Jesse Jackson's was the latest failure in the attempt to accomplish that. However, the potential is there, given a deep economic crisis to compound the everyday plight of American blacks, for an ideologically affected political movement to attract a mass black base. On the basis of that potential, there is the possibility that an ideologically affected black leadership, swollen by younger ranks bred on the university campus, could have a renewed impact on the political scene. If those elements are allowed to come together, the outcome could be a special black role in either fomenting anti-Israel feeling – or, more likely, in having an effect on general American foreign policy, which could be severely detrimental to Israel. That would be an ironic denouement for two natural allies on the American scene, the blacks and the Jews.

## Notes

1. *Crisis*, February 1919, p. 166.
2. *Amsterdam News*, 25 January 1941.
3. Begin, Menachem, *The Revolt* (Dell Publishing Company, 1978), p. 387.
4. Frantz Fanon, *The Wretched of the Earth* (first published in French in 1961). Published in Evergreen Black Cat edition, 1968).
5. Ibid., p. 314.
6. Ibid., p. 213.
7. Ibid.
8. In *Black Anti-Semitism and Jewish Racism*, edited by Nat Hentoff, Richard W. Baron, (New York: 1969) p. 3.
9. Kenneth Clark, 'Candor on Negro-Jewish relations', *Commentary*, February 1946, p. 8.
10. Gertrude Selznick and Stephen Steinberg, *The Tenacity of Prejudice* (New York), p. 119.
11. Ibid., pp. 119, 121.
12. Paul Jacobs, 'Negro-Jewish relations in America', *Midstream*, December, 1966, p. 3.
13. Earl Raab, 'The Black Revolution and the Jewish Question', *Commentary*, January, 1969.
14. *New York Times*, 24 May 1964.
15. Lincoln, C. Eric, *The Black Muslims in America* (Boston: Beacon Press, 1963), p. 129.
16. *SNCC Newsletter*, June-July 1967.
17. *American Jewish Yearbook* (1971) p. 149.
18. Gary T. Marx, *Protest and Prejudice* (New York: Harper and Row, 1967), p. 25.
19. Ibid., p. 27.
20. Ibid., p. 30.
21. Bureau of the Census, *Statistical Abstract of the U.S., 1984*, p. 144.
22. Marx, *Protest and Prejudice*, p. 56.
23. R. Searles, and J. A. Williams, Jr., 'Negro College Students' participation in sit-ins', *Social Forces*, 1962, pp. 215–20.
24. Marx, *Protest and Prejudice*, p. 78 ff.
25. See E. Franklin Frazier, *The Negro in the United States*, (New York: Macmillan Company, 1949), Chapter 14.
26. William Brink, and Louis Harris, *The Negro Revolution in America* (New York: Simon and Schuster, 1964), p. 100.
27. Marx, *Protest and Prejudice*, p. 101.
28. Ibid.
29. Brink and Harris, p. 103.
30. Marx, *Protest and Prejudice*, p. 26.
31. Robert G. Weisbord, and Richard Kazarian, Jr., *Israel in the Black American Perspective* (Greenwood Press, 1985), p. 39.
32. Ibid., p. 142.
33. Ibid., p. 145.
34. Ibid., p. 125.
35. *Afro-American*, 1 September 1979.
36. Weisbord and Kazarian, p. 125.
37. *New York Times*, 29 June 1984.
38. Edwin Epstein, and Earl Raab, 'The Foreign Policy of Berkeley, California', *Moment*, September 1984, p. 17.

39. American Jewish Congress report, January 1974.
40. Steven J. Rosen, and Yosef I. Abramowitz, *How Americans Feel About Israel* (AIPAC, Washington D.C., 1984, p. 1.
41. Ibid., pp. 6 and 12.
42. See, for example, Earl Raab, 'Blacks and Jews Asunder', *Midstream*, November, 1979, p. 8.
43. Weisbord and Kazarian, p. 55.
44. Seymour Martin Lipset, and William Schneider, *American Opinion Toward Israel and Jew*, unpublished Mss. They found a correlation of –.07 between conventional antisemitism and sympathy for Israel; a correlation of –.09 between conventional antisemitism and support of the PLO.

# 13 Western Anti-Zionism: The Middle Ground

## Shlomo Avineri

Discussing the issue of Western anti-Zionism within the so-called liberal 'centre' raises two preliminary problems. First, by its very definition, the 'centre' is a rather amorphous category. While both the 'left' and the 'right' are more or less identifiable, with organisations whose activities can be monitored and publications which can be quoted, the 'centre' is a much more nebulous entity; in a way it is coeval with 'Everybody Else'. Second, both 'left' and 'right' thrive on ideological and philosophical debates, have no problems in identifying right from wrong, are usually quite straightforward and truculent in their way of expressing their convictions and are therefore very quotable. In the case of the 'centre' we are dealing with something much more elusive: moods, general attitudes and nuances, all of which may be more of a shifting and tentative nature than the clear and unequivocal pronouncements coming from both extremes of the political spectrum.

On the other hand, another aspect should be kept in mind. If one should perhaps not be overly troubled by extreme 'left' or 'right' expressions of anti-Zionism because of their public marginality and limited appeal and scope, the case of the 'centre' is different. If we perceive here a constant and significant erosion of support for Israel or even the emergence of anti-Zionist attitudes, this should give us cause to pause. What we call the 'centre' has, after all, been consistent in its support of Israel for several decades; it also is the mainstream of Western, democratic public opinion. If Israel gets into trouble with this constituency – its most natural and friendly habitat – then something fundamental has gone wrong.

I will not try to define at any great length for the purpose of our analysis what 'anti-Zionism' is and to what degree – if at all – it is identical with, or different from, traditional antisemitism. Suffice it to say that the debate in recent years about the relationship of the two has brought out the complexity of that multifaceted relation. This debate has at least shown that one can be antisemitic without being necessarily anti-Zionist and, conversely, one may hold anti-Zionist ideas (as Noam Chomsky does) without being antisemitic. No blanket telescoping of these two terms is very helpful in our debate.

Furthermore, I would like to underline the fact that not every criticism of Israel or any aspect of its policies should be immediately construed as anti-Zionist and branded as such. Many Israelis, Zionists and Jews sometimes tend to express such an automatic reflex, yet it is extremely ill-advised. One may criticise Israel for its policies *vis-à-vis* the Palestinians, or take a dim view of the relationship between religion and state in Israel, or even advocate the establishment of a Palestinian state on the West Bank, without being anti-Zionist. After all, many Israelis, and this includes legitimate Zionist parties in Israel, hold such positions. It is true that criticism of Israeli policies is sometimes used as a cover for a much more fundamental negation of Israel and the delegitimisation of the whole Zionist enterprise. But we should be able to make a distinction between legitimate criticism of Israel – even if it is unpalatable and unacceptable to us – and a fundamental refusal to accept the legitimacy of Israel. Only the latter should be viewed as 'anti-Zionism' as such.

Another aspect of the complex of issues under discussion is to ask whether there has been an increase in anti-Zionist attitudes in 'centrist' Western circles in the last decade or so and if so, to try to identify its sources. Again, here we are faced with a dilemma which is sometimes unconsciously glossed over. On the one hand, there is no doubt that there has been an increase in such attitudes and it is immaterial for the moment whether they are fundamentally 'anti-Zionist' or merely critical of certain aspects of Israeli policy. The fact is that there is a general consensus that we have been witnessing a constant increase in the recurrence of such unfriendly attitudes. When the question is then asked about the causes of this increase, some Jewish observers blandly reply that antisemitism is endemic and accounts for the emergence of anti-Israeli or anti-Zionist attitudes.

Some of this is, evidently, true. But such an automatic response only begs the question. If antisemitic attitudes are an endemic factor in Western societies, why did they not rebound against Israel earlier? How does a constant factor appear, over time, with different intensity and frequency? Why was Israel the darling of Western liberal opinion during and immediately after the Six Day War of 1967 and yet had to face such grave problems in the Lebanon War of 1982? When we say that the memory of the Holocaust is fading, this again is evidently true: it may even be a truism. But is it the whole answer? Nor can the change be attributed to the power of Arab oil and petro-dollars: this could perhaps explain 1973, but not 1982.

What I am seeking is to come to grips with the realisation of one aspect of the complex relationship between Jews and non-Jews. I am not of the opinion that antisemitism as such is caused by what Jews are, do or say. In other words, Jews do not 'cause' antisemitism – the antisemites do. But when we discuss political attitudes towards Israel as expressed, over time, by organisations and individuals basically supportive of Israel – as the 'centre' has traditionally been since the Second World War – and we see an increase in critical attitudes towards it, can we divorce this development completely from Israeli behaviour? Can we separate the perceptions of Israel from its political actions, the statements of its leaders and its self-proclaimed ideology? There is no doubt that Israel has changed in the last decade, and some of these transformations have been quite profound. Would it be completely nonsensical to imagine that certain of these changes have been registered by 'centrist' Western liberal opinion and that they impinge on some aspects of how Israel is perceived by them and critically judged? Indeed, would it not be totally unrealistic to imagine that such profound changes as those which have taken place in Israel cannot fail to be reflected in the way the country – and Zionism – are perceived by Western liberal public opinion?

While not suggesting that these are the sole reasons for the shifts that have occurred in the perception of Israel – they obviously are not – two changes in the real context of Israeli life have, to my mind, been reflected in the way Israel is being perceived from the outside. These shifts in perception have contributed in some cases to a reorienting of sympathy and attitudes. Two dates are crucial in this respect – 1967 and 1977. Until 1967 the general view of Israel, which gained it basic support in liberal Western circles, held that it was a small, democratic pioneering country, surrounded by implacable enemies. Three million Israelis surrounded by almost one hundred million Arabs committed to their expulsion from the Middle East – this was an image projected by Israel which certainly corresponded to reality. Such a perception automatically generated warmth towards Israel and moral support for it, especially if the discrepancy was noted between Israel's democratic system and the combination of reactionary regimes and military dictatorships in the Arab world.

Since Israel's astounding victory of 1967, both reality and perception have changed. While, objectively speaking, Israel is still outnumbered by its enemies, its control since 1967 of 1.2 million Palestinians on the West Bank and Gaza has focused public attention on something else: so much of the news coming from the Middle East since the Six Day War has to do with the fact of Israel being the occupier of Palestinian territories. Whatever the rights and wrongs of the conflicting claims for Judea, Samaria and Gaza, there is no doubt that since 1967 television viewers in the West have seen hundreds of news items in which the projected image was that of Israeli soldiers in confrontation with a civilian Arab population under military occupation. Liberal as this occupation may be, the picture of Israel as the occupier and no longer as the threatened underdog has imprinted itself on Western minds. Even without the skilful exploitation of this role-change by Arab propaganda, it is not difficult to present to the liberal West a convincing picture in which Israel no longer appears as the threatened or victimised partner. This is not a question of the relative merits of Israeli or Palestinian claims but rather of simple, opposing images which determine people's attitudes even if they are not very knowledgeable about the facts in dispute. If the dominant images before 1967 in the Western liberal 'centre' were friendly to Israel, since 1967 they have been far more ambivalent, tending to present the Palestinians as being under foreign occupation. Israel is no longer David confronting an Arab Goliath; it is perceived as a powerful, militarily strong country, sitting on top of over a million 'Third World ' Palestinians.

The change of government in Israel after 1977 added a further dimension to this. While until 1977 criticism of Israel was usually limited to the extreme left, to expressly pro-Arab circles and Third World countries, the rise to power of Menachem Begin broadened the basis of anti-Israeli criticism. While many Western liberals might not have been overly happy with some aspects of Israel's policy even before 1977, the switch in language, terminology and rhetoric – let alone policy – inaugurated by the Likud government exacerbated these tendencies. If Western liberals might have questioned whether some sort of control over the West Bank was crucial to Israeli security, most people involved realised that the Israelis might take a different view of where their security lay than comfortably situated Western observers. But when the claim to Israeli control over the West Bank was no longer made in security terms – which are, after all, debatable – but produced historical and religious arguments to legitimise Israeli control, criticism greatly intensified. Insistence on the right of Jews to settle 'anywhere and everywhere in Eretz Israel' and the determination to put West Bank settlement at the top of Israel's agenda, immediately created antagonism among informed and moderate Western opinion. It was felt that by espousing such language the Begin government expressed a philosophy from which most Western liberals instinctively recoiled. The romantic, historicist arguments of Begin and the plans to settle 100 000 Jews in Judea and Samaria evoked among Western liberals unpleasant echoes of a chapter of European nationalism which most Europeans felt should be relegated to the history books.

When this appeared to be coupled with utter insensitivity to any Palestinian rights, even people whose whole political life was identified with support of Israel found it difficult to swallow. Such claims sometimes received enthusiastic support from right-wing, hawkish Christian fundamentalists: when a person like the Reverend Jerry Falwell received the Jabotinsky Prize from Prime Minister Begin, Israel simply became tarred with the brush of the Moral Majority. American liberal opinion, in opposing Falwell, criticised his friends and admirers alike. Such a policy did, indeed, generate support for Israel among Southern Baptists: but could one really marvel at the fact that middle-of-the-road supporters of Israel felt uneasy?

What has been said until now does not mean that Israel was to *blame* for the decrease in support for its policies among the middle ground liberals. It merely suggests that since there were changes in the reality of the relationship between Israel itself which had shifted the language and idiom of the conflict into another sphere, one should not be surprised at the altered liberal perception and judgement of the Jewish state. If an Israeli Prime Minister insists that Zionism means settling Judea and Samaria, can one really cavil at those who then voice doubts as to whether Zionism may perhaps have some colonialist aspects? In short, what Israel does and says exerts an impact on 'centrist' liberal opinion. When it comes to the extreme left and to Arab propaganda one may justly argue that nothing Israel does will make any difference, since it will in any case be condemned. But this is not the case with the middle ground. There is no doubt that the language used by official Israeli spokesmen during the Lebanon War created problems with this constituency. Without in any way exonerating some of the Western media and Western statesmen from inexcusable language with regard to Israel during the Lebanon War it must be admitted that some Israeli statements at that time helped to fuel the fire.

This had far-reaching consequences even for the tone of the relationship between Israel and the United States as can be seen from the following example. The AWACS controversy was one case where Israel and its friends appeared to have been pitted against what was presented as US national security interests in the Middle East. This was certainly one of the more extreme instances of such disagreement between Israel and the American Administration and the stakes – both financial and political – were exceedingly high. Yet never before had Administration officials in Washington reverted to impugning 'double loyalty' to the supporters of Israel as they did on that occasion. The slogan 'Reagan v. Begin' not only rhymed well; it became politically feasible because of the image which Prime Minister Begin succeeded in projecting of himself and of Israel. It is a sad fact that during the last years of Begin's leadership his name did provoke hostility in world public opinion. This cannot be attributed to 'constant' anti-Zionism, nor was it a consequence of Begin's tough political stance. Ben Gurion and Golda Meir were never easy partners to deal with and both did occasionally confront US administrations. But their names and, by implication, that of Israel, never acquired a negative association. Successive American administrations, even when conducting political campaigns aimed to offset Israeli influence on the policy-making of the United States, never could bank on exploiting negative images connected with these Israeli leaders.

Beyond these particular cases there are, however, instances where Israel is beginning to appear in a problematic light within the US decision-making process. This is mainly connected with what is called the 'Israel lobby' in the United States. The great influence of this lobby and the criticism to which it has been subjected in the last few years does raise the issue of a hidden agenda which occasionally may border on antisemitism – disguised as a legitimate expression of US national interests.

Listening to some of the accounts of the power of the pro-Israeli lobby in Washington, one might have been forgiven for thinking that this was the only lobby at work on Capitol Hill. It does not matter much whether these accounts of the exploits of the pro-Israel lobby are accurate or grossly exaggerated. What matters is that American policy is conducted in an open field in which different and conflicting lobbies inevitably overlap. I do not recall anybody objecting to the very existence of a pro-Taiwan, or pro-People's Republic of China, or pro-South Korea lobby (provided they are operating within the law). To single out the 'Jewish lobby' as the only lobby which may be deflecting US policy from its true course is to set up a separate standard by which Israel and the Jews are to be judged. This is unacceptable and should be branded as such. It should also be pointed out that despite the resourcefulness of the pro-Israeli lobby the US position is diametrically opposed to that of Israel on some very crucial issues: the status of Jerusalem (not only East but also West Jerusalem), the Golan Heights, Israeli settlements on the West Bank, some of the finer points in the interpretation of Security Council Resolution 242, the meaning of autonomy under the Camp David Accords. If the pro-Israel lobby were really as strong as its demonologised perception suggests how, could the United States withstand 'Jewish pressure' on such critical issues?

There are other points of an almost subliminal nature which crept into 'centrist' usage and which harp on sometimes unconscious and ambivalent issues (to say the least) *vis-à-vis* the Jews and Israel. The Western press occasionally refers to the 'Movement for Greater Israel'. There is no such movement. There is, rather, a movement which is called in Hebrew 'The Movement for the Complete (or Whole, or Undivided) Land of Israel'. I am not an advocate of this movement or of its philosophy, but an 'Undivided Eretz Israel' is very different from a 'Greater Eretz Israel'. To add the 'Greater' with its obvious historical associations is something which every Israeli and Jew, regardless of his opinions on the issue itself, should object to.

Another closely related example is the use of the adjective 'biblical' or 'Old Testament', sometimes injected into journalistic accounts of controversial issues in Israel. When the liberal Western press says that Mr Begin refers to the West Bank by its 'biblical name of Judea and Samaria', this is an adjectival use which is highly questionable. 'Judea and Samaria' are not the 'biblical' names of these areas: they are their *Hebrew* names, just as Jerusalem is not the 'biblical' name of *al-Kuds* but its Hebrew name. Similarly when during the Lebanon War some Israeli acts were referred to as expressing 'biblical' vengeance or 'Old Testament' fury, very insidious meanings were added to what were not objectively descriptive terms. To use 'biblical' or 'Old Testament' in this subliminally pejorative way is unacceptable to all but religious bigots of the worst kind.

What emerges from these remarks is that clearly there is no uniform, middle-of-the-road body of opinion or philosophy which can be construed as anti-Zionist or antisemitic: we are dealing here with nuances, continuities and fluidities. Basically, when we refer to the 'centre', we mean a rather diffuse camp which is not inimical to Israel. But it too may be prone to some of the pitfalls of latent, traditional anti-Jewish language. On the other hand, it is a group which because of its basic decency and lack of extremism is open to persuasion. It takes issues of liberty, equal rights and self-determination seriously and is responding in terms of its own liberal ideology to what it honestly perceives as the issues at stake. This group cannot be swayed by public relations gimmicks, though more adequate information never hurts. This group will support Israel if its *policies* appear to go hand-in-hand with its liberal values. If it sometimes demands from Israel more than from other nations, this is not always a double standard. Sometimes it is a sincere expression of its appreciation for Israel, uncomfortable as the consequences may be. To this group, what Israel does, how it is being done and the language used by the Jewish state to describe and defend its actions will greatly determine its attitudes towards Zionism. In other words, in most cases the key to its support lies in our hands.

# 14 Impugning Israel's Legitimacy: Anti-Zionism and Antisemitism
## Julius Gould

The long history of hatred toward and persecution of Jewish individuals and groups now fills entire libraries. It is true that the term 'anti-semitism' is little more than a hundred years old. It was coined in 1879 by Wilhelm Marr, a Judeophobe whose phobia was secular, populist and racist. He promoted his *Antisemiten-Liga* to propagate his message. Yet by now the word is probably as overloaded and overused as the acts to which it points are deadly and distasteful. It is certainly true that it would be hard to secure complete agreement upon its definition – on what it 'really' is. For the concept is a contested one and, in political use, the coverage of such concepts can be extended or narrowed to suit tactical convenience.

The historical record shows that Jews were the targets of defamation, hatred and persecution in many lands well before the term 'anti-Semitism' was coined. They had been variously assailed – well before the coming of 'scientific racism' – for holding religious views other than those officially approved in the countries in which they lived. And this was of special importance in Christian Europe during the centuries when Christians themselves held Christian beliefs with high seriousness. In general, in lands and at times when religious differences were grounded on deeply-held convictions, and where religious perspectives were, in part or in whole, the sources of legitimacy for the power of rulers, disputes over the Jewish religion could easily arise or be concocted. And intolerance over beliefs could (and often did) develop into social prejudice and political persecution. There is no general theory to explain these matters of somber historical record: neither a clash of economic interests nor the prevalence of an 'authoritarian personality' in society can provide a simple, let alone universal, explanation. And it should be said that Judeophobia was not, of course, an omnipresent feature in Christian Europe. A British writer can hardly fail to note that it was the Puritan Cromwell who, for a variety of reasons, approved the readmittance of the Jews to England in 1656. Cromwell had strong Christian preoccupations but they were not marked by any very general religious tolerance even toward (perhaps especially toward) his fellow Christians. And in the Christian heyday in Europe, Christians of various kinds were ambivalent about the Jews on theological grounds, finding – in the words of Jacob Katz – 'a rationale, in their anticipated conversion, for tolerating their existence'.

Looking back at Christian Europe (whether in anger, disbelief or horror) has its own fascination. But what, it might be asked, has this to do with the state of the Jews (let alone the Jewish state) today? A historical prelude was quite deliberate, though necessarily incomplete. For both the Jewish and non-Jewish perceptions of present-day Jewish life and prospects are inevitably coloured by historical memory, record and legend. Jewish relations with non-Jews over thousands of years, in great diversity of territories and social contexts, should not be seen as a uniform, unbroken stream of passions and events. There have been important gaps and ruptures in the traditions of coexistence, misunderstandings, conflict and atrocity. Yet there is a strong case for the view that the Jews are essentially a 'historical' people and that their past contacts with other peoples have left an indelible set of historical markings. After all, it was in 1215 that the Fourth Lateran Council enjoined that Jews should wear a distinguishing mark – a disk attached to their clothing coming to be a favoured sign of Jewish separateness. And less than fifty years ago that badge of difference was zealously reimposed by the Nazis and their European accomplices. Such deadly symbolism – as well as the myths about horrendous Jewish rituals and conspiracies – has very ancient roots. It antedates the controversies in which the eighteenth-century Enlightenment thinkers found fault with Judaism as an antecedent of the hated superstitions of established Christianity and regarded Jewish religious particularism as, *inter alia*, an obstacle to 'modernity'. It antedates the later preoccupations with Jews by, for example, 'Luddite' Catholic reactionaries who objected to Jews as *carriers* of that same 'modernity'. It antedates too the views of those many brands of socialists (including some Jewish socialists) who either dismissed Jewish identity and consciousness (religious or secular) as a form of particularism doomed to erosion and destruction or (sometimes simultaneously) criticised Jewish (and other) forms of the hated particularism from the standpoint of a secular ethical universalism whose Jewish basis was, genuinely or for polemical ends, highlighted and proclaimed. Many of these themes live on; few of them have lost all influence – even in the special circumstances of the late twentieth century.

Since 1945 hostility toward Jews – and Jewish reactions to that hostility – has been constantly modified *and* intensified by two major historical facts. One is the fact of the Nazi persecution. The other is the fact of the establishment of the State of Israel. At one level these facts by sheer repetition can turn into platitudes – truisms to adorn a peroration or a fund-raising speech. But they are much more than platitudes. For philosophers and theologians they raise the gravest of moral or metaphysical questions. For politicians, diplomats and political commentators they set the boundaries for a debate that never ends about issues which, though they may be transformed, still never disappear – 'the Jewish problem' or rather 'the problems Jews have with their neighbours'. For Jews themselves the Holocaust was the *almost* final dissolution – the ultimate, never-to-be-forgotten expression of their status as victims, as *objects* of history rather than its creators. It was followed by their one major political creation (or to be more exact, the creation of an adventurous pioneer elite and of refugees from persecution) – the State of Israel. That alone rescued world Jewry (what was left of it in the 1940s and beyond) from the status of a dispersed people without a national home – a people whose fragments, however large and, at times, prosperous, had figured for centuries in the pages of other peoples' histories and in the grim interstices of the relations between the great powers.

Again, after 1945 many felt that the record and memory of the Holocaust had firmly discredited anti-Jewish movements and ideas – especially in the opinion-forming elites of the Western world. Twenty years ago, writing in *Jewish Life in Modern Britain*, I noted the growth of cultural and other forms of pro-Jewishness in several Western countries – induced by a mixture of compassion, guilt and shame over Nazi atrocities. Israel too was a source of pro-Jewish sentiment. She basked in the warmth of much liberal opinion. The memory of her fight for independence (and for building a place of refuge for the victims of persecution); her democratic polity; the vitality of her cultural and social achievements – all this, on balance, outweighed Arabist and associated sympathies for dispossessed or refugee Palestinians. The Suez war of 1956, prosecuted alongside French and British moves against Nasser, did little lasting damage to Israel's image or reputation. Under American pressure the Israelis withdrew from their conquest in the Sinai – accepting (as several European nations did not do after the Second World War) that success in war does not guarantee territorial gains.

There was another source of gratification for Western Jews with a taste for history. In October 1965, after the earlier pressures canalised by Pope John XXIII, the Second Vatican Council, under Pope Paul VI, reversed centuries-old Catholic doctrine – conceding, in the document *Nostra Aetate*, that the blame for the crucifixion of Christ 'cannot be charged against all Jews, without distinction, then alive, nor against the Jews of today'. This declaration, like Paul VI's visit to Israel for twelve hours in January 1964, was of more than symbolic interest – even though the Vatican had not in 1964 (any more than now) formally recognised the Jewish state.

It cannot be claimed that these trends, and a general though far from universal post-war affluence, brought about a mood of extreme euphoria among Western Jews. But from the late 1940s until the late 1960s they did enjoy a sense of security and self-esteem not known to their parents or grand-parents. American Jewry in particular notched up many varied achievements. Not only did American Jews enjoy what by European standards appeared super-affluence. They became respected leaders in their country in matters of cultural taste and scientific advance. Social change, for once, was on their side. They were no longer afflicted by the social or religious hostilities – including those of populist and Christian fundamentalist extremists – that had, in the inter-war years, caused them so much embarrassment and difficulty. Like Jews in other liberal democracies they enjoyed a status vastly more agreeable in every respect than that available, for example, to Jews exposed to the economic and political vagaries of Latin American dictatorships. And their place as free citizens in Western society stood in marked contrast to the long night of Soviet and East European Jewry. The Prague trials of Slansky and other Czech Communists of Jewish origins had taken place in 1952. The Jewish Doctors' 'plot' in the USSR in 1953 was the culmination of many anti-Jewish acts (including murder) inspired by Stalin in his final years with the aim of exposing and removing 'homeless cosmopolitans' – i.e., Jews. These and other Eastern manoeuvres were a prelude to the subsequent pressures that were, by 1970, to have brought effectively to an end the long history of Czech and Polish Jewry – and to lead to the penalties now imposed upon those Soviet Jews who seek to leave the USSR or to practice a fuller Jewish life.

This assessment of Western philosemitism in 1964 was accompanied by the feeling that such things were too good to last. But who could have predicted the movement of opinion that was shortly to occur? Many factors were at work – but the catalyst was the Israeli success in the Six Day War in 1967 – a success which, by stages, led to the extraordinary campaign, in the United Nations and elsewhere, to delegitimise Israel. Twenty years ago this was a prospect to which little thought was given. Perhaps, even before 1967, Western Jews were too reliant on an enduring Gentile sense of guilt. Guilt, after all, is a wasting emotion – especially among the class of intellectuals and semi-intellectuals that has so much expanded in recent decades. Many semi-intellectuals were indeed recruited by the New Left radical movements of the 1960s: they were already in place by the time of the Six Day War, and they brought their own strands of ill-informed malevolence to the discussion of Jewish affairs. The end of guilt found many an expression. Among the most open – and significant in its German context – was the remark of the young radical, Dieter Kunzelmann who, according to a contemporary account, ' . . . went so far as to insist – in his explanation of why he had planted a bomb in Berlin's Fasanenstrasse Synagogue, rebuilt after the Nazis burned it down in 1938 – that his comrades just had to get over their *Judenknax*, by which he meant "their thing about the Jews"' (that is, their post-1945 German pro-Semitic liberalism). No doubt Kunzelmann was franker as well as more extreme than others of his generation; but the mood he expressed was to fuse with other currents of New Left opinion and to usher in a new age of disregard for Jewish sensitivities.

By the mid-1980s, Jews had seen their sensitivities openly affronted as well as disregarded. As a result, they developed an acute concern about the international campaign against Zionism – which had so many confluent political sources – and about the parallel charge (following the UN resolution in 1975) that Zionism is a form of racism. They felt that this campaign, and such charges, arose from antisemitic motives, were a continuation of historical antisemitism, and had occasioned (and will occasion) anti-Jewish activities in places quite remote from the Middle Eastern conflict between Israel and her Arab neighbours. They were, likewise, concerned about the intermittent revival in Western Europe of right-wing extremism whose exponents sporadically attacked Jewish people and properties and advanced new forms of anti-Jewish defamation through denying or falsifying the history of the Holocaust. At this stage two points of general interest can be made. First, the denial of the Holocaust was not only an offence against decency and objectivity. It was intended to be seen (and was so seen by Jews) as a way of undermining the legitimacy of Israel – founded as she was as a place of refuge. Second, while the falsifiers of history had their base in what can be dubbed right-wing circles the argument had been taken up and given much wider circulation by Arab and other Third World spokesmen, Soviet and Soviet-oriented communists and Western (including Jewish) Trotskyites – a plethora of groups that differed widely from each other on so many matters but seemed tacitly to converge on certain central obsessions about Jews and Israel.

A later section will return to some of these central themes, cutting as they do across boundaries, trumpeted as they have been through the UN system and the world's media by a variety of hostile voices. The difficult issue will also be considered whether these forms of contemporary nastiness could be fully or adequately under the rubric of 'antisemitism'. But to illustrate how *national* nuances are superadded to the more general themes, it is helpful to look first at some events and trends in three selected countries – the US, France and Britain. A comprehensive treatise would obviously also examine the very different situations that obtain in the USSR and in Latin America. But the choice of three liberal democracies, each of which has a sizeable and important Jewish community – is not an arbitrary one. For it was precisely such liberal democracies that were the main targets of the propaganda about Jews and Israel–propaganda that had a distinctly anti-Western as well as an anti-Jewish aspect.

## THE UNITED STATES

Over the last two decades black-Jewish relations in the US became the focus of delicate and interwoven tensions. In the early part of the century liberal Jews had begun to forge strong links with the emergent black political leadership. Jews had been actively involved in 1909 in the establishment of the National Association for the Advancement of Coloured People – and the common interest of Jews and blacks in the extension of equal opportunities was a principal source of strength for the Democratic coalition initially assembled by Roosevelt in 1933. Later on there was much Jewish support, in finance and other ways, for the black movement, via the courts and on the streets, for full civil rights in the 1960s. But by the late 1960s a rift was opening between the more self-confident and aggressive black leadership and the 'established' Jewish community – and a skein of animosity began to unravel. I recall trying to explain to highly intelligent black students in Atlanta in 1968 that, to a visitor, the recent ghetto riots at least *appeared* to contain an anti-Jewish element – for I had seen burned-out Jewish shops (notably but not solely liquor-shops) and was hearing complaints about Jewish ghetto-landlords. But acts of violence, whatever their complex motivation, were not the principal problem. The main concern developed over the growth of black claims (or claims on their behalf) for an equality not simply of *opportunity* but also for equality of *outcomes*. The early skirmishes were marked by the bitter clashes in 1968 when, in Brooklyn (at Ocean Hill-Brownsville), blacks laid claim to teaching positions held by Jews in the public education network. Before very long the principles in regard to the 'new equality' became a matter of nationwide debate. Inevitably Jewish interests as well as sensitivities were involved in the long contentious struggles that have since been pursued, through the bureaucracies and the courts, over *affirmative action* – forms of positive discrimination in favour of minorities (principally blacks, Hispanics and women) deemed to have been historically the victims of discrimination in education and employment. No disclaimers (e.g., that 'targets' are not 'quotas') could dissolve Jewish apprehensions that affirmative action is a sophisticated extension of the *numerus clausus* against which Jews, and their supporters, had so successfully fought hitherto. It was, of course, true to observe that Jews had, to their credit, been 'disproportionately' successful in matters of education and employment through the operation of meritocratic principles. But there was a genuine clash of interests between Jews and those who advanced 'group targets' as a way of rectifying the historical disadvantages of others. Such 'group-targets' did not overall have their origins in anti-Jewish motivation. But their proponents were seldom sympathetically moved by the prospect of *consequent* Jewish disadvantage. And Jews, like other relatively privileged Americans, would not be easily reconciled to an anti-meritocratic ethos which sought to establish an equality of outcomes that, more or less, corresponded to the numerical distribution of social groups in the population as a whole. Such a 'group equality' *would* be a source of Jewish disadvantage – however marginal – unlikely to detach Jews from their older concern for equality of opportunity based on individual talent and social mobility.

These controversies have been very lightly sketched. But enough has been said to foreshadow how Jewish and other concerns over the 'new equality' could collide with the political assertiveness of black activists, spokesmen and politicians. In those quarters (and, as we shall see, not only in America) there is also acute sensitivity geared to the rational further-ance of self-interest and group interest. The overall mantle of such endeav-ours is the elimination of 'racism' – a term that is as ill-defined as antisemitism and just as contested. Whatever its exact meaning racism has, in the contemporary idiom, a bad reputation – and when it is transmuted into 'institutionalised racism' its presence may be sought even (and perhaps especially) in places that are free from all apparent taint of subjective prejudice. These are complex matters – that have acquired a dialectic and rhetoric that is self-sealing.

But it was not only in relation to the new equality that the charge of racism unsettled American Jews. For example, in August 1979 Andrew Young, the black ambassador of the United States at the UN, resigned his post after the disclosure of his unauthorised meeting with a representative of the PLO. The Jews were at once blamed for alleged (but unverified) exercise of 'racist' political pressure. Not everyone in the black community joined in the chorus – nor was there any upsurge of black antisemitism. But the episode could be exploited by aspirant black politicians both directly and indirectly – the strand of support for the PLO merging into a further heightening of black radicalism, around such leaders as Jesse Jackson, within a mood of approval for Third World revolutionary ideas. In other words, there arose around the Andrew Young episode a melange of motifs in the contemporary idiom, a bad reputation – and when it is transmuted into 'institutionalised racism' its presence may be sought even (and perhaps especially) in places that are free from all apparent taint of subjective prejudice. These are complex matters – that have acquired a dialectic and rhetoric that is self-sealing.

Finally, in this selective tour d'horizon – the presidential election cam-paign of 1984. The issue of antisemitism had a place in that campaign despite the fact that poll data show that the post-war decline in antisemit-ism in the US has continued and, interestingly, that American popular support for Israel (despite recent acrimonious debate over the Lebanon) has remained remarkably high. There can be little doubt that the prime source of the antisemitism issue was the clearly pejorative use by the Reverend Jesse Jackson, aspirant to his Democratic presidential candidacy, of the words 'Hymie' and 'Hymietown' early in 1984. There was also a whole series of hostile references to Jews made by Jackson's prominent Black Muslim supporter Louis Farrakhan.

It should, however, be noted that it was in the Republican and not the Democratic platform that antisemitism was specifically condemned. This was not in itself proof that Republicans overall were more pro-Jewish than Democrats – or that the victorious Reagan administration's domestic or Middle East policies would follow at all points traditional Jewish expectations. Nor did the campaign issue of antisemitism, as I have indicated, flow from any suddenly heightened anti-Jewish sentiment. What I would call 'Jacksonism' became, however, an outlook with which many American blacks concurred – and to which white politicians will be bound to address themselves. Jacksonism in the Democratic party would survive the disappearance of Jackson himself. The complex of affirmative action and Third World ideology became an important and demographically increasing constituency within the Democratic Party which was no longer the Roosevelt coalition to which an earlier Jewish liberalism made so generous a contribution.

## FRANCE

For historical reasons France is another interesting context for insight into contemporary attitudes toward Jews. Thanks to the work of such scholars as Michael Marrus and David Pryce-Jones, we now have a frank view of French sentiments – both on the left and the right – on the wartime fate of French Jewry both in the occupied and in Vichy-controlled parts of France. A sense of guilt, ambivalence and *arrière-pensées* undoubtedly survives. In recent years France has been the scene of some more than ordinary anti-Jewish activities that involved damage to Jewish schools, synagogues and other buildings. Whatever their provenance, the outrage in the Rue Copernic (and that on the Goldenberg Restaurant) was to became a public focus of anti-antisemitism that cut across most normal party lines. It was small consolation to French Jewry to know that, so far as right wing vandalism and terror were concerned, non-Jewish targets had preceded the Jewish on some of the hit-lists. It must also be observed that in France (in marked contrast to the ethos of the 1930s) right-wing extremist movements were pursued through the law with extreme vigour. Some such organisations were obliged to disband; criminal acts were energetically investigated and their perpetrators, when convicted, given exemplary sentences. All the same, these phenomena – as well as left-wing ambivalence over anti-Zionism – aroused much Jewish anxiety over the years. That anxiety was further fuelled by the way in which in the French elections to the European Assembly in June 1984 the National Front, led by Jean-Marie Le

Pen, surprised both its opponents and the pollsters. With over two million votes, it secured 11 per cent of the votes and ten Assembly seats. Clearly – after its municipal and by-election advances in the previous two years – the Front had broadened its geographical and social sources of support. Its policies appeared amorphous and diffuse – centring upon what may be read into such slogans as 'France and the French First' – with a special emphasis on the suggested links between high unemployment and competition from immigrant labour. Xenophobia was in fact a crucial part of the Front's appeal – and French Jews could not be indifferent to its spread. It should be made clear that such xenophobia, stressing the real or supposed problems created by immigrant or non-French workers and their families, was not an invention of Le Pen. The French Communist party (which did very badly in the European elections) had also shown clear willingness to exploit such feelings and the underlying racism that those feelings both expressed and stimulated. There were indeed social resentments and tensions in France – even if the xenophobic response of left and right offered no realistic or sensible solutions. Jews were not the open target of the Front's propaganda. When Jewish politicians such as Simone Veil or Laurent Fabius were singled out for criticism there was no need to mention their origins. The hidden message was well-understood in the context of a heated election campaign – even though countered by Le Pen's insistence that he personally was well-disposed to Israel. French Jews could reasonably have been distressed when the taboos against racism appeared to have been relaxed – whatever the real resentments about housing or work prospects that assisted the relaxation. Further worries perplexed French Jews. There was the left-wing anti-Zionism only slightly masked by, for example, the Communist party's search for Jewish support against fascism – which seemed to many a diversionary tactic seeking to divert Jewish attention away from left-wing double standards about the Middle East conflict. And, as we shall see below, France has been a fertile source of quasi-intellectual revisionist history – as well as some influential, though cranky, groups of thinkers who, without endorsing antisemitism, revived, with some modern twists, the old lines of thought about European racial superiority.

## BRITAIN

The British National Front has discredited itself, split into factions and enjoyed electoral disasters in successive British general elections. Its spokesmen, in its various segments, leaped clumsily from hostility to British non-white immigrants, and their British-born children, to support for striking miners without in any sense relaxing their hostility toward the Jewish people or institutions. They were not a political success. Their significance lay not in what they did (which was generally deplorable) but in the role they occupied as a target for anti-fascism and anti-racism. These are among many good causes that are ill-defined and that become tarnished when taken up by the anti-democratic revolutionary left in Britain – or anywhere else. 'Anti-racism' is a blanket-term of the left – one with a very elastic definition. When the National Front type of agitation promoted or reflected racial hostilities toward 'blacks' (including native-born fully British citizens) it brought into being not just genuine outrage but also a synthetic, political anti-racism. The excesses committed under that banner occasion an opposing train of thought – a spectrum of anti-anti-racism. One end of that spectrum may, in fact, shade into the real racist feeling that caused the original offence. In general, there develops a cycle of reaction and counter-reaction, of sentiment and counter-sentiment.

It was tempting for many British Jews to seek to relive the battles of 1934 against Mosley and the fascists of that time. On the other hand, it seemed more prudent for Jews to recognise that, via an indiscriminate anti-racism, they could become marooned in an emotional and political swamp – a location in which they would have some strange companions. For anti-racism could easily be manipulated by left-wing politicians seeking to secure, at public expense, a Third World constituency in the furtherance of their political, or personal, ambitions; by Trotskyite and other communists in several parties who explicitly regard Zionism as just one department of racism that needs to be combatted. Some of these people openly said that British Jews were led by fascists; others compared Israelis or Zionists with Nazis as a prelude to describing British policies in Ireland as comparable with the Holocaust – this, no doubt, was done with an eye to their Irish supporters in London or other major cities. With this clatter of dishonest argument about an ill-defined racism and with allies who believed (and said) that their anti-Zionism is partly their anti-racism, Jews could have little in the way of common ground.

My own belief is that the campaign against Zionism in recent years has been nothing other than a thinly-coded expression of the fight against Israel. It has nothing in its origins that is in any way connected with the long-standing debates within Zionist circles or between Zionists and their intellectual opponents down the years. It also goes beyond matters about which there is bound to be legitimate dispute – for example, about the precise boundaries which, to general satisfaction, might be regarded as satisfying Israel's security needs. Anti-Zionism impugns the moral/ideological basis of *any* Jewish state in and around 'Zion'. Those who conduct anti-Zionist polemics may affect to believe that in attacking Zionism (or using the word 'Zionist' instead of 'Jewish') they will be absolved from any suspicion of antisemitism. In truth it would be hard to claim that *all* such usages are signs of antisemitism, but the suspicion can hardly be avoided. For most Jews, not just Israelis, the semantic disjunction was quite impossible. While Jews inside and outside Israel may have felt justified (even obliged) to dissent from declared policies of Israeli governments (or from motifs within these policies), they recognised attacks on Zionism as attacks on the rights of Jews to enjoy a *collective* emancipation as a people. They regarded this as a form of collective discrimination against the Jewish people that recalled past (or present) denials to *individual* Jews of equality of citizen-rights.

Argument over the legitimacy of Israel shifted and escalated sharply after 1967. Israel's control over the 'administered territories' increased the Arab population under Israeli forms of control – and made possible, under both Alignment and Likud governments (but especially under the Likud) the establishment of Jewish settlements in the West Bank area that, until 1967, had been under Jordanian occupation. One consequence in the international propaganda battle was the intensification of what must be called a Third World argument about the legitimacy of Israel. This took several forms – but the core claim was that Israel exercised colonial domination over all its Arab inhabitants but especially over the Arab inhabitants of areas of recent Jewish settlement. Israel was deemed a 'colonial settler-state' whose non-Jewish inhabitants needed to be liberated – part of a worldwide liberation by peoples in Africa, Asia and elsewhere hitherto exploited by alien Western rule. (The control of non-Western peoples inside and outside the USSR by Russian state agencies was, for familiar reasons, generally exempted from most Third World strictures.) American military or economic aid to Israel was considered further proof, if such were needed, of Israel's place in the colonialist-imperialist camp.

This could not be construed simply as an anti-Israeli argument – one that sought to weigh Israeli claims to the administered territories against those of its Palestinian inhabitants, judiciously finding that the Palestinian case was stronger . . . *Prima facie* such a judgement might be plausible though unacceptable. But it became suspect when accompanied (as it generally was in Third World circles) by the assertion that *no* collective Jewish existence in any part of former mandatory Palestine could be recognised. This was in fact the thrust of the hostile references to Zionism (or the 'Zionist entity') by the Arab states that have never recognised Israel. It was taken up by Western supporters of the Palestinian case. It echoed in the propaganda (for internal as well as external consumption) that issued from Soviet and other communist sources whose governments have never withdrawn their earlier recognition of Israel but who, for anti-American purposes, were zealously active in stirring the anti-colonialist pot.

This anti-Zionism aimed at damaging Israel's name among the nations – or, rather and more narrowly, among the liberal intelligentsia within the Western nations. It was in many ways remarkably efficacious. Its successes were reinforced by the Lebanon War of 1982 and by media responses to that war. It was seldom, if ever, based on any careful or reasoned attention to Zionist history. So far as Third World countries are concerned, many of them had little if any direct contact with Jews and, quite understandably, only superficial knowledge of – as well as scant experience with – Zionist or other aspects of Jewish history. They were, if blame is to be apportioned, less blameworthy for circulating inexpert nonsense than were the Western intellectuals (and journalists) who imbibe it with such abandon.

Anti-Zionism shaded into antisemitism when certain other arguments were introduced – those that called into question the Holocaust of European Jewry; those that deliberately used the language of holocaust and genocide to pillory aspects of Israeli policy toward Arabs; those that equated Zionism with racism; and those that operated a double-standard in reviewing Jewish–Israeli responses to Arab hostility.

In Arab countries there has been a long-standing complaint that in 1948 Palestinian Arabs were obliged by the international community to bear the burden of Hitler's persecution of the Jews of Europe and that subsequent Western (including West German) aid to Israel was a form of vicarious atonement for the injuries inflicted by Western Europeans on their Jewish fellow-citizens. Arabs who took this line (and their supporters) were generally impervious to the counter-arguments about the deprivations of Jews in Arab lands or to the well-documented evidence of Arab acts of support for Hitler's wartime drive into the Balkans and the Middle East. But this position did not, obviously, deny that there was a Nazi Holocaust campaign. It could only 'delegitimise' Israel to the extent that the *only* source of the Jewish state was the need to find a refuge for sufferers from the Holocaust. Facts suggest that Israel rests upon broader and more diverse, as well as older, grounds of legitimation. But to this long-standing Arab position – that which distances Arabs from Western attempts to atone for Western sins – there was superimposed a more deadly, sophistical (I cannot say more sophisticated) ploy, namely, that of denying that the Holocaust had taken place and/or the charge that what destruction of the Jews did take place under Hitler was on a small scale and of very different character from what is normally believed. This is a significant and distasteful innovation. Its origins are in the right-wing revision of the history of the Nazi period. One of the French pioneers in this curious field of literary endeavour, Paul Rassinier, published his *Le mensonge d'Ulysse* as early as 1950. But the spate of literature in the 1970s with the appearance of further work by Rassinier as well as the work *Did Six Million Really Die?* by Richard B. Harwood and, in the United States, A. R. Butz's *The Hoax of the Twentieth Century*. By 1984 there were some fifty such works – as well as semi- or quasi-scholarly journals devoted to these matters and cranky minor brochures with what purports to be a Christian patina.

No doubt these attempts to exonerate the Nazis had an obvious appeal to ageing former Nazis themselves – and to the small groups of their younger neo-Nazi or neo-fascist successors. But there was in fact no great difference between right and left when it came to these malevolent revisions of recent Jewish history. In recent years, leftist Third World propaganda took over this fresh theme and slotted it very squarely into the support offered to the Palestinian Arabs. But there was a further twist to this ugly tale – namely, the assertion that the Zionists conspired with the Nazis to use (if not to promote and stimulate) what quantum of Jewish persecution did occur. The alleged Zionist purpose was to promote Jewish and selectively Zionist emigration to Palestine. This line has had a special appeal to Soviet writers about Zionism and about current efforts by Soviet Jews to leave the USSR. Western Trotskyites – particularly Jews – also dwelled affectionately on this theme. They, and others utilised and distorted selected scraps of historical evidence, dismissing or ignoring the discussion among serious historians on such vexed matters as, for example, the transfer agreements with the Nazis, the conduct of different Judenräte in Eastern Europe and, of course, the well-documented pro-Allied, anti-Axis activities of the Yishuv.

The charge that Zionism is a form of racism is – I think intentionally – a peculiarly wounding accusation, for over the last century Jews have been the principal victims of racial ideology and racially-fuelled projects of genocide. It has already been mentioned that racism and anti-racism can lend themselves to odd and dangerous modes of definition. So far as Zionist endeavours are concerned, the claim that Zionists are racist, or have anything in common with so-called scientific racism could only be based upon a distortion or willful ignorance of Jewish history and practice. Certainly Zionists have always held fast to the 'uniqueness' of the Jewish people and to the demand that Jews, like other peoples, have the right to work for national liberation. But that could not constitute a racist stance. It is, of course, possible to enter into a debate about the nature of such Jewish uniqueness and about the active implementation of that right to national liberation. When any people, or any spokesman on their behalf, lays claim to such uniqueness, the claim does set it apart from other comparably unique and distinct entities. But to make such a claim and on its basis to build a nation-state, does not logically entail a belief in the fundamental inferiority of any or all such other unique entities or a supposition that such alleged inferiority has so-called racial grounds or origins. Again, an honest concern with these matters would involve a rational understanding of Jewish history and the basis of Jewish peoplehood. The Jewishness of the Jewish state and the criteria set out in the Law of Return (and its implementation) do, of course, place an emphasis on religion and descent. But such defining criteria are not the product of any racist ideology. No belief in Jewish 'racial' superiority is part of Zionist ideology or official Israeli practice. This can be confidently affirmed – despite two important yet easily over-emphasised sets of facts. First, it is true that in recent years a small number of Israelis have invoked what seem to be racist themes in their generally contemptuous discussions about the treatment of Arabs. Indeed, as is well known, in the 1984 Israeli elections one such group secured enough votes to enable its leader to be elected to the Knesset. But this outlook (and its political and moral dangers) have been widely condemned by Israelis of all shades of political opinion – and legislation against advocates of racialism was at once, and actively, canvassed. Second, there is no doubt that in what appears to them to be self-defence, Israeli Defence Forces inflicted heavy damage to life and property in some of their neighbours' territories – most recently in the territory of the disintegrated state of Lebanon. Argument has raged, and will continue, about the wisdom of such military campaigns. And, it has been frequently observed, Israelis themselves debated them with the utmost heat. But such acts – even when unwise, excessive, or counter-productive – do not constitute evidence of 'racism'. They need not (and are not) undertaken, nor should they be condemned, as an expression of any claims to Jewish 'racial superiority'.

Third-world polemicists – and their friends in the liberal democracies – who used the 'racist' argument were, in fact, denying that Jews had the right to satisfy their national aspirations – a right not denied to other such aspirants. It is worth considering whether this denial of Jewish rights (though those rights certainly conflict with the serious claims of others) seems itself to border on racism, insofar as that much misused term retains clear meaning and whether the anti-racism that centered so obsessively on the delegitimation of Israel (a process that in certain Arab eyes was a stated preliminary to her elimination) was not itself very close to racism in its antisemitic form. Why it might be asked, are Jews so special (i.e., inferior) that they – unlike the residents of, say, Mali or Ruanda-Urundi – should be denied the right to statehood? Why in the defence of that state should they be denied the 'normal' means of self-defence (not necessarily by means that are edifying or ennobling)? When Jews in Israel were stigmatised for claiming and exercising those rights it seemed designed to create for Israel a pariah status analogous to the inferior status of the Jews in the darkest days of their travail in Europe – and therefore it was interpreted as antisemitic.

After all, Palestinian claims for such national identity were validated in liberal-democratic (as well as other) parts of the world. They were of more recent origin than the much contested and often rejected claims of the Zionists. Palestinian leaders have discussed the Jewish question and the Zionist entity in terms that smack of a genocidal intent. And they have not been the subject of UN resolutions for so doing – even when they argued in the rhetoric of the bogus *Protocols of the Elders of Zion*, freely available in Arabic translation. It may appear pedantic to ask whether such a Palestinian position, glossed over by Western opponents of Zionism, was not just offensive to Jews – but also genocidal in its implications. Certainly most Israelis were in no hurry to commit national suicide by adhering to the position that *their* state, being racist, is not simply bound to make mistakes (including mistakes about its own interests) but embodied such a supreme form of wickedness that it should not exist.

These waves of argument, often hate-laden and malicious, may, some would say, be the price Jews must pay for political life; in politics hard words are often exchanged and it is often well to believe, or pretend to believe, that the hard words embody no underlying hatred or malice. The ritual of abuse is simply part of the political game. But Jews did not find this an easy or even possible posture. Accustomed to the types of vandalism (or worse) associated with the right-wing enemy, they were deeply hurt by the new attacks from their erstwhile friends on the left. Their pain is fully justified – but whether the insults are explained (or more easily combatted), by being attributed to antisemitism is, in many ways, a very open question. On balance I would say that delegitimising Israel was *in itself* offensive and a much greater threat to the Jewish people, and their interests, than many of the more familiar forms of Judeophobia. That must remain a matter of judgement. There seemed grounds to hold that the presentation of the Lebanon War to the Western public – and, indeed, of the whole Israeli–Arab conflict – was flawed by a strand of what even non-Jews (such as Conor Cruise O'Brien in his 1982 *Observer* article), regarded as antisemitism.

Antisemitism picks out certain traits of character or modes of conduct to which objection may properly be taken but labels them as peculiarly Jewish – even when and although the traits and the conduct are found across the board. It is also found when Jews are not accorded the right to do what others may do without censure or accusation. These are general observations – and apply to anti-Jewish discrimination whether it is reliant upon religious, social, moral or political criteria. As we have seen, the peculiarity of the charge of racism as applied to the Zionist enterprise was that Jews/Zionists are deemed to commit the ultimate sin of racism when they exercise the very rights of self-determination guaranteed to other people or when they resort to military measures in order to remove a major threat to national security. A dual standard is invoked on both counts. And, although what counts as a major threat to national security is a matter of subjective judgement, a claim that Israel *alone* was wrong to act to remove such a threat is clear evidence of a double standard. So, of course, is the prior judgement (held by rejectionist Arabs, non-rejectionist Arabs in their rejectionist moods, and assorted Western sympathisers) that no Jewish state in Zion can be recognised if it conflicts (which it does) with the Palestinian claim to have their state on the same territory.

When Israel is upbraided through lines of argument that *are* applied to all states that is not by itself a sign of anti-Jewish malice or prejudice; to recognise that Israel's leaders, through acts of commission or omission, deserve blame or censure is not antisemitism if what other Middle Eastern leaders do is judged by the same criteria. This uniformity of standards is not often secured. The events in the Lebanon in 1982 and after yielded countless instances of this dual-standard approach – especially in Western media reporting. For example, a concern with civilian casualties in the Lebanon in 1982 is entirely justified, as was concern over the atrocities in Sabra and Shatila. But it moves along an antisemitic track if the *differing* Israeli responsibility for these matters is likened to the conduct of the Nazis – with reference to Holocaust and genocide thrown in to drive the needle home. On the other hand, PLO responsibility for deliberately locating their military fixtures in civilian areas is ignored or played down, and Israeli steps – however less than complete – to avoid civilian casualties go unmentioned. Again, failure to report the extent of discovered PLO materiel in the Lebanon seemed a sign of bad faith among otherwise vigilant media people – as did their tendency to overestimate, sometimes ludicrously and credulously, the civilian death toll in Southern Lebanon as the Israelis advanced. Such reporting failures ran parallel with the under-reporting, for example, of President Assad's onslaught on 'enemy' Muslims in his own city of Hama or the casualties in the Iran–Iraq war – a catastrophe not attributable to Zionist origins or plots. These media presentations (and other failures to ask pertinent questions of the PLO) may have many causes, including fear of the PLO. But they also smack of double standards and of antisemitism.

It is necessary to be very exact in alleging antisemitism. Alas, all too many verifiable instances have occurred where motive, language, rhetoric and context pointed ominously to antisemitism. But when, for example, foreign statesmen object in diplomatic terms to acts of Israeli policy without in any way denying Israel's right to exist or invoking any double standard, it would be foolish and unproductive to accuse them of antise-mitism or of seeking to continue the Holocaust by other means. Indeed, paradoxically but obviously, to do so is to devalue that Holocaust. To invoke it lightly or angrily in the defence of the most worthy of causes is to rob it of its uniquely distinctive horror and to place oneself on a moral level perilously close to that of those who describe any of Israel's acts of self-defence, however cautious, limited, or justifiable, as instances of genocide against the Palestinians. This is an offensive as well as an explosive game in which no one, not even embattled Jews, can engage without serious moral contamination.

Despite the collapse of much liberal-left support for Israel since 1967 and the subsequent descent of opinion-formers into the muddle of dual stan-dards, it has yet to be shown that, in democratic countries, the anti-Zionist mischief may lead to an active, populist antisemitism. Perhaps there is a time-lag in such things and the overall result is not at present ascertainable.

But how bad it will be is not historically predetermined. From events since 1967 Jews the world over learned how closely their image and their future were linked with that of Israel. Some (though not all) of the honest unease felt in Diaspora Jewry about Israel's policies in Lebanon or the West Bank and how they are reflected in the Western press resulted from anxiety (perhaps misplaced) about how their non-Jewish associates would think of them. That was neither unnatural nor dishonourable. Nor can Western Diaspora Jews feel confident that any future disputes between their own government and that of Israel will absolve them from making the most agonising of reappraisals. Such anxieties are inevitable. It would be wrong to suppress them and pretend that they do not exist. For they are often conjoined with a real concern for Israel, its interests, and above all, its people.

This essay was first published in William Frankel (ed.), *Survey of Jewish Affairs 1985* (Cranbury, N.J.: Fairleigh Dickinson University Press, 1985).

# 15 Antisemitism and Anti-Zionism – New and Old

## Yehuda Bauer

Topical discussions on antisemitism, in order to be useful, have, I think, to be founded on a combination of approaches – historical, psychological and sociological. The historical approach is vital, unless one believes that antisemitism today has no roots in the past and is characterised by completely new phenomena. The problem really arises out of the fact that there is a discrepancy between our consciousness of ourselves as individuals who measure time by their own lives, and the objective time measures of human societies. We live a life-span of around seventy or eighty years, and delude ourselves into thinking that historical processes take place within such time-frames. In actual fact, historical developments in societies take very much longer than that; the time that has elapsed since the writing of the Book of Esther, in which radical anti-Jewishness is reported in the language of clear murderous intent – as is the Jewish response – is not that long. Modern psychology teaches us that human responses to social pressures are not that different today from what they were a few thousand years ago. When we discuss contemporary anti-Zionism, we are therefore thrown back to basic questions: Why the Jews? Why is this particular 'prejudice' so time-resistant as to have lasted for 2500 years and yet remained with a basic core of dislike, fear, unease, hatred or inflation of the power of Jews? Can contemporary anti-Zionism be explained without referring to such basic, historical problems? I do not think so.

The term 'antisemitism' is, of course, a very modern one. We have become accustomed to using it as a kind of shorthand for all kinds of anti-Jewishness, although we are fully aware of the fact that an undifferentiated usage may mislead us and others. Let me therefore deal with anti-Jewishness (*sin'at Yisrael*) first, though very briefly.

Jewish civilisation emerged as a 'counter-culture' in the ancient world. It rebelled against the prevailing hierarchical structure of religions, which itself reflected a hierarchical social structure. For Jews there was but one God, and therefore all human beings were essentially equal. The Bible presents contradictory attitudes to other religions, the prophet Micah, for instance, pleading for a *laissez faire* relationship between Judaism and the others ('For all people will walk every one in the name of his god', 4:5), but at the same time insisting upon the predominance of the one true Jewish deity. Religious pluralism as practiced in the ancient world was, in principle, abhorrent to a monotheistic approach. The Jewish approach, as evidenced in the biblical tradition, translated social realities and ideals into legal language. The Jewish tradition made clear statements of principle against slavery, in favour of equality before the law ('eye for an eye, tooth for a tooth') and against the overbearing behaviour of government, the aristocracy and the military leadership. In the context of antiquity, all this was bound to arouse intense dislike. For political reasons that had nothing to do with their religion, many of the Jews dispersed into what came to be known as their Diaspora, bringing their own culture and civilisation with them. As long as the general political and social culture around them remained tolerant of differences, dislike, fortified by economic or other jealousies, rarely led to physical violence. Nevertheless, Judaism frequently provoked intense animosity, fear and social rejection. On the other hand, Judaism was also a proselytising religion, and many joined it because of its clear and decisive answers to spiritual and social problems. This changed radically only with the rise of Christianity to predominance. A sharp difference developed between the new religion (which had to prove to a Gentile world that disliked Judaism that it was not identical with the latter) and the older nation-religion which obstinately stuck to its guns. Islam later adopted a similar stance of opposition to the two religions from which it sprang and from whom it had to differentiate itself.

Modern, secularised society has inherited these basic problems. The rebellion of rationalists and secularists against Christianity, along with the new interpretations that deists attempted of their religious traditions, generated opposition to the civilisation from which Christianity sprang. It was at times much simpler (as with Voltaire, for instance) to oppose the source of Christianity, Judaism, than to take on directly the powerful Catholic Church. Nazism built on previous traditions, though it opposed Christianity, just as the rationalists had done.

Shmuel Ettinger's insistence on the importance of stereotypes helps us to understand the way negative images of Jews were transmitted from generation to generation. Shorthand explanations of the world around us are a necessity today, but they were essential in the past as well. Images were thus formed and embodied in the culture of civilisations. As history developed these images became part of the culture transmitted from one age to another, even from one civilisation to another. Anti-Jewish stereotypes of this kind became part of the civilisation of Christian Europe and the world of Islam. From the lowliest folk culture to the highest achievements of these respective civilisations, from the customs of English villages to the plays of Marlowe and Shakespeare or the music of Bach, anti-Jewish traditions formed part of the cultural heritage. This cannot be expunged, any more than St John's Gospel can be; all one can do – and that is, of course, essential – is to reinterpret the traditions. What is extremely important to realise is that while these stereotypes changed slowly, the largely negative attitude to the Jews remained both central and constant because of the underlying historical elements mentioned above. The argument, therefore, about continuity and discontinuity in modern antisemitism seems to me to be based on a misunderstanding. The stereo-type is predominantly, but not necessarily or wholly, negative. Its many and important negative elements are not 'eternal', though there is a remarkable repetitiveness in the themes of anti-Jewishness. New elements are added as historical situations change, and then old ones are reintroduced, as and when they seem to fit again.

In this respect one must not lose sight of the fact that no discussion of contemporary antisemitism is possible without taking into account changes wrought by Nazism and the Holocaust. The first new element introduced by Nazism was the literal way in which the Nazi leadership interpreted previous anti-Jewish imagery. The second and ultimately decisive factor was the translation of pre-existing calls for the annihilation of the Jews into modern, bureaucratically-directed and total mass murder. The third new element was the way in which the Nazis combined pre-modern anti-Jewish images with modern, nineteenth-century antisemitism into one whole. Apart from these very crucial additions, all the old and modern anti-Jewish attitudes and statements were repeated. Basic to the Nazi understanding of 'the Jew' was the combination of the Christian image of the Jew as a parasite, derived from the misapplication of positivistic nineteenth-century science.

The devil myth, inspired by medieval Christianity, led to another very basic antisemitic stereotype, that of the Jewish world conspiracy, trans-lated into the infamous *Protocols of the Elders of Zion* at the turn of the nineteenth century. The Nazis took this over, but they did not talk merely of a Jewish conspiracy to seize control of the world in the future. Nazism saw the Jewish devil assuming different and contradictory forms. The Jews had invented capitalism and socialism (Marxism). Their present rule was in the main based on Bolshevism (which was their invention) but they were also in control of plutocratic America, democratic France and, if they were not stopped, they would soon complete their dominance of England as well. Thus Hitler explained England's turnabout in early 1939, when the British decided to oppose further German expansion, especially attributing their continued fight against Germany after the fall of France in 1940 to 'Jewish' machinations.

The theme of world domination was by no means unique to the Nazis. Their ideology was but the most extreme of a number of similar ideological fantasies. It is worth remembering that the Balfour Declaration was issued, at least in part, because the British thought that the Jews had a tremendous influence in both America and Russia; a declaration in their favour would, it was hoped, bring this extremely powerful international factor to the side of the Allies. 'International Jewry' was a living concept in early twentieth-century politics, and the Zionist movement seemed to provide proof of its reality. Zionism therefore appeared in a setting which, in a peculiar way, had been prepared for it. It fulfilled prophecies – both of well-wishers among the Gentiles, who saw in its rise the realisation of ancient predictions tied to Christian eschatology – and of antisemites, who saw in it the Jewish Cabal coming out of the closet. Zionists themselves used this antisemitic imagery in order to advance their political aims. Moderate antisemites, who merely exaggerated the power of Jewish 'international finance' or of 'Jewish worldwide connections', could be persuaded to support Zionism for quasi-practical reasons, because it was better to have these powerful Jews on your side. This was the consideration that had led the Germans in early 1918 to make a pro-Zionist declaration of their own to counteract the Balfour Declaration.

For the Nazis, Zionism was both an admission on the part of the Jews themselves of the correctness of the Nazi ideology, and also a threat. The Zionists admitted, in Nazi eyes, that Jews were a racially different group; the Zionist movement was a branch, or a part, of that Jewish world power against which the Nazis were fighting. During the 1930s the Nazi aim was to get rid of the Jewish devil-parasite poisoning the German nation. Jewish emigration would weaken the countries of reception, and thus make them either more amenable to alliances with Germany or less resistant to conquest. Zionism, which wanted to remove the Jews from Germany, was therefore not markedly hindered by Nazi bureaucrats. On the other hand, the Peel partition plan of 1937 aroused the practical possibility of a Jewish state being established in Palestine, and the Germans were anxious lest this become a Jewish Vatican, a centre for Jewish world-power and anti-German conspiracy. A Jewish state had therefore to be opposed. But emigration to Palestine was still supported until early 1941.

Antisemitism in the post-Holocaust world is, in principle, not that different from the pre-1939 variety, similarly combining continuity and new developments. The terminology used by some commentators, which tries to differentiate between 'classical' and 'modern' (or racist) antisemitism is much too rigid. We have already seen how the Nazis adapted old concepts to fit new realities. Hence, to differentiate 'classical' antisemitism from new versions is a dangerous and potentially misleading exercise. If by 'classical' antisemitism one means legal and formal discrimination against Jews; if one means accusations of sharp business practices, clannishness, etc., then indeed such phenomena are becoming rare. They exist, of course, but one has to note again that they are intertwined with 'new' twists in antisemitic ideology. Thus the oft-quoted speech by Jordanian Ambassador Nusseibah at the UN in 1980 combines anti-Zionism with accusations that the 'Zionists' control the price of gold. One can quote reams of similar stuff from Soviet antisemitic propaganda. Anti-Zionism uses such 'classical' themes whenever this appears appropriate. The point, however, is that 'old' or 'classical' antisemitism has been downgraded to a mere supporting position. The main role has been taken over by the world conspiracy theory and the devilish Jewish–Zionist character.

Any discussion of anti-Zionism in the contemporary world has to define what is meant by Zionism. For our purposes it will suffice to say that Zionism is the Jewish national movement, which defines the Jews as being one people dispersed over the globe, with a common heritage, and with a political centre in Israel with which those Jews who so wish may identify. In such a statement there are really two distinct parts. One posits the existence of a single Jewish people. The other states that Israel is the political centre for this people. There is also the implication that, as with other national groups, the identification is largely subjective (i.e. a Jew in Bradford or in Chicago can take or avoid certain steps which will take him or her out of the Jewish community). Considerable numbers of Jews, in fact a very large majority, would probably come under this definition. Those living outside of Israel may not wish to move there, but they will, while acting as loyal citizens of their respective countries, usually consider themselves as belonging to the Jewish community; they will identify as Jews in one way or another, and they will see themselves as part of a historical unit with an often vague and undefined yet quite strong attachment to the centre that is Israel.

If this is broadly what Zionism means, then anti-Zionism can be seen as the denial of the right of Jews to be part of a worldwide community or to constitute an independent political unit in Israel. This goes beyond the denial of the right to self-determination as understood in international politics. One may deny the right of the Basques to a separate state, yet still be in favour of Basque schools, even of autonomy. In the case of Israel, denial of the right to exist has clear genocidal implications. In the present state of the Middle East, nobody could believe that the abolition of the Israeli state would result in anything but the wholesale murder of its Jewish citizens. What would happen if Israel was effectively denied its right to exist is therefore abundantly clear. In the case of the Jewish Diaspora, the rejection of Zionism means first of all a clear discrimination between Jews and non-Jews. For pragmatic reasons, demands of nationalities or ethnic groups may be denied for a time or permanently. But there is no case in contemporary politics where such a right is denied on principle. In both cases, therefore, we are dealing with a basic anti-Jewish stance; the Jews, or a majority among them, define themselves in one way, and anti-Zionism denies their right to so define themselves. When this happens with Basques, such a position would be called anti-Basque. In our case, it is clearly anti-Jewish. Antisemitism today means a principled anti-Jewish stand. Anti-Zionism is therefore, in most cases, another form of antisemitism.

However, we must pursue our analysis further. First of all, the argument is presented that there are Jewish anti-Zionists who cannot be considered Jewish antisemites. In fact, there is no reason why there should not be anti-Jewish Jews. Historically speaking, the Jewish minority has always been under severe pressure to conform to majority values and to renege on former loyalties. Some of the foremost opponents of Judaism in the Middle Ages and in early modern times were converted Jews. There are similar examples with other nationalities – Slovaks identifying with Magyarisation campaigns in Hungary, Poles becoming agents of Russification, Welshmen anglicising Wales, etc.

In the case of Zionism, Jewish opposition to it comes from two main sources: Western or Communist assimilation and ultra-orthodoxy. Any connection with a worldwide Jewish nationality or ethnicity is denied, and any tie to Israel is usually repudiated by the first type of anti-Zionists. This attitude is then generalised and presented as a principle to be adopted by 'progressive' mankind. But in the case of the assimilationists in West and East, one can safely say that their attitude is the expression of an ardent desire to conform to what is perceived to be the prevalent view in the host society. These are therefore mainly Jewish individuals who identify with the anti-Zionist ideologies of their environment.

This is not the case with the ultra-orthodox opponents of Zionism. They range from the Satmarer Hassidim, whose headquarters are in New York, and the Neturei Karta of Jerusalem (the two are allied but not identical), to the more extreme wings of Agudat Israel, who participate in the government of Israel; the more moderate parts of the Aguda are non-Zionist – they do not support Zionism but recognise the Israeli government for purely pragmatic purposes. Orthodox anti-Zionism does not question the first part of our definition: it fully agrees with the proposition that the Jews are one people with a common history. Indeed, that to them is a minimal statement and they would add religious sanction to it. Nor do they disagree with the idea that Eretz Israel is the country of the Jews, to which the Messiah will lead them in the fullness of time. They oppose Zionism as a political movement of a basically secular character which derives its legitimation not from religious law but from democratic procedures. Jews, in orthodox thinking, are not permitted to establish a political structure of their own and thereby challenge 'the nations', or engage in a political Ingathering of the Exiles, as long as the Messiah has not come. Religious Zionists, by contrast, find justification in religious traditions for the opposite approach. Ultra-orthodox opposition to the Zionist movement, though often expressed in violent terms and occasionally going to the extreme of collaboration with Israel's enemies, is not really opposed to Zionism in the sense of denying the Jewish right to self-determination. Though calling themselves anti-Zionists, the ultra-orthodox are obviously qualitatively different from Gentile anti-Zionists in East and West.

Anti-Zionism in the Soviet Union (and in Czechoslovakia and East

Germany) is today the most dangerous and deadly opponent not only of the Jewish national movement and the State of Israel, but of Jews generally, and through them of Western democracy. Antisemitism in the socialist movement of the nineteenth century can be documented from the founding fathers of socialism: Proudhon, Marx, Engels and Bakunin. The devil image of the Jews was transformed, in this case, into the image of the capitalist exploiter. The characteristic features of such exploiters in popular socialist literature of the second half of the nineteenth century were based on medieval Christian imagery. In the late nineteenth century, however, with antisemitism becoming a tool in the hands of right-wing political movements, socialists turned against it, calling it the 'socialism of fools'. In the first part of our century, social-democratic parties became often the only or last centres of opposition to antisemitism.

The Soviet Union inherited this mixed tradition, but it had to confront a much older tradition as well: Russian society, including the Russian peasantry and townspeople, had been heirs to an antisemitic heritage going back hundreds of years. This antisemitic tradition was religiously motivated, and served as one of the cultural symbols uniting Russian society before the overthrow of the Tsarist regime. After the victory of the Revolution in Russia all national movements were suppressed, including Zionism, even though it did not demand any national territory in the USSR, only in Palestine. However, from the mid-1930s, with the increasingly blatant turn towards a Great-Russian chauvinism, discrimination specifically against the Jews began to take shape. Jewish schools and other forms of cultural life were gradually suppressed. The Second World War saw open antisemitism in many partisan units behind German lines, though the Soviet High Command issued orders prohibiting antisemitic actions. Popular antisemitism seems to have risen considerably in the Soviet hinterland, while massive collaboration in the murder of the Jews took place in areas under German control, especially in the Ukraine. The Soviet leadership under Stalin began to see in the Jews a hostile element, and during the 'Doctors' plot' in early 1953 a mass pogrom against the Jews was in the offing.

Zionism had always been regarded as a bourgeois-nationalist deviation, but then so were other movements of nationalities in the USSR. The difference in the Zionist case was that the Jews were identified with concrete 'imperialist agencies', and in the 1950s this became clear throughout the Soviet bloc when show trials were held in most Soviet-controlled countries. A disproportionately large number of the accused were Jews, all of them old, tried and loyal communists. They were charged with being part of a Zionist–Trotskyite–Titoist conspiracy, and having served as 'agents' for the CIA and the American Jewish Joint Distribution Committee (a purely philanthropic social agency). It is true that Israel was already perceived by the Soviet leaders in the early 1950s to be a Western client state, but this was a secondary motif. The main purpose of the trials and of the antisemitic propaganda which was renewed with tremendous force after the Six Day War, was internal. Zionism, a dangerous imperialist plot based on a world conspiracy of bourgeois-nationalist Jewry, was the mortal enemy of the Soviet regime.

The vast propaganda that has spewed forth from the USSR since 1967 has several characteristics built upon the foundations I have tried to describe. Zionism, in Soviet eyes, is not only a 'world conspiracy' directed specifically against the socialist countries, but it increasingly controls imperialism and its aim is to dominate the world in the interests of the Jewish–Zionist ruling clique of bankers and industrialists. Zionism, in Soviet eyes, is based on Judaism, which itself is a religious theory which forms a basis for fascism and racism. Indeed, popularisers of antisemitism such as Vladimir Begun or Lev Korneyev (to mention two of the most notorious) trace the evil character of Judaism to the First Temple period. The Jews carry with them the unfortunate heritage of a base and reactionary culture that predisposes them to fill the role of a corrupting agency in all civilisations which have had the misfortune of coming into contact with them. Of course, there are good Jews too. They are the ones who abandoned all their Jewish characteristics and, presumably, their Jewish connections. Soviet anti-Zionism, therefore, is an attack on a world conspiracy, on Jewish religion and culture, and of course on the State of Israel which embodies these characteristics. Soviet neo-antisemitism introduces some novel elements such as Jewish–Zionist control of 'imperialism', Zionist encouragement of fascist and racist ideologies, and the like. But much of it is 'old', such as the attack on Jewish religion, or else it is directly descended from Nazism. For example, the universally corrupting influence of the Jews, or the world conspiracy thesis, which we have briefly traced from its Christian origins through modern antisemitism, to Nazism, and finally to the Soviets.

Arab and Third World anti-Zionism is undoubtedly influenced by Soviet propaganda. But it also has additional and different ingredients. With the Arabs there is a realistic political element. The struggle between Israel and the Palestinians is a struggle over a piece of land. The Arabs oppose the Jewish national movement that fights against Palestinian nationalism over Eretz Israel. In a way, it is almost a relief to face this nationalist kind of anti-Zionism which is openly hostile and denies the Jews their right to self-determination. But the implications of this hostility are clearly genocidal and anti-Jewish. True, in the present-day PLO version they do not see world Jewry as a major problem without whose solution there is no future or progress. However, the abstention of the PLO from openly anti-Jewish propaganda is the exception rather than the rule in the Arab world. In Sunni Egypt as well as in Shi'ite Iran, anti-Jewish propaganda is very marked, often seeing Israel as the centre of a Communist–Jewish conspiracy. The Soviet model is followed, except that the Jews here become Communist rather than capitalist–imperialist plotters, as in the USSR. Jews are frequently seen as a sect or a conspiratorial group, not as a nation or a people. Generally, they are depicted as malevolent – sometimes as absolutely evil. This anti-Zionism is not only primitive but very clearly antisemitic. 'Classic' antisemitic images are copied from European antisemitism and super-imposed on existing Islamic stereotypes of Jews.

The Third World countries of Africa and Asia copy stereotypes from the Northern hemisphere; they accept them in the same way as they accept washing machines, television and political slogans. Antisemitism here is part of the package, because it is an integral part of the European heritage. The problem becomes acute because these countries are dependent on the Northern hemisphere – whether it is the USSR or the US – not only for material goods but also for political concepts. For these countries the West, and to some extent the East as well, have failed to deliver their promises. 'Northern' civilisation, whether Western or Eastern, promised material advance, political freedom or economic equality between poor and rich. Democracy was presented by the West as a solution, and the Soviets preached socialism. In the meantime, there is starvation, over-population, internal strife, military dictatorships, abject poverty. Who is responsible? According to Soviet anti-Zionist propaganda, it is the Jews in and outside their State of Israel. The Jews may well become the symbol of the failure of the West to provide solutions for the Third World. This tendency was utilised by the Soviets when they engineered the 1975 'Zionism equals racism' resolution at the UN.

The UN resolution has an importance that should not be underestimated. Through the delegitimation of Israel, the USSR hoped to achieve a major blow against the democratic West; antisemitic anti-Zionism was undoubtedly seen by the Soviets as a mobilising agent for their interests and Israel as a symbol of the West that failed to keep its promise to the Third World countries. The identification of Zionism with racism, the major expression of evil in the eyes of the Third World, would make Israel an outcast that could be legitimately attacked and destroyed whenever this became feasible. The resolution, once adopted, provided a legitimation for the continuation and increase of antisemitic propaganda all over the world. Such propaganda in the West is a welcome destabilising agent in Soviet eyes. It acts as a stabilising and mobilising agent in the Soviet bloc. The fact that this tactic does not always work, that in Poland or Hungary such Soviet propaganda is viewed with considerable suspicion, if not distaste, is not due to lack of trying by the Soviets. The 'Zionism equals racism' resolution was the result, in many ways, of the Soviet antisemitic offensive. In turn, the resolution was to provide a continued momentum for the domestic campaign.

It has been pointed out by many observers that the UN resolution, by ostracising Israel, seeks to place the Jewish state in a position analogous to that of the individual Jew in pre-modern society. The attack now is on the *collective* rather than the individual Jew, and that is a special feature of this antisemitism. The State of Israel is new, of course, but the attack on the Jewish collectivity has precedents. Jews could convert in the Middle Ages to escape persecution, which was directed against Judaism and the Jewish collectivity. The major difference is that now the Jews can fight back, be it in ever so limited a fashion. The spectre of real as opposed to imaginary Jewish power has become fact. The attack is therefore very determined.

Anti-Zionism is not a preserve of Communist or Third World countries. Extreme right and left movements in the West and even segments of liberal opinion have fallen for it as well. On the right, anti-Zionism is very marked in marginal neo-Nazi movements which (like the Soviets) see in Zionism a world conspiracy whose centre is in Israel. There the antisemitic content is clear. What is more dangerous, however, is the denial of the Holocaust, now propagated by intellectuals and quasi-intellectuals in the US, Britain, France and elsewhere. The aim, whether conscious or unconscious, is the same as with Soviet propaganda: the destabilisation of democratic societies in order first to justify Nazi Germany and then to create a society in its image. In order to achieve that the horrendous deeds of the Nazi regime have to be denied. Anti-Zionism is an integral part of this campaign, because the reason why the Jews invented the Holocaust (according to the deniers) is to establish their world conspiratorial centre in Israel, with the money squeezed out of West Germany. This is really a rehash of Nazi ideology in contemporary conditions. The problem is that this propaganda is gaining ground precisely because the Holocaust is too horrendous a reality to be accepted, and any theory denying it may find fertile psychological ground.

The Old and New Left, rebelling against liberal and democratic society, take a not dissimilar line. Building on older antisemitic images, the New Left especially, often led by guilt-ridden Jews who try to escape their Jewishness through universalism (as did their Old Left fathers and grandfathers), see Zionism as the embodiment of the values they oppose. In addition their identification with the Third World leads them to identify the Palestinians with the 'good' victim and the Jews with the 'evil' oppressor. The devil stereotype is reawakened in a new form. But while the extremes of right and left may be potentially bothersome, a major danger lies in the middle, from an unconscious antisemitism posing as opposition not necessarily to Zionism or Israel as such but to policies of the Israeli government.

It is abundantly clear, of course, that criticism of the policies of the Israeli government is not anti-Zionism or antisemitism. By analogy, one can be pro-American or pro-British without agreeing to Mr Bush's or Mrs Thatcher's policies. But liberal, democratic, social democratic or moderately conservative opinion can suddenly flare up against Israel in an unmistakably antisemitic fashion. The electronic and printed media seem to be particularly prone to this affliction. A classical case in point is the story of the Lebanese war and the Western media in the summer of 1982. Even the social-democratic press in a neutral country such as Sweden returned to unambiguous antisemitic imagery in reporting the war. American and British television audiences were also treated to selective reporting which emphasised the equation of Jews and Nazis. The imagery again was antisemitic, exuded an irrational hatred of Jews and the denial of the right of Israel to anything – be it self-defence or a trust in its word equal to the bulletins of the PLO or the Shi'ites today. The images of Israelis dropping booby-trapped toys to kill children from their airplanes or of them poisoning Arab girls on the West Bank fit so neatly into unconsciously preserved stereotypes inherited from the past.

It is typical that such excesses of antisemitic propaganda in anti-Zionist garb subside almost as quickly as they arise. From late 1982 on, media reporting has not been exactly friendly to Israel but a minimum of balance has been preserved in most cases. Occasionally there is a vicious case reminiscent of June 1982, such as the uproar about the accidental killing of two CBS reporters by an Israeli tank in South Lebanon. CBS would not dream of accusing Kampuchea, Britain or Nicaragua of any harm that may come to its reporters without first checking the facts. Certainly no blanket accusations would be presented. But in the Israeli case the army was *a priori* guilty: the reporters had been close to the tank that fired on them, they were clearly unarmed, the killing was premeditated murder. Why? Well, Israelis are not like other human beings apparently. The important thing to remember is that it is only towards Israel that CBS would have dared behave with this kind of *chutzpah*. An investigation by a senior CBS functionary, with Israeli officialdom behaving in an impeccably friendly way, then showed that the tank had been 2.5 kilometres away from the crew, that a camera pointed from the roof of a private car, which had no business being in a combat area, looked just like a missile pointed at the tank, that the CBS crew did not bother to tell the Israeli army that it was going to film them from the Lebanese side (the enemy side from the Israeli perspective) and so on. CBS could not be expected to apologise. Instead they punished the Jews by not showing a presumably friendly programme on Israel which they had prepared. This is a kind of modern-style *Kulturantisemitismus*, directed against the Zionist state and unconsciously using stereotypes that date back generations.

How far is anti-Zionist antisemitism influenced by what Israel does? Or by what Diaspora Jews do? In this case it is mainly the behaviour of Israel that has an input into antisemitism. It is important to note that antisemitism has always been influenced not only by the world in which the Jews lived, but by the Jews themselves. Antisemitic arguments were always caricatures of Jews and their behaviour, but there had to be some Jewish behaviour or situation that could be caricatured.

The establishment of the State of Israel, and the Six Day War, could be cited as examples of how positive images are in part created by actions that the Jews undertake. Zionist ideology posited the gradual disappearance of antisemitism as a result of the 'normalisation' of the Jews in their own country and the Ingathering of the Exiles. This has not happened. Instead, as we have seen, the collective Jew has taken the place of the individual Jew as the target of antisemitism. Nevertheless, positive as well as negative attitudes are influenced by what the Jews or Israel do; the question is, to what extent is this so? Here again, the Lebanon war can serve as an example. Opposition in Israel to the war arose from the very beginning and increased as time went on, but very little of it was motivated by a desire to find favour with world opinion or in order to combat antisemitism. Opposition was voiced on moral and practical grounds that arose out of the Israeli social and political constellation. Yet this opposition was, to put it simply, flabbergasted by the wave of hostility to Israel *as such*, not only to the government that had initiated the war but against the Jewish people. In this case it was clear that the antisemitic reaction was triggered rather than caused by what Israel did. But, we all asked, if this is what is latent in the Western intelligentsia as exemplified in the media, what can we expect at any point of crisis involving or not involving Jews and Israel in the future? On the other hand, had it not been for the invasion, this antisemitism might have remained latent and a slow process of counter-education might have decreased its danger. In this sense, Israeli behaviour may well have influenced antisemitic reaction.

Israeli behaviour on the West Bank (or Judea and Samaria, according to one's political inclinations), and the rise of the Kach movement of Meir Kahane on the lunatic right-wing fringe of Israeli politics, can serve as additional examples. The tarnished image of the Israeli egalitarian and humanist, now turned soldier imposing curfews and worse upon a population of Arabs who have no political rights, certainly does not *cause* antisemitism; but it probably triggers it by arousing public opinion against Israel. The precarious objective situation of Israel makes it incumbent upon Israeli politicians to decide carefully whether their policies are so essential to the security of the state and to its future role as the focal point of Jewish hopes and aspirations as to justify the disenfranchisement of the Palestinian Arabs. The price paid for this in terms of an encouragement of antisemitism dressed up as anti-Zionism may be relatively cheap in the eyes of the Israeli right-wing parties. But there hardly seems a doubt that there is a price to pay, and that Israeli political and social behaviour does influence antisemitic and anti-Zionist propaganda; the problem one can argue about is the extent to which this takes place. To those of us on the left and centre of Israeli public life, it is not primarily a matter of influencing potential antisemites that makes us unhappy about certain aspects of Israeli politics. Rather, it is the self-image that matters and it is not just an image either. It is a problem of the type of Israeli society and morality that we have, as contrasted with what we want. Both wings of Israeli public opinion should realise, however, that the anti-Zionist wave is big enough and dangerous enough to warrant careful weighing of Israeli policies that may affect it one way or the other.

To sum up: anti-Zionism today is very largely another way of propagating antisemitism. There may be those who advocate an abolition of nationalism and national aspirations altogether and include the Jews in this as a matter of course. I do not think that this is a very widespread view. Other anti-Zionists are, whether they realise it or not, antisemites. Anti-Zionism is a destabilising, basically anti-democratic trend. It poses a danger to Jews and to Israel. But it is also a threat to democracy, liberalism and to all the values that make life worth living. Can it be fought? I think so. I do not pretend that antisemitism in any guise can be eliminated in a few decades, but there are movements afoot that militate against antisemitism. One should note the deep change that is slowly taking place in the Christian churches, among Catholics and Protestants. Vatican II and statements by bishops' conferences in Germany and France, as well as parallel moves in some Protestant churches, might well cut the ground from under the oldest existing antisemitic stereotypes. For example, by recognising the Jewish religion as equal to their own, by denying the deicide accusation and by introducing or discussing the introduction of other basic reforms. In the West large numbers of people seem to be beginning to understand the inherent danger to democratic society from antisemitism. Soviet antisemitism does not work very well in some Soviet-controlled countries. Thus the outlook is by no means hopeless. Political movements have a role to fulfil in this fight, but so do academics. They have the task of analysing the situation and suggesting lines of thought that will lead to effective action.

Finally, while antisemitism is unique, it is nevertheless a certain type of prejudice, moreover, one often held in conjunction with other types of prejudice. In this sense, we are still in the same boat as others against whom hatred is preached or discrimination is practiced. Our natural allies are all those who fight intelligently against all types of prejudice, because there can be little doubt that the different types feed each other.

# Index

Made in United States
Troutdale, OR
10/30/2024

24294260R00126